Constitutionalism, Democracy and Religious Freedom

In both Europe and North America it can be argued that the associational and institutional dimensions of the right to freedom of religion or belief are increasingly coming under pressure. This book demonstrates why a more classical understanding of the idea of a liberal democracy can allow for greater respect for the right to freedom of religion or belief.

The book examines the major direction in which liberal democracy has developed over the last fifty years and contends that this is not the most legitimate type of liberal democracy for religiously divided societies. Drawing on theoretical developments in the field of transnational constitutionalism, Hans-Martien ten Napel argues that redirecting the concept and practice of liberal democracy toward the more classical notion of limited, constitutional government, with a considerable degree of autonomy for civil society organizations, would allow greater religious pluralism. The book shows how, in a postsecular and multicultural context, modern sources of constitutionalism and democracy, supplemented by premodern, transcendental legitimation, continue to provide the best means of legitimating Western constitutional and political orders.

Hans-Martien ten Napel is Associate Professor of Constitutional and Administrative Law at Leiden University in the Netherlands. During the academic year 2014–2015 he was a Research Fellow in Legal Studies at the Center of Theological Inquiry in Princeton, New Jersey.

Law and Religion

The practice of religion by individuals and groups, the rise of religious diversity, and the fear of religious extremism, raise profound questions for the interaction between law and religion in society. The regulatory systems involved, the religion laws of secular government (national and international) and the religious laws of faith communities, are valuable tools for our understanding of the dynamics of mutual accommodation and the analysis and resolution of issues in such areas as: religious freedom; discrimination; the autonomy of religious organisations; doctrine, worship and religious symbols; the property and finances of religion; religion, education and public institutions; and religion, marriage and children. In this series, scholars at the forefront of law and religion contribute to the debates in this area. The books in the series are analytical with a key target audience of scholars and practitioners, including lawyers, religious leaders, and others with an interest in this rapidly developing discipline.

Titles in this series include:

Religious Expression in the Workplace and the Contested Role of Law
Andrew Hambler

Women's Rights and Religious Law
Domestic and International Perspectives
Fareda Banda and Lisa Fishbbayn Joffe

The Collective Dimension of Freedom of Religion
A Case Study on Turkey
Mine Yıldırım

Constitutionalism, Democracy and Religious Freedom
To Be Fully Human
Hans-Martien ten Napel

The Legal Architecture of English Cathedrals
Norman Doe

Religion, Law and the Constitution?
Balancing Beliefs in Britain
Javier García Oliva and Helen Hall

Forthcoming titles in this series include:

State and Religion
The Australian Story
Renae Barker

Law, Religion and Love
Seeking Ecumenical Justice for the Other
Paul Babie and Vanja-Ivan Savić

Distinguishing between Islam, Islamism and Violent Extremism
A philosophical-legal guide
Matthew Wilkinson

Constitutionalism, Democracy and Religious Freedom

To Be Fully Human

Hans-Martien ten Napel

Routledge
Taylor & Francis Group
LONDON AND NEW YORK

First published 2017
by Routledge

2 Park Square, Milton Park, Abingdon, Oxfordshire OX14 4RN
52 Vanderbilt Avenue, New York, NY 10017

Routledge is an imprint of the Taylor & Francis Group, an informa business

First issued in paperback 2019

British Library Cataloguing in Publication Data
A catalogue record for this book is available from the British Library

Library of Congress Cataloging in Publication Data
A catalog record for this book has been requested

ISBN: 978-1-138-64715-2 (hbk)
ISBN: 978-0-367-22420-2 (pbk)

Typeset in Galliard
by Keystroke, Neville Lodge, Tettenhall, Wolverhampton

Contents

Preface

Throughout my professional career, my passion has been the question of how liberal democracies can be designed to meet the demands of religiously and otherwise divided societies. Thus, while teaching at a Department of Political Science, I chose to specialize in Religion and Politics, among other things. My Ph.D. thesis dealt with the origins of the Dutch Christian Democratic party, whose predecessors were major architects of the pluriform democracy which characterized the Netherlands throughout the greater part of the twentieth century. Since my transfer to Leiden Law School, in 2000, Law and Religion has become one of my fields of expertise. In 2007 I also participated for the first time at two inspiring international gatherings on this topic: the Atlantic Conversation on Religion and Public Life, organized by St George's House, Windsor Castle, in association with the Center of Theological Inquiry (CTI) in Princeton, New Jersey, and "From Silver to Gold: The Next 25 Years of Law and Religion," the Silver Jubilee Conference of Emory University's Center for the Study of Law and Religion.

My research interests in the field of Law and Religion acquired their current focus largely as a result of a stimulating conference on "Religion and Civil Society: The Changing Faces of 'Religion' and 'Secularity'" held at Harvard Law School in 2012. The paper on "State, Civil Society and Religious Freedom" that I presented on that occasion was published in the *Oxford Journal of Law and Religion* in October 2013. It also formed the basis of my own contribution to a research proposal, co-authored with Dutch-American historian James Kennedy as principal applicant, that was granted a major subsidy by the Dutch Association for Scientific Research (NWO) in the summer of 2013. With the subsidy for this project, entitled "Religion Renegotiated: Faith-Based Organizations and the State in the Netherlands Since the 1960s," Leonard van 't Hul and Mart Rutjes have been appointed as Ph.D. Fellow and Postdoctoral Researcher respectively at the University of Amsterdam. The current book serves as my own contribution to this project, to the extent that it aims at providing some of the international and legal context in which the developments in the Netherlands can be better interpreted.

Since finishing my doctoral dissertation, I have published some 20 edited volumes, 150 book chapters and journal articles as well as numerous book reviews, case notes, etc. Increasingly, these publications were written in English. What was missing was a monograph in English. A research fellowship at CTI afforded me the opportunity to lay the foundations for such a monograph during the academic year 2014–2015 at Princeton. I am immensely grateful to CTI for this opportunity, and indeed to my home institution for allowing me to be on leave for such a considerable time. The subsidy from NWO helped to make it possible for me to finish the manuscript back at my regular desk at Leiden University, for which I am obviously equally thankful.

Nor do I wish to forget those who were present during presentations of the various chapters at academic conferences in the course of the past few years. A first draft of the first chapter, for example, was presented during the XXI Quinquennial World Congress of the International Association for the History of Religions (IAHR) held in Erfurt, Germany, August 23–29, 2015. At this conference my colleagues from the NWO project and I had organized a panel "Religion Renegotiated," where we all presented the progress of our work. A draft of the second chapter had been presented a year earlier, at the IXth World Congress of Constitutional Law held at the University of Oslo, Norway, June 16–20, 2014. The chapter on democracy was originally presented at the second annual conference of the International Society of Public Law held at New York University School of Law, July 1–3, 2015. Even while finishing the manuscript for the book, I took the opportunity to test parts of its argument during, for example, the Cardiff Festival of Law and Religion in Wales, May 5–6, 2016. An earlier version of the fourth chapter was presented at the conference "Christianity and the Future of our Societies," jointly organized by the Evangelische Theologische Faculteit, Leuven, and the Association for Reformational Philosophy in Leuven, Belgium, August 15–19, 2016. I am grateful to all my audiences on these occasions and for the feedback they graciously provided.

The same goes for my students, who over the years have attended various courses during which I have been able to develop ideas for parts of the book, notably my Bachelor of Laws Elective Course on Dutch Parliamentary Democracy and my Master Elective Course on Comparative Constitutional Law. They probably do not realize how important it is to be able to try out arguments and ideas in front of a motivated student audience, and how much there is to be learned from their responses both in writing and during class. It is my hope that this book will have an even larger audience than the (remarkably growing) group of direct colleagues and students in this field. For example, the book might also be helpful to practitioners working for either governments or non-governmental organizations in the field of religious freedom. To the extent that this goal is achieved, my students deserve due thanks for this because it is with them in mind that I have tried to write this narrative.

At least, I hope what follows will indeed be perceived to be a story, despite its primarily academic ambitions. If so, I will have succeeded in finding my voice, thanks also to my editor at Leiden University, Wendy Rodger. In that case I might also want to continue the narrative now that this one is finished. As will have become clear from the above, although in at least one sense this book has been long in the making, it is also actually based on a couple of recent presentations. As such, it is not so much the end of a period in my academic life, but I hope it marks the beginning of a new, even more fruitful, one. New courses and presentations are already in the making.

Introduction

Negotiating Amish–State Relations

Tuesday September 2, 2014 marked the official start of my Research Fellowship in Legal Studies at the Center of Theological Inquiry (CTI) in Princeton, New Jersey. Part of the mission of CTI is to seek the dialogue between theology and other disciplines. During the academic year 2014–2015, thanks to a generous gift from the John Templeton Foundation, a group of 12 resident fellows could be appointed. Approximately half of these were theologians and ethicists, the other half legal scholars. The overarching theme of this particular inquiry was law and religious freedom.

Some of the work I would be carrying out during the fellowship, including the current book project, had, however, unexpectedly already taken shape in the weeks running up to the start of the fellowship. During part of August we had been enjoying a holiday in Lancaster County, Pennsylvania. Lancaster County is just a two-and-a-half-hour drive from Princeton University. Yet it feels as if you are in a different country.

One reason why Lancaster County feels so different is that it is one of the strongholds of the Amish. As soon as one takes the highway exit, it is noticeable because of the slow-moving vehicles on the road: Amish horse-drawn buggies. Nor does it require much effort to determine on which farms the Amish live, because of the numerous black and white garments hanging out to dry on the washing lines. It is actually possible to encounter the Amish, and also Mennonites who belong to the same "Plain People," in local shops, some of which are run by members of the group.

The Amish are a conservative Christian group. In the early eighteenth century they were forced to flee European countries such as Switzerland and Germany where they were persecuted because of their religious convictions. In the Province of Pennsylvania, William Penn, himself an English Quaker, offered them hospitality in exchange for their willingness to farm the fertile soil.

Ever since, the Amish have attempted to stick to their traditional lifestyle as far as possible, because of what they regard as their biblical task—that is, to be *in* the world but not *of* the world. For this reason they largely refrain from using electricity and cars, among other things. But it is not the electricity and cars as such that they are against, just the fact that these could connect them too closely to the outside world. In a similar vein, the Amish are generally hesitant to use the judicial system or to engage in political activities. At the same time, they are widely considered to be about the best neighbors one could possibly wish for. They are also connected economically to the people around them, because of the fresh produce and other goods they trade.

Although it may seem counterintuitive, the Amish constantly interact with the outside world and adapt slowly but steadily to new developments occurring there. In turn, the Amish present a test case for the outside world, which has to frequently consider which concessions should be made in legislation and otherwise to accommodate the distinctive lifestyle of the Amish in areas such as military service and conscription, education and schooling, social security and taxes, health care, land use and zoning, and other First Amendment issues (Kraybill 2003a). Although this tolerance does not always come easily, the fact is that the Amish have been able to live in Lancaster County and elsewhere in the United States according to their religious convictions for centuries.

As historian of modern Christianity Martin E. Marty has put it, the Amish "negotiate, while appearing not to negotiate" (2003: x). As a result, Amish–state relations can be characterized as "a dynamic process of give and take, compromise and concession, a process that continually redraws the symbolic lines between church and state" (Kraybill 2003b: 20). The same holds true for other religious groups which find themselves in, what at least in the West appear to be, increasingly secular, majoritarian contexts (Lind, Lövheim, and Zackariasson 2016; González and D'Amato 2017; Guesnet, Laborde, and Lee 2017). Whether they are aware of it or not, these negotiations all take place against the backdrop of the right to freedom of religion or belief.

In addition to its clearly crucial individual aspects, this right also protects what have been called the associational and institutional dimensions of religious freedom. As Johan D. van der Vyver has explained, the associational dimension of the right to freedom of religion or belief concerns

> a collective group right (it vests in individuals as members of the religious community) and includes (i) the right to practice one's religion, in association with other members of the religious community, and (ii) the right to form, join and maintain religious associations.
>
> (Van der Vyver 2011: 1)

Institutional religious freedom, on the other hand, "is an institutional group right (the right vests in a religious institution as such) and . . . requires of the State not to interfere in the internal affairs of religious institutions" (ibid.; see also Langlaude-Doné 2016).

This book focuses on these associational and institutional dimensions of the right to freedom of religion or belief, and their significance for the proper functioning of our Western liberal democracies. More specifically, it asks the question to what extent in both Europe and North America communal religious freedom continues to be protected. According to at least one observer,

> There is no more important issue in law and religion today than institutional religious autonomy. . . . This area of law is the source of growing contestation and will likely prove a more important site of law and religion debate than traditional religious freedom and religion-state relations questions.
>
> (Calo 2014: 15; see also Scolnicov 2011; Norton 2016; Schwartzman, Flanders, and Robinson 2016)

Another observer rightly noted that what is at issue in communal religious freedom is more than immediately meets the eye. It also involves a fundamental question regarding the role of religious and other associations, groups, and institutions in society:

> Does civil society consist of a set of institutions that help the government achieve its purposes as it defines them when their doing so might be more efficient or convenient than the state's doing so itself, or does civil society consist of an assortment of efforts by citizens to band together in pursuit of mutual aims and goods as they understand them? Is it an extension of the state or of the community?
>
> (Levin 2012)

Levin regards the potential pressure on institutional religious autonomy as "perhaps the gravest threat to freedom in American life today" (2012; cf. Sherratt 2012). It is not without reason that Secretary-General Ban Ki-moon of the United Nations called civil society "the oxygen of democracy" (UN News Centre 2015; see also World Movement for Democracy 2012).

The "New Critics of Religious Freedom"

Before I left for Princeton I already had the sense that, as the United Nations Special Rapporteur on freedom of religion or belief Heiner Bielefeldt noted, religious freedom was globally becoming "a human right under pressure" (2012). Political scientist Allen D. Hertzke, the editor of a recent volume on the future of the right to freedom of religion or belief, speaks about "a profound paradox of our age," in the sense that "at the very time that the value of religious freedom is mounting, the international consensus behind it is weakening. . . . Indeed we see not only widespread violations around the world, but looming threats in the West that jeopardize previous gains" (2013: 3).

Still, the thing that without doubt has struck me most during my fellowship is how relatively fast and comprehensively the right to freedom of religion or belief has indeed already come under pressure across the West, at least in theory. It is true that in my home country, the Netherlands, a debate already arose a decade ago on whether to continue guaranteeing, or instead abolish, this right (Ooijen *et al.* 2008). Also more generally in Europe, respect for this fundamental right appears to have been eroding for quite some time, certainly in some of the courts (Trigg 2013). In the meantime, however, also in the United States, which can globally still be considered to be one of the main advocates of religious freedom (Su 2016), the traditional consensus concerning the significance of this right has weakened if not disappeared altogether. As one author put it,

> [f]or the first time in nearly 300 years, important forces in American society are questioning the free exercise of religion in principle—suggesting that free exercise of religion may be a bad idea, or at least, a right to be minimized.
> (Laycock 2011: 407; see also Reno 2014; Smith 2014; Tushnet 2015)

It is difficult to give a single and clear-cut explanation for this. One important factor is without doubt the political polarization that has come to be associated with religious freedom. Thus, Democrats blame Republicans for claiming a near-monopoly with respect to the right to freedom of religion or belief, thereby interpreting it in a conservative manner when it comes to topics such as same-sex marriage. On their part, as they themselves would be the first to admit, the Obama administration has not always dealt in a sensitive manner with issues regarding the inclusion of abortion and anticonception in the healthcare legislation it has introduced.

In academic circles, the "new critics of religious freedom" is a term which refers to a group of legal and other scholars that criticizes the right to freedom of religion or belief as such (Philpott 2014: 4; 2016; Philpott and Shah 2016). Obviously, it is possible, and indeed common, for academics to be critical about specific interpretations and applications of the right in particular cases. In this sense, I also consider myself a critic of the right to freedom of religion or belief as, later on in the book, I will argue that the liberal individualist paradigm that one can sometimes see at work in the case law of, for example, the U.S. Supreme Court, can easily place pressure on communal religious freedom.

The criticisms by the new critics go much further, in that they question virtually all elements of the phrase "the right to freedom of religion or belief." Thus, a *first question* they ask is whether a right is a suitable way to protect religious freedom. The notion of rights is, of course, one of the pillars on which Western liberal constitutional orders are based. Globally, however, other types of constitutionalism can be discerned, which cannot necessarily accommodate the notion of rights so easily (Thio 2012). Also questioned is the idea that by attempting to guarantee religious freedom by means of a right, freedom is actually enhanced. To the extent that the protection of a liberal-style right is biased in a particular way, one's religious freedom can actually be limited rather than enlarged.

In fact, according to the new critics of religious freedom, there is reason to believe that the protection that the right to freedom of religion or belief provides is biased. This is because they regard the concept of religion itself as a Western invention. As a result, the concept is heavily influenced by, for example, Christian theology. Therefore, to the extent that the right aims at providing equal protection to believers, this is only possible within the terms of this framework. If Judaism, for example, is based on ethnicity, rather than a universalist religion such as

Christianity, legal protection of the religious rights of Jews is likely to be negatively influenced.

Finally, the idea of religion as a belief is perhaps what causes the bias in the first place. This is seen as a Christian, and more particularly a protestant, bias. Protestant is usually written with a small "p" in this context, so as to stress that the term is not used in a narrow denominational sense. Still, the reference to Protestantism is clear. In the process, Protestantism is depicted as a largely individual and private type of religion, which is focused on doctrine rather than practice. The same is said to apply to Christianity as a whole, when looked at from a comparative point of view. In this view, it is Christianity which is largely responsible for the distinction between a public and a private sphere, with "belief" being relegated to the latter (e.g. Sullivan 2005; Sullivan, Shakman Hurd, Mahmood, and Danchin 2015; Petty 2016).

The adjective "new" in "new critics of religious freedom" is a reference to the fact that there have been earlier critics of the right to freedom of religion or belief as such. These past critics of religious freedom were generally conservative in outlook. Thus, the Roman Catholic Church had not wholeheartedly embraced the idea of there being such a thing as religious freedom until the Second Vatican Council in the 1960s. Before then, the Church was critical of liberal democracy in general and the right to freedom of religion or belief in particular, because of the relativism that was believed to be at the heart of both. This was also the position of other, for example orthodox Protestant, churches. The new critics of religious freedom, on the contrary, appear to be mostly progressives who now might well believe religious freedom to have been an idea of conservative origins in the first place.

Of course, the new critics of religious freedom do not all contend exactly the same things, and in fact there are notable differences between them. As we have seen, however, what the critics do have in common is that they criticize the right to freedom of religion or belief as such. Their criticisms are therefore minimally of interest to human rights scholars in general and specialists in religious freedom in particular. Yet sometimes the implications of the criticisms, or of secularism more generally, for liberal democracy as a whole are also spelled out (see e.g. Rosenfeld and Mancini 2013; Cohen and Laborde 2015). Secularism, among other things, refers "to different normative-ideological state projects, as well as to different legal-constitutional frameworks of separation of state and religion and to different models of differentiation of religion, ethics, morality, and law" (Casanova 2011: 66). It is here that the topic takes on an even broader relevance and becomes also of interest to constitutional lawyers and political scientists more generally. Whereas the criticisms referred to above hold that the protection which the right to freedom of religion or belief provides is too limited, in the West religious freedom is arguably currently granted too much protection according to this latter line of thought.

Thus, one of the questions raised is whether recent case law in the United States has witnessed the resurgence of an almost medieval, "jurisdictional," approach to the right to freedom of religion or belief. Characteristic of this approach is that, besides the obvious sovereignty claim of today's national states, other—more controversial—sovereignty claims by religious associations, groups, and institutions are increasingly being acknowledged. The latter sovereignty claims are regarded by their critics as being incompatible with the idea of state sovereignty being the only legitimate source of sovereignty in society. Thus, it is presented as though a clear choice will have to be made between the jurisdictional approach to religious freedom and the view that sees sovereignty within the liberal democratic state as essentially monistic in nature (Cohen 2015).

In a similar vein, it is sometimes considered "sectarian" to grant special protection to religion or comparable beliefs at all. One way the right to freedom of religion or belief could be made more inclusive is by transforming it into, for example, a general right to ethical integrity (Laborde 2015). Another option, as we saw already, is to abolish the right to freedom of religion or belief altogether and henceforth deal with religious rights in the context of, for example, the freedoms of expression and assembly and association.

The points made by the new critics of religious freedom raise a *second question* which has given rise to the current book, in addition to the question of to what extent in Europe and North America the communal dimension of religious freedom continues to be protected. This second question is whether the recognition that there are multiple sources of sovereignty in society can actually help to achieve legitimacy of the democratic constitutional order rather than putting its political legitimacy under pressure. Legitimacy is used here in the descriptive sense of "people's beliefs about political authority and, sometimes, political obligations" (Peter 2016). Whereas the first question is of an empirical nature, the second question is more normative. To the extent that the answer to the first question will, although provisionally, have to be in the affirmative, the second question obviously gains in weight.

Main Thesis and Synopsis of the Book

Although I rather fundamentally disagree with them, I am at the same time grateful to the new critics of religious freedom, some of whom I had the privilege of meeting personally during my year at Princeton. Perhaps unintentionally, they have provided at least some of the inspiration for this book and made it clear to me what its thesis would have to be: that no matter if one argues that the protection provided by the right to freedom of religion or belief is too wide or too limited, there is always more at stake than this right in itself—that is, constitutionalism and democracy (cf. Joustra 2016). Although it is obviously possible to disagree about concrete interpretations and applications of the right to freedom of religion or belief, to argue that the protection provided by this fundamental right is generally too limited suggests that religious freedom within the framework of a liberal democratic state has become an impossibility altogether. Similarly, to argue that the protection provided by the right to freedom of religion or belief is generally too wide because it puts the monopoly of the state on sovereignty under pressure, which is characteristic of a democratic constitutional order, is to question the political legitimacy of the same order. There are likely to be many members of Western societies who, for religious reasons, are unable to subscribe to the idea that all sovereignty is concentrated within the state and the worldly authorities which public law constitutes.

More specifically, the main thesis of the book is that no legitimate liberal democracy is feasible without there being the type of protection of religious freedom offered by the right to freedom of religion or belief as it has historically developed. In turn, a more classical understanding of the idea of a democratic constitutional state than many of the new critics of religious freedom appear to adhere to leads to a generous interpretation of in particular the associational and institutional dimensions of the right to freedom of religion or belief, in addition to its clearly also crucial individual aspects. The reason for the principled interconnectedness of these principles is that it is possible to argue that the purpose of all three—constitutionalism, democracy, and religious freedom—is ultimately to allow citizens to become "fully human."

"To be fully human" is a quotation from Professor Emeritus in Christian Ethics at the North-West University (Potchefstroomcampus) Koos Vorster. The full quotation reads as follows:

> The attitude of the Christian towards other religions can be served best where room is created for all to be fully human in the public and private spheres. To be fully human means to cradle the spirituality of one's religion and to build one's life on the foundation that the religion offers.
>
> (2010: 179)

As is clear from this quotation, Vorster indeed takes for granted the arguably Christian idea of, for example, the separation of a public and a private sphere, yet believes that this still can be beneficial to "other religions" as well. Equally, although Vorster addresses primarily his fellow Christians in this instance, the notion that it is important with a view to human flourishing to make room for all to build their lives on the foundation of their religious—or other—worldviews is also one that can be adhered to more generally by many faiths.

The book is divided into four chapters and a conclusion. Chapter 1 analyses what three relatively recent actual court cases—one from Europe, one from the United States, and one from Canada—can teach us about how the right to freedom of religion or belief, and in particular its associational and institutional dimensions, is currently being interpreted and applied. Is the protection that religious freedom is granted indeed too broad, or is it perhaps the case that also in the case law the right to freedom of religion or belief is gradually coming under pressure? It will be concluded that, although at first sight the various high court rulings seem to suggest otherwise, the cup of religious freedom is indeed gradually becoming half empty rather than half full.

An obvious explanation that has remained unmentioned thus far is the change in religious convictions taking place among, for example, the American population. Changes in the religious maps of Europe and North America cannot simply be equated with secularization. The concept of secularization "usually refers to actual or alleged empirical-historical patterns of transformation and differentiation of 'the religious' (ecclesiastical institutions and churches) and 'the secular' (state, economy, science, art, entertainment, health, welfare, etc.) institutional spheres from early-modern to contemporary societies" (Casanova 2011: 54). However, as sociologist of religion José Casanova has pointed out, secularization is also sometimes held to comprise "the progressive decline of religious beliefs and practices as a concomitant of levels of modernization" as well as the "privatization of religion as a precondition of modern secular and democratic politics" (2011: 60; see also Casanova 1994). According to the so-called theory of secularization, developed within the social sciences, all three processes have inevitably progressed during the past couple of centuries up to the point that, at least in the West, we have now entered a "secular age." Canadian philosopher Charles Taylor describes this change as "one which takes us from a society in which it was virtually impossible not to believe in God, to one in which faith, even for the staunchest believer, is one human possibility among others" (2007: 3).

On the contrary: what, according to at least some literature, seems to emerge is rather a postsecular constellation. As German philosopher Jürgen Habermas points out, it really only makes sense to apply this term to societies which since at least the Second World War have become relatively secularized also in the second and third meanings of the term as distinguished by Casanova, such as various Western European countries and Canada, not so much with respect to the United States. In the former countries, religion then arguably "maintains a public influence and relevance, while the secularistic certainty that religion will disappear worldwide in the course of modernization is losing ground" (2008: 21). In the context of this book the term postsecular is, in addition, used to indicate that there are not just more secular people in society, but that there is also more diversity among the equally significant part of the population that remains religious or spiritual (cf. Commission on Religion and Belief in British Public Life 2015: 6). Some authors even hold that it makes more sense to do away with the religion/secular divide altogether, as the question is not so much whether but *how* people are religious (Paul 2014).

The notion of a postsecular society is without doubt a valuable perspective, as it draws attention to the fact that historically religion has proved to be a lasting characteristic of the human condition. This does not exclude the possibility, however, that when looking specifically at developments in the West in recent decades, first of all a process of secularization can be discerned. This has recently also come to include the United States, although still maybe not to the extent that is the case in certain European countries such as the United Kingdom (Bagehot 2016). As a result, the renegotiations that are taking place between in particular Christian organizations and the state are rather of a defensive nature. A religion which in many countries used to enjoy a majority status now has to slowly but steadily become accustomed to being in the minority (Bottum 2014). For Islam the story is different, as in many instances it is for the first time negotiating a status for its followers, next to religions which in the West are more established.

One advantage of there being a right to freedom of religion or belief is, however, that it ought not to make much difference whether a religion enjoys a majority status or is in the minority. Of course, in practice both legislation and case law can become influenced themselves by the majority religion, as has in the past without doubt been the case with Christianity in the West. Similarly, a (developing) secular majority will be able to legitimately influence legislation and case law in its own way. Still, to the extent that religious freedom is a fundamental right and even, as some hold, a natural right preceding the state, the various renegotiations between Christian organizations and the state should not be as comprehensive as otherwise might have been the case. Also, a more recently established religion such as Islam should be able to enjoy basic protection of its associational and institutional religious rights under a secular majority as well.

Some of the criticisms voiced by the new critics of religious freedom without doubt contain a considerable amount of truth, such as that the concept of religion employed by courts in the West is not as "transhistorical and transcultural" as is sometimes tacitly assumed (Petty 2016: 15), but instead is heavily influenced by Christianity (Trigg 2010: 18). It would indeed be quite a sensation to somehow discover that the legal conception of religion in the West had not been influenced by Christianity. As will be argued in Chapter 2, a close relationship exists also more generally between classical liberal principles for the constitutional order and theological notions such as original sin, the separation of church and state, conscience protection, and the fundamental equality of all human beings before God.

Partly under the influence of the social and cultural revolution of the 1960s, however, liberalism has arguably developed from a means of managing diversity in the direction of an ideological agenda of its own. In a postsecular society a more limited type of government thus appears to be required once again, in order for it to remain legitimate. Such so-called social pluralist constitutionalism extends the idea of the separation of powers from the statal powers to non-state actors. The purpose of the doctrine of the separation of powers is to prevent tyranny. However, especially now that the state has grown so much bigger, a type of separation of powers between the state powers only may no longer suffice. It will be argued that certain (theoretical) developments taking place in the area of transnational constitutionalism can lead the way with respect to the—in this view—desired existence of multiple sources of sovereignty in society.

Contrary to what legal and political theorist Jean L. Cohen and others suggest, it will indeed be argued in Chapter 2 that the debate on where the ultimate source of sovereignty lies has historically never been answered by Western democracies. What is more, liberal democracy is not even able to legitimately settle this issue in an unequivocal manner given its own principles, such as the right to freedom of religion or belief. Thus, the individual dimension of this right actually creates a solid foundation for the associational and institutional dimension of the same right. Institutional religious autonomy is, in turn, foundational for the notion of limited government and as such for liberal democracy as a whole. Of course, it remains the case that "[n]o private group residing in a liberal democracy enjoys sovereign immunity from the actions of government, even for its internal affairs.

Given a sufficiently important reason, government can and does intervene in 'internal' religious group matters" (Gedicks 2013: 17).

Expanding upon the line of thought developed in Chapter 2, Chapter 3 argues how in our present time, in which Western societies, despite a clear degree of secularization, have at the same time become perhaps more divided than ever, according to social pluralist thought a democracy needs to be characterized by a generally accessible and as a result truly pluralistic public square. As Aristoteles once taught, the essence of politics consists in ethical debate about what constitutes "the good life." The Achilles heel of liberal democracy is that by itself it is not able to formulate an answer to this question, and because of the lack of substantial public and parliamentary debate on the matter has become largely dysfunctional. To the extent that there is still substantial public and parliamentary debate, this tends to focus on issues such as the economy and security. Also, paradoxically, there appears to be less tolerance of views that do not belong to the—new—mainstream than there used to be even some 20 years ago (Mansvelt Beck 2015).

A resurrection of democracy, to borrow the phrase from theological ethicist Luke Bretherton (2015), is not feasible without generous protection of (also) the more associational and institutional dimensions of the right to freedom of religion or belief, however (Van den Brink and Ten Napel 2013; Ten Napel and Van den Brink 2014). It is submitted that precisely within faith and other communities mature visions of the good life can develop, which simultaneously contribute to the notion of the common good. At first sight, there is a contradiction between the notion of a truly pluralistic public square and the desire that several minorities feel that they also contribute to the common good. This tension can be resolved to the extent that the said faith and indeed other communities also teach that good citizenship implies the idea of liberal democracy as a moral engagement. The more citizens look at the political decision-making process in this way, the more they will respect the vital interests of others. Moral engagement also makes it possible to translate differing visions of the good life into the pursuit of policies that are in the interest of all.

As will be set out in Chapter 3, several thinkers who believe in the need to translate the pluralism in society into a truly "equal political voice liberalism" (Wolterstorff 2012) accord much weight in particular to the freedoms of assembly and association. In order for different voices to be heard, there is a need for places where people can find their voice, even if this implies that some of these ideas will not be in conformity with the majority opinions in society. In such cases, it is furthermore required to be reluctant to interfere in the internal affairs of religious and other associations. At first sight this may seem to imply that the new critics of religious freedom are also right when they argue that the protection provided by more general political rights—such as those of speech, press and assembly—suffices. It is submitted, however, that in these cases the more general political rights and communal religious freedom can complement and strengthen one another (Inazu 2014).

Crucially, however, at the same time boundaries will need to be set in order to keep the public square indeed generally accessible and pluralistic and thus to maintain the foundations of a pluriform democracy. As Chapter 3 will argue, however, these boundaries are markedly different from those advocated by adherents of the currently still dominant, yet arguably by and large worn-out, concept of a public reason. The difference is that, in the case of an equal political voice liberalism, the boundaries are confined to existing constitutional limits, notably those set by classical fundamental rights. In the case of public reason liberalism, additional limits are added on top of these, which according to the critics make it next to impossible for various minorities to join the conversation, with the result that they will opt out instead of joining in.

Chapter 4 goes on to outline the implications of a return to a more limited form of government and the development towards a truly pluriform democracy for the associational and institutional dimensions of the right to freedom of religion or belief in particular. In so far as both democratic constitutionalism in general and the right to freedom of religion or belief in particular aim at enabling citizens to become "fully human," as we have seen, it is clear that a generous interpretation of this right is advisable in order to achieve or maintain legitimacy. In their interpretation of the right to freedom of religion or belief, courts and legislatures sometimes tend to narrow it down to its individual dimension.

Still, there is not really the need for a radically new theory of this right. This is because the associational and institutional aspects of religious freedom have traditionally constituted an integral part of the right to freedom of religion or belief, and it is perfectly possible to build on this legacy in a manner that is both pragmatic and principled. It may be the case that, this way, both democratic constitutionalism in general and the right to freedom of religion or belief in particular retain a distinctly Western and even Christian character. It is submitted that this should be regarded as an asset rather than a weakness that needs to be done away with as thoroughly as possible for the sake of "true" religious freedom, however. The fact that an idea has originated in a particular cultural or religious context does not imply that it cannot serve the interests of people in different parts of the world or belonging to other faiths or no faith.

It may sound rather pragmatic not to begin the search for a radically new theory of the right to freedom of religion or belief for our present time. Paradoxically, however, in the light of some of the criticisms of the right to freedom of religion or belief currently voiced, it almost becomes as radical to suggest that a gradual further development—and indeed improvement—of existing practice with regard to the interpretation and application of this universal fundamental right is to be preferred over a new beginning. It remains difficult to see, moreover, how a political order could maintain its legitimacy for long by legally ignoring the deepest convictions of at least sections of the population.

The Conclusion will wrap up the argument of the book. Of course, the position of religious and other minorities in the increasingly secular, majoritarian contexts of Western liberal democracies cannot be safeguarded by the associational and institutional dimensions of the right to freedom of religion or belief alone. In addition, a particular type of constitutional design in the broadest sense of the term may be needed, which is suitable for the present-day perhaps predominantly secular, but at the same time still religiously and otherwise divided, societies (Choudhry 2008). This book, however, focuses on the idea that, in such a post-secular context, modern sources of constitutionalism and democracy, supplemented by a touch of premodern, transcendental legitimation, might well continue to provide the best means of legitimating Western political orders. It may not sound very democratic, or even academic, to suggest that some form of transcendence might even in modern times remain of relevance to a political order. Still, the fact that to some the right to freedom of religion or belief can be regarded as a natural right preceding the state proves that there is already a transcendental dimension at work regarding human rights and its underlying notion of human dignity. After all, according to the United States Declaration of Independence, "[w]e hold these truths to be self-evident, that all men are created equal, that they are endowed by their Creator with certain unalienable Rights, that among these are Life, Liberty and the pursuit of Happiness" (Emon, Levering, and Novak 2014; Holzer 2015; Muňoz 2016).

Gratitude for what has historically grown is perhaps more generally the most effective answer to the skepticism that a postsecular age can also give rise to. A reorientation of liberal democracy towards the common good is one main contribution that world religions such as Christianity, Islam, and Judaism can help achieve in an otherwise religiously violent world (Volf 2016). The constitutional significance of in particular the associational and institutional dimensions of the right to freedom of religion or belief is that they facilitate this contribution. To put into question the possibility to realize this right is to doubt whether liberal democracy itself is possible. Or so it will be argued in what follows.

Approach

As will already have become clear from the above, the book applies an interdisciplinary method, by combining insights from (comparative) constitutional law and political science on the one hand with elements of other disciplines, notably ethics and theology, on the other hand. As has rightly been argued,

> [t]heologians have been trained in a deep history of thought about the nature of our life with and without God. It is possible to disagree with their perspectives on our society, and they certainly disagree with each other. But we dare not dismiss the depth of their thinking by assuming religion is no longer a significant player in our life together.
>
> (Barnes 2016; cf. Storrar 2007; Skeel 2008)

To do so is very much in line with, and indeed inspired by, the "fresh" approach to the issue of law and religious freedom which CTI has pursued during the academic year 2014–2015. It should be noted, however, that the current book will engage these other disciplines in an indirect manner only—that is, in so far as ethics and theology are necessary to develop and apply the social pluralist framework which the study uses and will be set out below. Each time I have been involved in interdisciplinary endeavors, I have—after the initial excitement—also experienced how difficult it is to actually translate the original ambitions and intentions into convincing results. It is for this reason that, although some will perhaps not even think this is worth calling interdisciplinary research, I consider a combining of insights from different disciplines already quite useful. In any case, I have found that some of the most worthwhile books on liberal democracy that have been published in recent years have been authored, for example, by ethicists and philosophers.

Such an interdisciplinary method also fits in well with what leading scholars in the field of comparative constitutional law, such as Armin von Bogdandy (2012) and Ran Hirschl (2014), in recent years have been pleading for, although they have largely restricted themselves to pointing out the relevance to law of history and the (other) social sciences. These authors have argued that the discipline of constitutional law ought to become more comparative, more theoretical, and more interdisciplinary in character. It is certainly the case that, because of this, the field of constitutional law has become much more interesting and lively since the founding of the *International Journal of Constitutional Law* some 15 years ago, to mention just one milestone (cf. DeGirolami 2015). Apart from making an interdisciplinary effort, the book is also theoretical in that its aim is not to offer a comprehensive overview of the latest case law regarding the right to freedom of religion or belief, but rather to develop a theoretical framework with the help of which developments in this area can be meaningfully interpreted and evaluated.

Finally, an interdisciplinary effort like this is, according to at least one observer, really only the very minimum of what would be needed in order to restore at least something of the previously existing intellectual and societal consensus regarding the significance of the right to freedom of religion or belief for liberal democracy—that is:

> a broad-based, multidisciplinary effort, comprised of many scholars and policy experts, many universities, and many research centers, both in the United States and abroad. It must involve economists, sociologists, psychologists, and anthropologists alongside philosophers, theologians, political theorists, policy makers, and, ultimately, the general public.
>
> (Farr 2012: 49)

As the same observer has noted, "[t]he stakes are high. They implicate human dignity, social harmony, political stability, economic growth, and world peace" (ibid.). The idea that ultimately what is at stake in debates regarding religious freedom is peace, both societal and international peace, can also be found in the preambles of various human rights declarations and treaties. What is more, as Professor Emeritus of the Practice in Religion, Ethnicity, and International Conflict at Harvard Divinity School David Little has pointed out, "[t]here is strong empirical support for the proposition that human rights compliance in general, and religious freedom compliance in particular, increase the prospects for peace" (2015: 4). This is known as the idea of a "Liberal Peace."

In addition to its principally interdisciplinary nature, the approach of at least some scholars at CTI has in the past been characterized by making explicit the philosophical background of one's writings, not just as a matter of academic integrity (everyone who looks at the fundamental questions of our constitutional and democratic order will bring their own set of convictions to the table, even—or maybe in particular—when these are "secular") (cf. Sandel 2014) but also in the hope and trust that precisely by doing so the dialogue with researchers who start from different theoretical frameworks will be facilitated instead of complicated (Waldron 2011: 7–13). The ensuing discussion might well bring the solution of the problems involved a step further, more so than when the participants in this discussion were forced to keep their deepest convictions hidden from their conversation partners.

In this sense an interesting parallel can be discerned between academia and the democratic process. In both cases it is considered politically correct to stick to "neutral" and "reasonable" arguments and positions (e.g. Espinoza and Rayner 2015). Just as it will be argued in this book that the notion of public reason actually contributes to the dysfunction of our political system, the same might hold true for academic debate. It is only when students and their teachers are provided with the opportunity to make explicit the background suppositions behind their theoretical frameworks that a real understanding and a real debate can begin. If academics are required to limit themselves to "neutral" arguments, any debate that nevertheless will take place runs the risk of remaining superficial. Apart from this paradoxically being a matter of academic integrity more generally, although many will disagree, getting to know students and other fellow academics better in this sense is often a precondition to further knowledge and understanding.

In light of the above, the book is not just meant for readers who could be expected to sympathize with some or all of the theoretical starting points set out here, but also as a modest invitation precisely to dissenters to engage in a "respectful academic conversation" similar to what Founding Director of the Center for Christian Studies at Gordon College (now the Center for Faith and Inquiry) Harold Heie calls a "respectful political conversation" (2014). Should this not, or no longer, be possible, then it will also prove difficult to uphold the ideal of a pluralistic public square as part of one's democracy conception, as advocated in what follows. To the extent that I have had the opportunity to put this model into practice myself, it was in academic settings such as academic conferences. Although it admittedly sometimes turned out to be difficult there as well, I have nevertheless concluded that it is worthwhile to stick to the ideal even in the undoubtedly still more difficult circumstances of practical politics.

Thus, a central tenet of the book is that both the questions surrounding the right to freedom of religion or belief and those surrounding constitutionalism and democracy can generally best be addressed by seeking guidance from the theory of social pluralism. At least three views of social pluralism can be distinguished: what could be called an argument from history (Edmund Burke, Guillaume Groen van Prinsterer, Otto von Gierke, John Neville Figgis); the recent Catholic tradition (Pope Leo XIII, Pope Pius XI, Jacques Maritain, Bishops of the Second

Vatican Council); and progressive Calvinism (Abraham Kuyper, Herman Dooyeweerd, H. Evan Runner, Bernard J. Zylstra). So much has been written on each of these three strands of social pluralist theory that there is no need to elaborate on the theory more than is strictly necessary in view of the argument of this book. The reader who would like to learn more about the theory itself can refer to more specialist literature such as the volume by political scientists James W. Skillen and Rockne M. McCarthy from which the above categorization stems in the first place (1991).

May it suffice to note here that a major starting point for the latter view of social pluralism, better known as neo-Calvinism, is the doctrines of associational and directional pluralism, which will be set out in Chapter 3. It is these doctrines which lie at the basis of the conception of a pluriform democracy as referred to above. The doctrines of associational and directional pluralism are regarded by their adherents as relevant to all cultures and all times, because they are believed to correspond "with the way things really are in terms of God and the nature of human being" (Heslam 2002: 26). As Skillen (2000: 368) puts it:

> Kuyper's way of seeking to discover and honor the integrity of creation's diversity illuminates one of the central social challenges people will always face in all parts of the world. . . . If individualism, collectivism, and secularism are all misleading in one direction or another, then the need for a God-centered, pluralist social vision will remain strong throughout the world.

These may at first sight appear to be strong statements. However, it is quite possible to come across similar claims and statements in the case of, for example, liberal theory. It has increasingly come to surprise me how it is considered perfectly acceptable to prescribe literature on such liberal theory and its internal debates, whereas even referring to other strands of thought such as social pluralist theory may easily be regarded as sectarian or even not fully appropriate in an academic context. Yet, just as it is probably not wise to exclude religious arguments from the public and political debate, there is no apparent reason why, for example, religious forms of constitutionalism should be ignored in academia. In fact, "the larger conversation of contemporary constitutional theory can only be deepened and clarified by treating them as legitimately within its domain" (Dane 2015: 476).

Interestingly, Catholic social teaching's recently more positive attitude towards democratic constitutionalism remains slightly more conditional than that of neo-Calvinism and by no means can be taken as an all-out acceptance of its (Enlightenment) liberal presuppositions. Thus, the handbook of this second view of social pluralism identified earlier, the *Compendium of the Social Doctrine of the Church*, "values" democracy (Pontifical Council for Justice and Peace 2005: 406). It adds (407), however, that

> an authentic democracy is not merely the result of a formal observation of a set of rules but is the fruit of a convinced acceptance of the values that inspire

> democratic procedures: the dignity of every human person, the respect of human rights, commitment to the common good as the purpose and guiding criterion for political life. If there is no general consensus on these values, the deepest meaning of democracy is lost and its stability is compromised.

As a result, this tradition can well serve to help formulate the boundaries that are needed to maintain the accessibility and the pluralistic nature of the public square.

Another contribution that the recent Catholic tradition can make to current debates on constitutionalism and democracy has to do with the notion of the common good which we came across earlier as well. Of the three strands of social pluralist theory, the notion of the common good is perhaps best developed within Catholic social teaching. It is certainly more developed here than within neo-Calvinism, which has a more individualist tendency, although generally the differences between neo-Calvinism and Catholic social teaching should no longer be exaggerated either. As has rightly been remarked in this connection:

> [U]nder contemporary sociological conditions, the Augustinian philosophical wellspring is likely to yield more than the Thomist one. . . . Augustine's late classical world was highly pluralistic: paganism, Donatism, Pelagianism, and Arianism all vied with Catholicism on the battlefield of ideas, and sometimes on the actual battlefield as well. In sharp contrast, Thomas' late medieval world was characterized by an ambient Catholic public culture that provided a common constellation of political languages, concepts, and frames.
>
> (Latham 2013)

Given the relative prominence of these first two traditions within social pluralist theory, one could of course wonder which consequences the apparent decay of at least organized Christianity in the West will have for the prospects of social pluralist constitutionalism and pluriform democracy. The current book project could easily be—and indeed has occasionally already been—almost written off as a pervasively sectarian undertaking, which will not succeed in reaching the audiences to which it is geared in the first place. This book will argue, however, that there is "a pessimistic case for hope" in this respect (Levin 2014). Among other things, this hope stems from the existing links between the neo-Calvinist and recent Catholic views on social pluralism and the first, more general strand of social pluralist theory identified above—that is, the argument from history or Conservatism. In the course of my year in the United States I became increasingly convinced of both the relevance and the vitality of the Conservative tradition. Obviously, it helped that in the United States the tradition appeared to be much more alive intellectually than back home in Europe, let alone in the Netherlands where it remains something of a taboo word. Of course, for example, Edmund Burke's natural law-based constitutionalism "is both consonant with, and indebted to, a series of Christian theological convictions" (Burgess 2016; cf. Kirk 2002; Regnery 2012).

It equally helped to find authors who specifically had attempted to apply Conservative thought to questions of religious freedom and the state. Thus, it has been argued that

> to be "conservative" is at least and among other things to join Burke in rejecting Rousseau's assertions that "a democratic society should be one in which absolutely nothing stands between man and the state" and that non-state authorities and associations should be proscribed. . . . [N]ear the heart of anything called "conservatism"—of any temperament, worldview, or set of ideas that stands opposite or reacts against the French Revolution—should be an appreciation for the place and role of non-state authorities in promoting the common good and the flourishing of persons and a commitment to religious freedom for individuals and institutions alike, secured in part through constitutional limits on the powers of political authorities.
>
> (Garnett 2016: 164)

When applied in a contemporary manner to problems such as those dealt with in this book, the tradition might well continue to be able to make an important contribution, in addition to other intellectual traditions. Moreover, there is no reason why it would not have the potential to appeal also to younger generations, including so-called "nones" who no longer consider themselves to be adherents of an organized religion, yet remain "spiritual" (Ingraham 2016). They might well feel attracted to a Culture War 2.0, which aims at reviving the culture in at least four ways:

> We need to be more communal in an age that's overly individualistic; we need to be more morally minded in an age that's overly utilitarian; we need to be more spiritually literate in an age that's overly materialistic; and we need to be more emotionally intelligent in an age that is overly cognitive.
>
> (Brooks 2016)

It is important to note, however, that, despite its clear affinity with Conservatism, social pluralism is not a theory for, say, rural Pennsylvania and populations such as the Amish only. Nor is it something of the past. Not long ago, for example, neo-Calvinism was listed by *Time* as one of "10 Ideas Changing the World Right Now" (Van Biema 2009). To the extent that I had a particular location in mind while writing this book, it was New York City. At just a one-hour train ride away from Princeton, the "greatest city on earth" occasionally formed a welcome and highly inspirational escape from the sometimes rather too peaceful and quiet Princeton campus during the year in which I worked there. Obviously, New York City has its own fair share of problems and there is no reason to idealize life in the city, or in the United States for that matter, whatsoever. Still, to my mind, there is no better test case for social pluralist theory than this diverse place. If it can make it there, it can make it anywhere, so to say. And that it has at least the potential to make it in New York City is demonstrated, for example, by the approach of Mayor De Blasio, a progressive liberal (Grynbaum and Otterman 2015).

There is an increasing academic fascination with cities, both in theology and law and political science, and rightly so. The reason for this lies without doubt in part in the prognosis that, globally, during the twenty-first century ever more people will be living in cities. As a result, the urge is felt to develop a theology for the city, with the help of which urban populations can be reached. An example is provided by the ministry of Tim Keller in New York City. His Redeemer Presbyterian Church, which celebrated its 25th anniversary in 2014 and can already in many ways be regarded as a success story, recently adopted an even more ambitious plan to reach a still larger part of the population of Manhattan. Also more in general, New York City can, contrary to what many people would expect, best be characterized as a religiously vibrant place (Bradley 2015; Roberts 2016). In political science, attention is paid to the increasing importance of cities in terms of governance. It almost seems as though cities are taking over the role previously played by national states—for example, when it comes to foreign policy (Daalder 2015).

Academically speaking, the infusion of ethical and theological insights can contribute to the so-called neo-institutionalism gaining more ground within the legal discipline as well. Institutionalism is a well-known school of thought within political science which, in part as a reaction to behavioralism, emphasizes the importance of both traditional and newer institutions. The legal neo-institutionalism does not imply full-blown pluralism, and its accompanying incommensurability of authority, but rather a weaker form of pluralism called subsidiarity (Muniz-Fraticelli 2014: chapter 3). Still, the more "the institutional turn" would be taken, the more, for example, a tendency should also become discernible, as one author recently put it, to "treat . . . religious entities as largely sovereign institutions, immunizing them from the application of civil rights laws and other statutes" (Horwitz 2013: 10). Subsidiarity is, of course, a governing concept which has its roots in social pluralist theory, notably its Catholic strand of thought.

What this means is that although within social pluralist theory there is certainly room for opinions such as Cohen's which emphasize the monistic character of sovereignty in the liberal democratic state as well, it clearly considers the jurisdictional approach to religious freedom to be at least equally legitimate and even plausible. The approach is thus also pluralist in the sense that it does not agree with Cohen that a choice will necessarily have to be made between these two approaches, but rather leaves the question of where the ultimate sovereignty is to be located within the liberal democratic state principally open. This can be called conservative, to the extent that, as was already noted above, historically this question has also not been "settled" once and for all—for example, during the American Revolution. On the contrary, the Founding Fathers differed significantly among each other on this topic.

Once again, this approach is not something which only Conservatives might agree with, however. For example, it also resembles in a sense the so-called minimalist interpretation theory advocated by legal scholar Cass Sunstein (2001), a progressive liberal. This theory holds that judges ought to stick as much as possible to the facts of the case and if possible avoid ruling on the deeper questions involved. More generally, the book will point to liberal pluralism as a plausible model to manage diversity also in a postsecular society (Galston 2002, 2005). It will also raise the question, in this context, if and to what extent social pluralist theory differs from liberal pluralism in a practical sense, although differences remain at the theoretical level. Former policy advisor to President Clinton and presidential candidates William A. Galston's alternative of political pluralism, for example,

> understands human life as consisting in a multiplicity of spheres, some overlapping, with distinct natures and/or inner norms. Each sphere enjoys a limited but real autonomy. It rejects any account of political community that creates a unidimensional hierarchical ordering among these spheres of life; rather, different forms of association and activity are complexly interrelated.
>
> (2004: 46–7)

What is more, although grounded at least in part in Christian theology, the approach is in a sense also remarkably similar to constitutional lawyer Asifa Quraishi-Landes's account of Islamic constitutionalism inspired by classical, premodern, Islamic regimes (2015). As colleague Perry Dane summarizes her account in his foreword to a symposium on religious constitutionalism, Islamic constitutionalism "is rooted in the pluralistic nature of *fiqh*—the necessarily human, imperfect, and widely diverse interpretation of Shariah." This characteristic idea of legal pluralism then leads to what Quraishi-Landes calls "a fundamental constitutional bifurcation":

> On one side of that divide is a community of communities, a collection of thick normative jurisdictions, each adhering to one of the various schools of *fiqh* or—crucially—to one or another non-Muslim faith. These communities would govern most of the details of life, individual conduct, and terms of social co-existence comprehensively governed by a religion of law. But they would also be volunteeristic. On the other side of the bifurcation is a much thinner, democratically-governed, state apparatus devoted, not to religious hermeneutics, but to *siyasa*, the pragmatic pursuit of the public good. (The central government would also—an important detail—craft its own set of rich but secular rules as a default option for anyone unwilling to commit to one of the volunteeristic schools of interpretation.) That state apparatus, in turn, would be subject to a further constitutional check, grounded in the fundamental purposes of Shariah to guarantee the common good broadly understood.
>
> (Dane 2015: 471)

Whether one agrees with such proposals or not, it seems difficult to deny

> the importance of engaging in an ongoing and open conversation about how to organize constitutional theories and actual states—whether religious or secular or some combination of the two—that can try to promote our highest and best aspirations as social beings while also respecting the divergent communities that any state will contain and treating each individual person justly and humanely.
>
> (477)

Bibliography

Bagehot (2016), "This Sceptic Isle," *The Economist*, August 13.

Barnes, M. Craig (2016), "The Missing Theologians," *The Christian Century*, July 8.

Bielefeldt, Heiner (2012), "Freedom of Religion or Belief—A Human Right under Pressure," *Oxford Journal of Law and Religion*, 1(1): 15–35.

Bogdandy, Armin von (2012), "National Legal Scholarship in the European Legal Area," *International Journal of Constitutional Law*, 10(3): 614–26.

Bottum, Joseph (2014), *An Anxious Age: The Post-Protestant Ethic and the Spirit of America* (Colorado Springs, CO: Image).

Bradley, Anthony (2015), "New York City is Post Secular and Highly Religious," *Acton Institute PowerBlog*, June 9.

Bretherton, Luke (2015), *Resurrecting Democracy: Faith, Citizenship, and the Politics of a Common Life* (Cambridge: Cambridge University Press).

Brink, Jaco van den and Hans-Martien ten Napel (2013), "The State, Civil Society and Religious Freedom," *Oxford Journal of Law and Religion*, 2(2): 354–70.

Brooks, David (2016), "Let's Have a Better Culture War," *The New York Times*, June 7.

Burgess, Samuel (2016), "Conservatism and Christianity: The Six Political Principles of Burkean Conservatism," The Kirby Laing Institute for Christian Ethics Working Papers, No. 2, April.

Calo, Zachary R. (2014), "Constructing the Secular: Law and Religion Jurisprudence in Europe and the United States," EUI Working Paper RSCAS 2014/94.

Casanova, José (1994), *Public Religions in the Modern World* (Chicago, IL: University of Chicago Press).

Casanova, José (2011), "The Secular, Secularizations, Secularisms," in: Craig Calhoun, Mark Juergensmeyer, and Jonathan VanAntwerpen (eds), *Rethinking Secularism* (Oxford: Oxford University Press) 54–74.

Choudhry, Sujit (ed.) (2008), *Constitutional Design for Divided Societies: Integration or Accommodation?* (Oxford: Oxford University Press).

Cohen, Jean L. (2015), "Freedom of Religion, Inc.: Whose Sovereignty?" *Netherlands Journal of Legal Philosophy*, 44(3): 169–210.

Cohen, Jean L. and Cécile Laborde (eds) (2015), *Religion, Secularism, and Constitutional Democracy* (New York, NY: Columbia University Press).

Commission on Religion and Belief in British Public Life (2015), "Living with Difference. Community, Diversity and the Common Good," Published by the Woolf Institute, Cambridge, December 7.

Daalder, Ivo (2015), "A New Global Order of Cities," *Financial Times*, May 26.

Dane, Perry (2015), "Foreword: On Religious Constitutionalism," *Rutgers Journal of Law and Religion*, 16(3): 460–77.

DeGirolami, Marc O. (2015), "The Ideological Fragmentation of Public Law," *Center for Law and Religion Forum*, January 12.

Emon, Anver M., Matthew Levering, and David Novak (2014), *Natural Law: A Jewish, Christian, and Islamic Trialogue* (Oxford: Oxford University Press).

Espinoza, Javier and Gordon Rayner (2015), "Politically Correct Universities 'Are Killing Free Speech,'" *The Telegraph*, December 18.

Farr, Thomas F. (2012), "Back to the Beginning: Rebuilding an Intellectual Consensus for Religious Freedom," *The Review of Faith & International Affairs*, 10(3): 43–50.

Galston, William A. (2002), *Liberal Pluralism: The Implications of Value Pluralism for Political Theory and Practice* (Cambridge: Cambridge University Press).

Galston, William (2004), "Religion and the Limits of Liberal Democracy," in: Douglas Farrow (ed.), *Recognizing Religion in a Secular Society. Essays in Pluralism, Religion, and Public Policy* (Montreal and Kingston, London, Ithaca, NY: McGill-Queen's University Press) 41–50.

Galston, William A. (2005), *The Practice of Liberal Pluralism* (Cambridge: Cambridge University Press).

Garnett, Richard W. (2016), "The Worms and the Octopus: Religious Freedom, Pluralism, and Conservatism," in: Sanford V. Levinson, Joel Parker, and Melissa S. Williams (eds), *American Conservatism*: NOMOS LVI (New York, NY: New York University Press) 160–96.

Gedicks, Frederick Mark (2013), "Religious Group Rights: Four Analytic Touchstones," in: Pasquale Annicchino (ed.), *Freedom of Religion or Belief in Foreign Policy: Which One?* (San Domenico di Fiesole: European University Institute) 15–20.

González, Francisco Colom and Gianni D'Amato (2017), *Multireligious Society: Dealing with Religious Diversity in Theory and Practice* (London and New York, NY: Routledge).

Grynbaum, Michael M. and Sharon Otterman (2015), "Mayor de Blasio Emerges as an Unexpected Champion of Religion," *The New York Times*, March 18.

Guesnet, François, Cécile Laborde, and Lois Lee (eds) (2017), *Negotiating Religion: Cross-Disciplinary Perspectives* (London and New York, NY: Routledge).

Habermas, Jürgen (2008), "Notes on Post-Secular Society," *New Perspectives Quarterly*, 25(4): 17–29.

Heie, Harold (2014), *Evangelicals on Public Policy Issues: Sustaining a Respectful Political Conversation* (Abilene, TX: Abilene Christian University Press).

Hertzke, Allen D. (2013), "Introduction. Advancing the First Freedom in the Twenty-First Century," in: Allen D. Hertzke (ed.), *The Future of Religious Freedom. Global Challenges* (Oxford: Oxford University Press) 3–27.

Heslam, Peter S. (2002), "Prophet of a Third Way: The Shape of Kuyper's Socio-Political Vision," *Journal of Markets and Morality*, 5(1): 11–33.

Hirschl, Ran (2014), *Comparative Matters: The Renaissance of Comparative Constitutional Law* (Oxford: Oxford University Press).

Holzer, Shannon (2015), "America Divided: Positive vs. Natural Law," *The Imaginative Conservative*, January 9.

Horwitz, Paul (2013), *First Amendment Institutions* (Cambridge, MA: Harvard University Press).

Inazu, John D. (2014), "The Four Freedoms and the Future of Religious Liberty," *North Carolina Law Review*, 92(3): 787–854.

Ingraham, Christopher (2016), "The Non-Religious Are Now the Country's Largest Religious Voting Bloc," *The Washington Post*, July 14.

Joustra, Robert (2016), "Is the Problem Really Religious Freedom?" *Arc of the Universe*, May 17.

Kirk, Russell (2002), "The Essence of Conservatism," Adapted from *The Intelligent Woman's Guide to Conservatism* (New York, NY: The Devin-Adair Company, 1957), available at www.kirkcenter.org/index.php/detail/essence-1957 (accessed November 24, 2016).

Kraybill, Donald B. (ed.) (2003a), *The Amish and the State* (Baltimore, MD, and London: Johns Hopkins University Press).

Kraybill, Donald B. (2003b), "Negotiating with Caesar," in: Donald B. Kraybill (ed.), *The Amish and the State* (Baltimore, MD, and London: Johns Hopkins University Press) 3–20.

Laborde, Cécile (2015), "Religion in the Law: The Disaggregation Approach," *Law and Philosophy*, 34(6): 581–600.

Langlaude-Doné, Sylvie (2016), "Religious Organisations, Internal Autonomy and Other Religious Rights before the European Court of Human Rights and the OSCE," *Netherlands Quarterly of Human Rights*, 34(1): 8–40.

Latham, Andrew A. (2013), "Pursuit of Felicitas," *First Things*, November.

Laycock, Douglas (2011), "McElroy Lecture. Sex, Atheism, and the Free Exercise of Religion," *University of Detroit Mercy Law Review*, 88(3): 407–32.

Levin, Yuval (2012), "Religious Liberty and Civil Society," *National Review Online*, January 30.

Levin, Yuval (2014), "A Pessimistic Case for Hope," *First Things*, September.

Lind, Anna-Sara, Mia Lövheim, and Ulf Zackariasson (eds) (2016), *Reconsidering Religion, Law, and Democracy: New Challenges for Society and Research* (Lund: Nordic Academic Press).

Little, David (2015), "Human Rights, Religious Freedom, and Peace," a lecture delivered at the opening session of the 22nd Annual Symposium on Religion and International Law, October 4, at the BYU Law School.

Mansvelt Beck, Floris (2015), *How We Do Things Here: Moral Communities, Integration, and Toleration in the Netherlands: Competing Interpretations of Liberalism in Parliamentary Practice, 2000–2013* (Leiden: Ph.D. Thesis).

Marty, Martin E. (2003), "Foreword," in: Donald B. Kraybill (ed.), *The Amish and the State* (Baltimore, MD, and London: Johns Hopkins University Press) ix–x.

Muniz-Fraticelli, Victor M. (2014), *The Structure of Pluralism* (Oxford: Oxford University Press).

Muñoz, Vincent Phillip (2016), "Two Concepts of Religious Liberty: The Natural Rights and Moral Autonomy Approaches to the Free Exercise of Religion," *American Political Science Review*, 110(2): 369–81.

Napel, Hans-Martien ten and Jaco van den Brink (2014), "Towards an Institution-Sensitive Religious Freedom Conception," in: Mary Ann Glendon and Alvira Rafael (eds), *Religion and Civil Society. The Changing Faces of Religion and Civil Society* (Religion and Civil Society No. 5; Hildesheim, Zurich, New York, NY: Georg Olms Verlag) 65–80.

Norton, Jane Calderwood (2016), *Freedom of Religious Organizations* (Oxford: Oxford University Press).

Ooijen, H.M.A.E. van, L.F. Egmond, Q.A.M. Eijkman, F. Olujić, O.P.G. Vos (eds) (2008), *Godsdienstvrijheid: afschaffen of beschermen?* (Leiden: Stichting NJCM-Boekerij).

Paul, Herman (2014), "Let's Do Away with the Religion/Secular Divide," *The Religion Factor*, July 31.

Peter, Fabienne (2016), "Political Legitimacy," *The Stanford Encyclopedia of Philosophy* (Summer 2016 Edition), Edward N. Zalta (ed.), forthcoming, available at http://plato.stanford.edu/archives/sum2016/entries/legitimacy (accessed November 24, 2016).

Petty, Aaron R. (2016), *The Legal Conception of "Religion"* (Leiden: Ph.D. Thesis).

Philpott, Daniel (2014), "In Defense of Religious Freedom," Presented at the Annual Meeting of the American Political Science Association, August 28.

Philpott, Daniel (2016), "Culture War or Common Heritage? On Recent Critics of Global Religious Freedom," *Lawfare*, June 30.

Philpott, Daniel and Timothy Samuel Shah (2016), "Engaging the 'New Critics' of Religious Freedom: A Review Essay," a lengthier and more annotated draft version of a review essay forthcoming in the *Journal of Law and Religion.*

Pontifical Council for Justice and Peace (2005), *Compendium of the Social Doctrine of the Church* (Washington, DC: USCCB Publishing).

Quraishi-Landes, Asifa (2015), "Islamic Constitutionalism: Not Secular, Not Theocratic, Not Impossible," *Rutgers Journal of Law and Religion*, 16(3): 553–79.

Regnery, Alfred S. (2012), "The Pillars of Modern American Conservatism," *The Intercollegiate Review*, Spring.

Reno, R.R. (2014), "Our Secular Future," *The National Catholic Review*, February 24.

Roberts, Kyle B. (2016), *Evangelical Gotham: Religion and the Making of New York City, 1783–1860* (Chicago, IL: University of Chicago Press).

Rosenfeld, Michel and Susanna Mancini (eds) (2013), *Constitutional Secularism in an Age of Religious Revival* (Oxford: Oxford University Press).

Sandel, Adam Adatto (2014), *The Place of Prejudice: A Case for Reasoning within the World* (Cambridge, MA: Harvard University Press).

Schwartzman, Micah, Chad Flanders, and Zoë Robinson (eds) (2016), *The Rise of Corporate Religious Liberty* (Oxford: Oxford University Press).

Scolnicov, Anat (2011), *The Right to Religious Freedom in International Law: Between Group Rights and Individual Rights* (London and New York, NY: Routledge).

Sherratt, Timothy (2012), "Civil Society after the Fall," *Capital Commentary*, May 4.

Skeel, Jr, David A. (2008), "The Unbearable Lightness of Christian Legal Scholarship," *Emory Law Journal*, 57(6): 1471–525.

Skillen, James W. (2000), "Why Kuyper Now?" in: Luis E. Lugo (ed.), *Religion, Pluralism, and Public Life: Abraham Kuyper's Legacy for the Twenty-First Century* (Grand Rapids, MI: William B. Eerdmans Publishing Company) 365–72.

Skillen, James W. and Rockne M. McCarthy (eds) (1991), *Political Order and the Plural Structure of Society* (Atlanta, GA: Scholars Press).

Smith, Steven (2014), *The Rise and Decline of American Religious Freedom* (Cambridge, MA: Harvard University Press).

Storrar, William (2007), "2007: A Kairos Moment for Public Theology," *International Journal of Public Theology*, 1(1): 5–25.

Su, Anna (2016), *Exporting Freedom: Religious Liberty and American Power* (Cambridge, MA: Harvard University Press).

Sullivan, Winnifred Fallers (2005), *The Impossibility of Religious Freedom* (Princeton, NJ: Princeton University Press).

Sullivan, Winnifred Fallers, Elizabeth Shakman Hurd, Saba Mahmood, and Peter G. Danchin (eds) (2015), *Politics of Religious Freedom* (Chicago, IL: University of Chicago Press).

Sunstein, Cass R. (2001), *One Case at a Time: Judicial Minimalism on the Supreme Court* (Cambridge, MA: Harvard University Press).

Taylor, Charles (2007), *A Secular Age* (Cambridge, MA: Harvard University Press).

Thio, Li-Ann (2012), "Constitutionalism in Illiberal Polities," in: Michel Rosenfeld and András Sajó (eds), *The Oxford Handbook of Comparative Constitutional Law* (Oxford: Oxford University Press) 133–52.

Trigg, Roger (2010), *Free to Believe? Religious Freedom in a Liberal Society* (London: Theos).

Trigg, Roger (2013), "Threats to Religious Freedom in Europe," *Public Discourse*, June 28.

Tushnet, Mark (2015), "Accommodation of Religion Thirty Years On," *Harvard Journal of Law & Gender*, 38(Winter): 1–33.

UN News Centre (2015), "UN Marks International Day by Stressing Vital Role of Civil Society for True Democracy," September 15.

Van Biema, David (2009), "3. The New Calvinism," *Time*, March 12.

Vyver, Johan D. van der (2011), "Constitutional Protection and Limits to Religious Freedom," Second ICLARS Conference, Santiago de Chile, September 10 (provisional).

Volf, Miroslav (2016), "Religion's Place in a Religiously Violent World," *Christianity Today*, March 17.

Vorster, J.M. (2010), "Current Options for the Constitutional Implementation of Religious Freedom," in: A. van de Beek, E.A.J.G. Van der Borght, and B.P. Vermeulen (eds), *Freedom of Religion* (Leiden and Boston, MA: Brill).

Waldron, Jeremy A. (2011), *A Religious View of the Foundations of International Law* (NYU School of Law, Public Law Research Paper No. 11–29).

Wolterstorff, Nicholas (2012), *Understanding Liberal Democracy: Essays in Political Philosophy* (Oxford: Oxford University Press).

World Movement for Democracy (2012), *Defending Civil Society: Report* (Washington, DC: World Movement for Democracy, 2nd edn).

1 *In Medias Res*: Communal Religious Freedom under Pressure

Introduction

In the spring of 2015 I attended a lecture by Mary Ann Glendon at the Catholic Center at New York University on "Religious Freedom: Yesterday, Today and Tomorrow." In the lecture Glendon, a Professor of Law at Harvard University and a former U.S. Ambassador to the Holy See, argued that in the United States religious freedom is well on its way to becoming a second-class human right (2015; see also Evans, Petkoff, and Rivers 2015).

At first sight this may seem unlikely, as the United States can in many respects be regarded as the birthplace of the modern right to freedom of religion or belief. Also, religious freedom is not just regulated in the so-called First Amendment to the U.S. Constitution, but also more generally often referred to in America as the "first freedom." This was what I expected to find out once again when I traveled to the United States to study the topic of "Law and Religious Freedom." Obviously, the United States is an open society, characterized by a considerable degree of pluralism from the time it was founded. Still I believed that the importance of the right to freedom of religion or belief would be at least one thing that Americans had continued to hold in common; that the sense that this is a special right, as it is foundational to various other rights such as the freedoms of expression and assembly and association, would somehow remain stronger here than back home in Europe.

Glendon mentions several reasons as to why the right to freedom of religion or belief can nevertheless be regarded as being on its way to becoming a second-class right in the United States. One reason is that increasing hostility towards religion can be discerned among opinion leaders, especially in the media and academia. In so far as academia is concerned, to which I will limit myself, this was to a certain extent already noted in the introductory chapter. In all fairness, however, it needs to be added that some of the new critics of religious freedom certainly do not exhibit any hostility towards religion itself.

A second reason that Glendon mentions for the development of the right to religious freedom towards becoming a second-class right, and which is worth singling out here, is that support for this right among the population at large is also eroding. In her opinion, this has to do with the cultural and social revolution that took place during the 1960s, which led to the rise of what Canadian philosopher Charles Taylor calls "expressive individualism" (2007: 473–95). Symbolic of this development is that increasingly at funerals the song "(I Did It) My Way," made famous by Frank Sinatra, is played (Glendon 2015: 7).

Somehow, this expressive individualism does not sit easily with the right to freedom of religion or belief as it has traditionally been defined. Of course, this right is certainly also, as many would argue and I agree with in the first place, an individual right. Still, even with respect to its individual dimension it was often invoked in the context of membership of more or less established and institutionalized world religions such as Judaism, Christianity, and Islam. This means that there has also, from the beginning, been a communal dimension to the right.

In so far as our current, postsecular age is characterized precisely by a decline of such institutionalized religions among the population, this could eventually also impact on the way the right to freedom of religion or belief is interpreted by, for example, the courts. This holds all the more true for the associational and institutional dimensions of religious freedom that this book is concerned with in particular. In a postsecular age, of which expressive individualism has become a salient feature, the right to freedom of religion or belief of individuals in its individual dimension can, for example, sometimes clash with the rights of religious associations, groups, and institutions. The question then becomes which of the two should prevail.

Earlier Case Law

Thus, in a 1991 article entitled "Structural Free Exercise" Glendon and Yanes were already arguing that, as far as the United States was concerned, a conception of religious freedom starting from the ideal of individual autonomy had become influential. After a comprehensive survey of the U.S. Supreme Court's Religion Clause jurisprudence from the 1940s onwards, their conclusion read that "in retrospect . . . the Court was fairly consistent in pursuing an individualistic, secularist, and separationist approach to religion cases" (Glendon and Yanes 1991: 536; see also Glendon 1991).

In a lecture delivered exactly 20 years after her article on "Structural Free Exercise," moreover, Glendon had to concede that the right to freedom of religion or belief in the West was "at heightened risk from, inter alia, the erosion of conscience protection for religious individuals and institutions, restrictions on the autonomy of religious institutions, and inroads on the rights of parents regarding the education of their children" (2012: 975). Indeed, according to Glendon (978),

> [The American] legal system's neglect of the associational and institutional dimensions of religious freedom, though punctuated with some notable exceptions, seems to be accelerating. As freedom of religion comes into conflict with claims based on nondiscrimination norms, abortion rights, and

> various lifestyle liberties, the freedom of religious entities to choose their own personnel, and even to publicly teach and defend their positions on controversial issues, is coming under increased attack.

It is important to see that such observations mainly concern the interpretation of the right to freedom of religion or belief by one high court. This court is, moreover, under an obligation to uphold the individual dimension of the right, as religious freedom is in the first instance an individual right. The observation that the U.S. Supreme Court, at least during the first couple of decades after the Second World War, was "*fairly* consistent" in emphasizing the individual dimension of the right to freedom of religion or belief over its associational and institutional dimensions, among other things, does not necessarily hold true for other courts and international organizations.

Recently, for example, the positions of the European Court of Human Rights (ECtHR) and the Organization for Security and Cooperation in Europe (OSCE) regarding the rights of religious organizations have been analysed. The conclusion of this analysis reads that such organizations enjoy

> a clear set of rights under European human rights law. The ECtHR and the OSCE have confirmed the importance of freedom of worship and meeting together through cases involving, amongst others, persecution of believers, imprisonment, interruption of meetings, and confiscation of religious literature. They have also confirmed the importance of legal personality in order for religious groups to be able to function properly. This position also shows that restricting religious freedom because of other concerns, for example the protection of individual rights such as privacy or sexual orientation, or the protection of national security, must be taken very cautiously.
>
> (Langlaude-Doné 2016: 40)

At the same time, and equally relevant in the context of this study, the analysis also demonstrates (40) how

> [t]ensions can however be seen in conflicts involving the dismissal of individuals working for religious organisations. There is not always agreement on whether and the extent to which religious groups have obligations and responsibilities under human rights law. The ECtHR and the OSCE recognise that both sides have interests that are in tension. To a large extent, despite a focus on balancing the interests at stake and the application of the principle of proportionality, the ECtHR so far has been very generous to religious autonomy in deciding such matters and in applying doctrinal issues in the employment context. However, the fact that religious organisations are not given complete free reign, as well as the recent narrow majority in *Fernández Martínez v Spain*, demonstrate that such decisions could change in the future.

Also relevant is law and religion scholar Zachary R. Calo's observation about the ECtHR's "identification of religious freedom as a tool for protecting and advancing the goods of democratic pluralism" (2010: 262). Calo concludes (268), on the basis of an analysis of the religion cases, that

> [e]ven as the Court defines religious pluralism as the hallmark of the liberal democratic order, this pluralism is locked within the bounds of a secular political narrative. Pluralism thus remains in a tenuous position, easily sacrificed when the Court encounters cases that challenge the predominance of this secular narrative.

Interestingly, the solution he proposes is "pluralization, in particular by opening the idea of human rights to theological perspectives, as one way to overcome the limitations of the secular tradition" (279).

Returning to the United States, leading First Amendment scholar Paul Horwitz, like Glendon and Yanes, discerns as "a common thread" in the First Amendment's literature and jurisprudence: that "they routinely emphasize the individual and deemphasize the institutional" (2013: 27). Earlier, colleague Frederick Schauer had in this regard already spoken of an "institutional agnosticism" (1998: 107). The most compelling recent formulation of the phenomenon I have come across is by international constitutional and human rights lawyer and religious freedom expert Iain Benson, according to whom the currently dominant "liberal individualistic approach manifests itself in two ways":

> 1. It defines or tends to describe the right of religion as an *individual* right merely, [and]
> 2. It defines or tends to describe the public sphere in ways that exclude full participation and religious involvement in that sphere. *Individualism* and *exclusionism* persist.
>
> (2013b: 8).

What makes this formulation so compelling is not just the fact that it is empirically grounded, as it stems from Benson's Ph.D. research regarding religious employer exemption cases in two jurisdictions, Canada and South Africa. It is also that it links two topics that at first sight may seem to differ, but which are also dealt with in this book as two interrelated symptoms of the same problem. First of all, the formulation deals with a specific interpretation of the right to freedom of religion or belief and as such it corresponds with the analyses by Glendon and Yanes, Schauer, and Horwitz referred to above. Second, however, the formulation also applies the liberal individualistic approach to the discussion about whether the public square can be considered sufficiently inclusive.

The latter question is dealt with in Chapter 3 of this book, but there is a clear connection with the current chapter. To the extent that religious freedom is interpreted as merely an individual right, the chances are that the potential contributions of religious associations, groups, and institutions to the public and parliamentary debate will also be underestimated. Indeed, a link between the liberal individualistic approach and constitutionalism, as dealt with in Chapter 2, also exists, in that it will lead to an emphasis on the state and the individual, and less so on mediating structures. This is why this book deals with religious freedom, constitutionalism, and democracy in an interconnected way. This is also why the current chapter is not the only chapter in which the question of whether communal religious freedom is under pressure is being explored. Although the case law in religion cases may be the most direct source to search for an answer, analyses with respect to developments within constitutionalism or the state of our democracy are also relevant. In fact, developments in these domains may have gone further already, so that it is more rewarding to look for clues there than in the case law.

Of course, what ought to be repeated here is that the formulation and criticism of a possible liberal individualist common thread in the literature and jurisprudence regarding religion cases is not intended to call into question in any way the fact that the individual dimension of the right to freedom of religion or belief is an essential, and arguably indeed the primary, dimension of this human right. It only wishes to convey the message that there is also a second dimension to the right, and that when the right is interpreted and applied in a particular—individualist—way, this communal dimension can easily come under pressure. This is, however, a matter of interpretation and application of the right, and in theory it is perfectly possible, although naturally not always easy, to balance the two dimensions of the right.

Interestingly, the relative neglect of the institutional religious autonomy principle is usually combined with a conception of the state as the holder of what is ultimately unfettered, sovereign executive power. As Emeritus Professor of Philosophy Roger Trigg has pointed out,

> [t]he more the role of the individual is extolled, the more powerful the state has to become, since the role of any protective institutions, even that of the family, to act as buffers between the state and the individual is eroded.
> (2012: 12; cf. Schall 2012)

This applies at present perhaps in particular with respect to equality. The paradox at work here is that the more the importance of equality and individual freedom are being emphasized, the more government interference and regulation become necessary to realize these ideals. As a result, freedom is diminished, to the extent that all are now required to subscribe to these ideals, even if this was not the case before the state became involved (Trigg 2012: 51; cf. Garnett 2014: 198; Shah, Farr, and Friedman 2016). As one observer noted,

> individual rights to religious liberty and equality, important though they undoubtedly are, do not represent an adequate grounding of principle for the law of organized religions. They fail to capture central parts of the subject-matter, they distort the underlying social reality, they are inherently weak,

> and they risk capture by a statist agenda that subjects all of civil society to its own ethos.
>
> (Rivers 2010: 322; 2007)

For example, in the report *Peaceful Coexistence: Reconciling Nondiscrimination Principles with Civil Liberties* (2016), published by the U.S. Commission on Civil Rights, five of the eight commissioners write that new laws and proposals which are being introduced in order to seek exceptions to laws prohibiting discrimination of lesbian, gay, bisexual, and transgender people "represent an orchestrated, nationwide effort by extremists to promote bigotry, cloaked in the mantle of 'religious freedom'" (160; see also Bachiochi 2016; DeGirolami 2016; Epstein 2016).

Looked at from this perspective, the difference of opinion does therefore not so much concern the importance of the individual dimension of the right of freedom of religion or belief. Nor does the difference of opinion concern the importance of the principle of equality. To a certain extent, classical rights such as the right to freedom of religion or belief are themselves grounded in the idea that all human beings are equal. Also those who regard religious freedom as a natural right preceding the state would probably agree that every person is equally entitled to respect for their human dignity. In so far as in the past the idea of equality has been qualified, so as to exclude particular categories of human beings from their entitlement to equal treatment by the law, this is not just generally but certainly also by many religious traditions regarded as progress. The fact that not all circumstances and situations are equal, so that sometimes difference in treatment is justified and even more desirable than equal treatment, is not something that only these religious traditions tend to emphasize but a more general constitutional principle (Garnett 2012: 197).

The problem then rather appears to consist of the fact that a similar philosophical grounding within the liberal framework as it has developed cannot be found for the associational and institutional dimensions of the right to freedom of religion or belief. As a result, legislatures and courts may be tempted to give priority to the individual dimension of this right, as well as to other individual rights, in cases where these conflict with communal religious freedom. In fact, this is one argument that some of the so-called "new critics of religious freedom" put forward, and, as with particular other points they make, they certainly have a point. It must be noted, however, that we have just seen that, for example, the ECtHR and the OSCE have thus far demonstrated this tendency to a significantly lesser extent than the U.S. Supreme Court has done. Also, it remains the case that the associational and institutional dimensions of the right to freedom of religion or belief are part of the positive law and therefore need to be taken into account, no matter how the right to religious freedom may be interpreted and applied in a particular case.

At a more fundamental level, the question seems to be how the liberal democratic tradition as a whole is being interpreted. By some, the liberal democratic order is regarded as a break from all or most societal and legal arrangements that existed before the American and French revolutions of the late eighteenth century. This point of view is likely to result in an emphasis on the individual dimension of religious freedom, as the notion of individual rights is foundational to progressive liberalism. This progressive or Enlightenment liberalism is rooted, among other things, in the legal and political theory of the social contract. According to this theory, individuals enter into a contract with the state whereby, in exchange for protection, they hand over part of their autonomy to the state under the condition that the state guarantees certain fundamental rights.

There is also a different interpretation possible, however, according to which the liberal democratic tradition is rather the culmination of a centuries-old, gradual development. This interpretation makes it possible to look for similarities between, for example, the Magna Carta (1215) and later human rights codifications. The use of the very word "codifications" is relevant here, as it suggests that something is turned into positive law which previously existed already. In the context of this study, one example of something which pre-existed is the notion of the "freedom of the church." In fact, the idea of there being a separation of church and state, in the sense that worldly authorities (also those preceding modern states) do not possess all power, can be seen as foundational to the later idea of limited government. We will come back to this point in the next chapter. For now, it is important to see that those holding this view will tend to interpret the modern right to freedom of religion or belief in the light of this longer constitutional development and history. To the extent that the notion of the freedom of the church forms part of this Western tradition, they will more naturally be inclined to attribute weight to the associational and institutional dimensions of religious freedom as well, in addition to its—in this perspective—more recent yet also important individual dimension.

A case in point in this regard is the Netherlands. For the better part of the twentieth century, Dutch politics and society have been characterized by a relatively large degree of "associational autonomy" ceded to private organizations in general and religious ones in particular. Although in certain respects the process of secularization in the Netherlands had already started around the turn of the nineteenth and twentieth centuries, until the 1960s the Dutch population was overwhelmingly Christian. Politically speaking, however, there were relatively sharp divisions between Protestant, Catholic, Liberal, and Socialist groups. In order to maintain societal peace, the leaders of these groups more or less pragmatically worked together, while agreeing that the ordinary members of these groups in society could live as much as possible according to their own religious or other convictions.

This was without doubt an arrangement born out of political necessity, as none of the groups was ever able to gain a parliamentary majority on its own. This "agreement to disagree" was made possible, however, by the more or less implicit adherence to the second interpretation of the Western liberal democratic tradition distinguished above. This interpretation made it easy to accept the idea not just that the worldviews in society differed, but also that the different groups were entitled to a fair measure of institutional religious autonomy from the state. It is interesting to note that the overwhelmingly Christian character of the nation did not prevent this conservative or classical type of liberalism, as it could be called, from gaining ground again during the twentieth century. Provided the conditions are right, such as there being only minorities in parliament and society, Christianity may even have been conducive to this kind of liberalism. The minimum that can be said is that theological justifications have been provided for this particular model of church–state relations, in which faith-based organizations are generously accommodated and also facilitated by the state, usually referred to as "principled pluralism" (Hiemstra 2015).

Since the 1960s, however, the shift from a "Christian" society to a more secular one has arguably the potential to turn the ideal of individual autonomy into a leading paradigm in both legislation and jurisprudence. In particular the non-discrimination principle, with which the Dutch Constitution has opened since 1983, is increasingly perceived as being in direct conflict with the traditional freedom to exercise the associational and institutional dimensions of religious freedom.

For example, on April 9, 2010 the Dutch Supreme Court ruled that the state was obliged to take effective measures to put an end to the Political Reformed Party's (Staatkundig Gereformeerde Partij; hereafter SGP) almost century-old refusal to grant women passive suffrage on biblical grounds. Subsequently, the party submitted an application to the ECtHR. In its decision on July 10, 2012 the Court declared the application to be manifestly ill-founded, however, and therefore inadmissible (Ten Napel 2011; Van den Brink and Ten Napel 2013; Ten Napel and Van den Brink 2014).

The example of the SGP case will probably not be equally convincing to all readers. Admittedly, the case is not as clear-cut as has sometimes been argued, because it does not involve a "normal" association but a political association. So it is more part of the structure of the state in the broadest sense of the term, though at the core remaining a private association. As a result, the state has a slightly stronger interest in maintaining the principles of equality and non-discrimination with respect to a political party than in the case of normal associations. It should also be acknowledged that many of the initiators of legal action against the SGP were driven by ideals. There is hardly any doubt in my mind that they sincerely believed they were acting on behalf of female members of the SGP who they believed ought to have the opportunity to become candidates in local government and other elections. Some of them will also have been convinced that they were acting in the broader interests of society. Although there was no imminent threat of the SGP gaining a majority, even in the Dutch bible belt, they thought it was possible that sooner or later an Islamic majority might take the same position regarding women's political rights. Thus, it became imperative to initiate legal action against the SGP, as otherwise it would become difficult to take legal steps against an Islamic party, which might pose a bigger threat.

The important point to make here, however, is that the idealism by which many of the initiators of legal action against the SGP were driven was inspired by the first interpretation of liberalism identified above. Characteristic of this Enlightenment liberalism is that it tends to give priority to the individual dimension of the right to freedom of religion or belief, and other individual rights for that matter, over the associational and institutional dimensions of religious freedom. Equally characteristic of Enlightenment liberalism is that it regards liberal democracy itself as an ideological programme, based on distinctive values such as equality, that deserves to be implemented even against the opinions of religious and other groups in so far as they differ from these liberal values.

What can be noted is that Enlightenment liberalism appears to have (re)surfaced, at least in the Netherlands, precisely at the point at which the process of secularization seems to intensify. In general, it is possible to see the cultural and social revolution of the 1960s as marking the start of this acceleration in the process of secularization, which, as we have seen, had already been underway for quite some time. Even after this cultural and social revolution, it was a couple of decades before consequences were seen in, for example, the political and legal spheres. In the 1990s, apparently the time was ripe to initiate legal action against the SGP, just as after the parliamentary elections of 1994 the first cabinet in recent Dutch political history was formed in which none of the (mainstream) Christian political parties—since 1980 unified in the Christian Democratic Appeal (CDA)—participated.

It is difficult to assess what caused the change. Was it the fact that the Netherlands had by now become less a country of minorities, or was it caused by the rise of a different kind of liberalism? What seems plausible is that the process of secularization, which had accelerated after the 1960s, led to a different societal constellation, in that—as historian James Kennedy already noted at the turn of the century (2001: 253)—slowly but gradually a secular majority had been formed. This secular majority had then led to the rise of a different kind of liberalism. It should be pointed out that there is nothing illegitimate about this by itself. In fact, although the Christian population had been divided among Protestants and Catholics, and the Protestants divided among themselves, it is perfectly possible to argue that there had been a Christian majority at work in Dutch politics and society for most of the twentieth century. Nor is it the case that Enlightenment liberalism is somehow less legitimate than classical liberalism. Finally, although it could be argued that classical liberalism was more suitable in the country of minorities that the Netherlands was during the better part of the twentieth century, the model did not always live up to its expectations. Thus, Christian groups in the past have on occasion probably been just as intolerant towards Liberals and Socialists as the secular majority is now sometimes accused of being towards the religious groups in society.

Still, what can be witnessed is that there is a change in tone and style in both Dutch politics and the legal system (cf. Mansvelt Beck 2015). Concerning the legal system, it is possible to argue that a case such as the SGP case would not have been conceivable while the country was still predominantly Christian in character. Although there is not a direct correlation with Christianity, and Christianity certainly does not automatically lead to the kind of classical liberalism identified above, what can be determined is that Christianity did not prevent such classical liberalism from being (re)introduced in the Netherlands at the turn of the century. On the other hand, the acceleration of the process of secularization in Dutch society since the 1960s appears to manifest itself politically in the form of a resurgence of Enlightenment liberalism. To the extent that classical liberalism favors a more inclusive model of church–state relations than Enlightenment liberalism, in the sense that faith-based organizations are generously accommodated and also facilitated by the state, it can therefore be argued that, paradoxically, Christianity has led to a greater tolerance than secular liberalism. Some would argue, however, that precisely because of the greater diversity in society than in the past, classical liberalism would no longer work the way it did during the better part of the twentieth century. We will come back to this point in Chapter 3.

As will be clear from the above, the question of how to shape the relationship between faith-based organizations and the state in a postsecular age is a political and scholarly debate that is hardly unique to the Netherlands. This makes it worthwhile to attempt to determine on the basis of even more recent case law the degree to which communal religious freedom is indeed currently coming under pressure in the case law of three different high courts (see also Ten Napel 2016).

Two Hypotheses

Before looking at three recent rulings in communal religious freedom cases, it should be pointed out that in the literature rather different views are expressed with respect to the question of whether institutional religious autonomy is indeed currently coming under pressure.

On the one hand, some authors stress that what we are witnessing at the moment is at best "free exercise by moonlight" (DeGirolami 2015). This quotation first of all indicates that free exercise of the right to freedom of religion or belief is naturally still possible. The addition of the words "by moonlight," however, implies that the clock is ticking and that we might soon enter the darkness of night. What this refers to, among other things, is that the idea of reasonable accommodation in matters of belief is gradually becoming more controversial in the United States (cf. Tushnet 2015). A recent illustration of this trend appears to be the fact that in 2015 a registrar in Kentucky, who had conscientious objections regarding the legal recognition of same-sex marriages, was even jailed for a couple of days. This development indeed came as a surprise, in the sense that in a country such as the Netherlands, despite probably being more secularized and radicalized in matters of religion than the United States, initially at least many municipalities sought somehow to accommodate civil servants who had conscientious objections regarding the conclusion of same-sex marriages (see, however, Loof 2008).

Another author in this first category puts it a little stronger by suggesting that what is actually going on is a general attack by Western law on religion across different jurisdictions (Benson 2013a; see also Eberstadt 2016). Like Glendon, Benson adopts a more long-term perspective and believes that the cultural and social revolution of the 1960s forms an important explanation regarding the alleged attack on religion taking place across the West today.

This thesis of a general trend stands even more in contrast with the second view that can be discerned in the literature, which holds that "the sky isn't falling" (Carlson-Thies 2015). The main reason why it is unlikely that a general attack on religion across the West is taking place, according to these authors, is precisely that the state of religious freedom is dependent on the specific time and place that one is looking at, in addition to the particular circumstances of each case.

Both Marc O. DeGirolami, a professor at St. John's University School of Law, where he is associate director of the Center for Law and Religion, and Benson are fine legal scholars. In fact, above I have praised Benson's Ph.D. research for being empirically grounded, among other things. Nevertheless, it can be observed that this second view is at least at first sight more what one would expect to be the position of a legal scholar, as lawyers tend to focus on the peculiarities of each case. It is obviously also more in line with a historian's approach, given the attention that historians usually pay to the context and details of a particular phenomenon. By looking at the merits of each individual case, the second view is also likely to be the more optimistic of the two. It is indeed to be expected that, by looking carefully at a court ruling, it will almost always be possible to find one or more elements that justify hope for a better decision next time, if desired (see e.g. Langston 2015). Also, it is rather unlikely that one would find unfavorable outcomes in each and every case that in recent decades, across the West, has come before a court.

At the same time it remains the case that adherents to this second view are typically also aware of certain negative trends with respect to communal religious freedom. Therefore, this view can be summed up by the slogan that the glass is half full. The first view is, in that case, the equivalent of the slogan that the glass is half empty. This metaphor already indicates that the differences between the two views should not be exaggerated. Still, the intriguing question is which view is the better of the two. This is what the next section will be concerned with.

Three Recent Cases

So which view is the better of the two: that what we are currently witnessing is at best "free exercise by moonlight" or that "the sky isn't falling"? In other words, when it comes to communal religious freedom, is the glass half full or half empty? We will try to determine the answer to this question by focusing on three reasonably comparable cases that have recently come before the high courts of various Western jurisdictions. These courts are, respectively, the U.S. Supreme Court, the European Court of Human Rights and the Supreme Court of Canada. Although the three cases are comparable, the ECtHR differs from the other two high courts in that it is a supranational or even an international court, whereas the U.S. Supreme Court and the Supreme Court of Canada are national high courts.

The first case, *Hosanna-Tabor Evangelical Lutheran Church and School v Equal Employment Opportunity Commission et al.* (132 S. Ct. 694), was decided by the

U.S. Supreme Court in 2012. The case concerned a religious school that wished to dismiss a teacher. The teacher had fallen ill and had taken recourse to a court when she wanted to return to her position after the school had made it clear that they had already appointed a successor. Taking recourse to legal proceedings in such a case was not in conformity with the philosophy of the school. Normally, in the case of an employment conflict like this, non-discrimination legislation would apply. However, the teacher in question was regarded by the school not as a lay but as a "called" teacher, because of the theological training she had received among other things. Therefore, the question arose as to whether the so-called "ministerial exception" would apply in this case. Such a ministerial exception means that with respect to someone who can be considered a minister the regular non-discrimination provisions do not apply. Interestingly, this question had already come up before lower courts in the past, but this was the first time it had reached the Supreme Court.

The second case, decided by the European Court of Human Rights in 2014, is *Fernández Martínez v Spain* (Case no. 56030/07; ECtHR 12 June 2014). This case concerned a religious education teacher employed by the Catholic Church, who had publicly demonstrated his disapproval of the Church's position with respect to celibacy. The Church had implicitly agreed with the teacher being married himself, despite the fact that he had been ordained as a priest, but believed that by seeking this type of publicity the teacher had caused a "scandal." As will be clear from this brief description of the case, the facts were rather similar to those in *Hosanna-Tabor Evangelical Lutheran Church and School v Equal Employment Opportunity Commission et al.* Therefore, the legal question the European Court of Human Rights had to answer was whether something like a European version of the "ministerial exception" existed. The Court had dealt with this question before, but only in Chamber judgments, and its position had not yet quite crystallized (Koffeman and Koffeman 2008; Van der Vyver 2012). It was anticipated that the Grand Chamber would seize the opportunity to clarify the position of the Court with respect to a "ministerial exception," despite the fact that it concerns a supra-national and even an international court rather than a national high court, and questions regarding church–state relations tend to be answered quite differently across almost 50 States Parties to the European Convention of Human Rights (Evans and Thomas 2006).

The third and final case to be considered, *Loyola High School and John Zucchi v Attorney General of Quebec*, was decided by the Supreme Court of Canada in 2015 ([2015] 1 SCR 613). The case concerned the introduction of a new religious education curriculum in the province of Quebec. Loyola High School, a private Catholic school, applied for an exemption from this curriculum, which was refused by the Ministry of Education. In a sense, the new curriculum marked a next step in the process of the secularization of the Quebec school system. This process had started some 20 years earlier and had resulted in the gradual substitution of the former religious schools by public schools. The government wanted the new religious education curriculum to apply not just to these public schools but also to the (remaining) private schools.

The interesting thing is that, in all three cases, the courts eventually ruled in favor of the religious organizations. Thus, in *Hosanna-Tabor Evangelical Lutheran Church and School v Equal Employment Opportunity Commission et al.*, the U.S. Supreme Court confirmed that such a thing as a ministerial exception did exist. It also applied this doctrine to the case at hand, to the effect that the school could dismiss the teacher without having to worry about applicable non-discrimination legislation. In *Fernández Martínez v Spain*, the ECtHR equally ruled in favor of the Catholic Church, which had dismissed a teacher because he had caused a "scandal." Finally, in *Loyola High School and John Zucchi v Attorney General of Quebec*, the Supreme Court of Canada granted the school at least a partial exemption from the new religious education curriculum.

At first sight these three recent cases therefore call into question the idea that what is going on is a general attack by Western law on religion. Since in all three cases the religious organizations were the winners, it would appear to be more the case that as far as religious freedom is concerned "the sky isn't falling." As a recent policy brief puts it: "In Europe and North America, there are concerns over increased Islamophobia and anti-Semitism as well as to a lesser degree over restrictions on new religious movements and marginalisation of conservative Christian groups" (Petito, Philpott, Ferrari, and Birdsall 2016: 2).

However, on closer inspection, things turn out to be more complicated than that. Thus, it is already telling in itself that in a relatively short period of time three similar cases have come before the high courts of three different Western jurisdictions. As we saw, it was the first time that the U.S. Supreme Court itself had to answer the question whether something like a ministerial exception existed. The same applies to the European Court of Human Rights, whose Grand Chamber had to clarify the position of the Court after a series of Chamber judgments.

Second, although the three high courts all ruled in favor of the religious organizations, in all three cases there had been earlier decisions by lower courts that had sometimes ruled against the same organizations. Apparently, it was possible to reach a different conclusion on the basis of the same legislation and precedents in the case law. This means that in a new case, and with possibly a slightly different composition of the court, the high court itself could easily also rule against the religious organization.

Third, in two of the three cases only the smallest possible majority ruled in favor of the religious organizations. The U.S. Supreme Court unanimously ruled in favor of Hosanna-Tabor Evangelical Lutheran Church. However, the European Court of Human Rights decided in favor of a European "ministerial exception" by a mere 9:8 majority, although this was technically achieved by holding that the non-renewal of the applicant's contract of a religious education teacher had not constituted a violation of his right to private life. Also, in a controversial dissenting opinion the Russian judge went so far as to question the organizational autonomy of the Roman Catholic Church with regard to, for example, celibacy. Finally, the Supreme Court of Canada granted an exemption to Loyola High School by a 4:3 majority, whereby the majority proved not willing to order the minister to grant an exemption to Loyola as suggested by the minority, but instead insisted on sending the matter back to the minister for reconsideration.

Fourth, it is worthwhile—as is usually the case in legal proceedings—to take a closer look at the contents of the different rulings. Thus, what is striking when the entire ruling in *Hosanna-Tabor Evangelical Lutheran Church v Equal Employment Opportunity Commission et al.* is considered is that the U.S. Supreme Court on the one hand acknowledges the fact that a "ministerial exception" exists; on the other hand, it also remarks that it is difficult to define who qualifies as a minister and who does not (132 S. Ct. 707–708). Although this may to a certain extent be understandable, as it would not be easy to provide a definition here either, what this means is that whether the ministerial exception applies or not in a particular case depends on the circumstances of that case as well as—once again—on the composition of the court. As a result, the case is not of much concrete help to faith-based organizations in their relations with the state in general. Uncertainty remains.

Similarly, in *Fernández Martínez v Spain*, the European Court of Human Rights on the one hand recognized the existence of a European ministerial exception and as a result a particular degree of "church autonomy." However, in the same judgment a crucial paragraph can be found dealing with the limits to the same church autonomy (para 132). Although, generally speaking, this may make sense, the limits in question are quite real because in this paragraph a proportionality test is introduced. Such a test means that the degree of church autonomy granted in a particular case must not be disproportionate compared with the possible harm caused by it to the plaintiff, in this case the married priest who had arguably caused a scandal by seeking publicity and had subsequently been dismissed as a religious education teacher.

Finally, in *Loyola High School and John Zucchi v Attorney General of Quebec*, the Supreme Court of Canada granted an exemption to the school. On closer inspection, however, this concerned only a partial exemption. Henceforth, the school was only allowed to teach about Catholicism from a Catholic perspective (para 81). With respect to other religions, the religious education curriculum of even this private Catholic school had to be secular in character. It is true that in the Canadian context in general, and in Quebec in particular, the term "secular" means something very different from, for example, the French term "*laicité*"; it is intended rather to mean something like "neutral." As the school understandably argued, however, it is quite a challenge for a Catholic teacher to teach in a neutral way about all other religions besides Catholicism. Moreover, the Canadian concept of a "multicultural democracy," to which the Court refers as well (para 48), at least in practice turns out to be a fairly different ideal for the state than Catholicism proposes.

The last point deserves some closer attention as it is obviously a highly relevant point in the context of this book. At first sight, it would seem as though a multicultural democracy would make it possible for faith-based organizations such as Catholic schools to act as much as possible in accordance with their distinctive identity. It is clear that its ensuing model of church–state relations could never be the first choice of the Roman Catholic Church, at least not in theory. Christian constitutionalism in its pure form is characterized by a privileged position of the Roman Catholic Church and its affiliated institutions (Brennan 2015). It is conceivable, however, that the Roman Catholic Church would regard a principled, pluralistic type of church–state relations as a second-best solution. This has arguably been the case in the Netherlands during the better part of the twentieth century, in which Catholics were encouraged by the Dutch episcopate to participate in political and social life, albeit as part of separate, Catholic organizations. There are no examples from the heyday of Dutch pluriform democracy of the state interfering with the internal autonomy of faith-based organizations in general and Catholic organizations in particular.

The more recent experience of faith-based organizations in Canada differs from that of Catholic organizations in the Netherlands, as the case of Loyola High School illustrates, but more examples could be added to this. It has also proved rather difficult for a Christian law school to become accredited, for example (Benson 2013c). One explanation for this difference is that in Canada the notion of a multicultural democracy has been enshrined in constitutional documents such as its Charter of Fundamental Rights. The Netherlands is sometimes criticized for not possessing a clear constitutional identity. The Dutch Constitution does not have a preamble or contain an explicit list of values on which the constitutional and political system is founded. Not even the fact that the Netherlands is a democratic constitutional state can be found in the constitution as such, although this can be deduced from a number of provisions, and a general provision expressing precisely this idea is being considered by the legislature.

What by some is regarded as a weakness might on second thought be considered a strength, however. Apparently, the fact that multiculturalism is referred to, and indeed specified, in Canadian constitutional documents and case law limits the internal autonomy of faith-based organizations. In this sense, Canadian culturalism is not very different from, for example, French laicism, in that both represent a range of values of their own. These values will subsequently be guaranteed by the various legislatures and the courts. Instead of the state acting as a neutral organizer of the pluralism in society, as the European Court of Human Rights has put it, the state becomes a major player that acts from a similar, yet different, set of values as the faith-based organizations are based on. Although the European Court of Human Rights would probably still regard this as the neutral organizing of societal pluralism by the state, just as it respects the role of the state in laicist jurisdictions such as France and Turkey, the question is to what extent this can really be seen as the state acting neutrally. Compared with the traditional role of the Dutch state in accommodating and also facilitating faith-based organizations, it could be argued that this was even more neutral in that it created room "for all to be fully human in the public and private spheres" and thus "to cradle the spirituality of one's religion and to build one's life on the foundation that the religion offers" (Vorster 2010: 179).

On the whole, therefore, the glass of religious freedom may be more empty than a superficial reading of the three cases suggests after all. Although it can be conceded that "the sky isn't falling," and on the basis of the three cases discussed here it is certainly not possible to conclude that what in fact is going on is a general attack by Western law on religion, the hypothesis that what we are witnessing is "free exercise by moonlight" is certainly not to be discarded too easily either. The next section will discuss how this, rather surprising, finding can be interpreted in the light of the concrete outcomes of the three cases, which after all were all in favor of the faith-based organizations involved.

Interpretation

How do we make sense of this development? Why would the glass of religious freedom be half empty rather than half full? How do we explain that what we are witnessing might indeed turn out to be "free exercise by moonlight"?

There are two possible ways to look at the development. One way is to point to the fact that constitutional law and courts inherently have a secularizing effect. This is a line of thought pursued by Ran Hirschl (2010), among others (see e.g. Reuter 2009). Hirschl, a comparative public lawyer and political scientist, has looked at dozens of jurisdictions worldwide and found that, universally, constitutional law impacts the "free" exercise of religion simply by structuring it. In addition, courts are staffed by people who have been professionally trained to apply precisely these laws and categories, and therefore run the risk of acting as a caste of high priests serving the "higher" cause of the law rather than the interests of citizens who, for example, want to practice their religion as freely as possible.

It has to be conceded that there is at least some truth to this observation, as many sociologists of religion would probably affirm. At the same time, a statement like this does not just apply to constitutional law, or to religion for that matter. In fact, the reasoning can easily be extended to states in general and liberalism in particular. Looked at this way, the thesis becomes that the very fact that state authority is being exercised over a particular territory, concerning a group of people living on that territory, limits their personal autonomy. Liberalism in a sense aggravates the problem, because it consists of a set of doctrines. These doctrines have sometimes been presented as neutral and procedural, but they are in reality considerably more substantive than such labels suggest. In so far as concepts such as constitutionalism and democracy, for example, belong to the family tree of liberalism, it is clear that these may paradoxically limit the autonomy of people nearly as much as they make the same autonomy possible. As we have seen, this is a point that some of the new critics of religious freedom also make. This, however, puts them outside the liberal tradition, a position this book clearly wishes to avoid.

Moreover, pointing to constitutional law and courts in general does not explain the recent development in the direction of "free exercise by moonlight." In fact, this very metaphor suggests that a time element is at work, that the clock keeps ticking, and that moonlight is approaching. Yet this is precisely what at least some of the material highlighted above suggests. In their 1991 article Glendon and Yanes referred specifically to modern Religion Clause jurisprudence in the first place. In 2012, and again in 2015, Glendon observed that the situation was rapidly deteriorating in the United States. The three recent cases are illustrative of a broader trend, in so far as they also involve Europe and Canada, although it was also noted that this does not represent a general attack by Western law and courts on religion. So how can this apparent development be explained?

It is submitted here that for this purpose a second type of explanation is needed: one that does not look at the state and its laws as the source of imminent restrictions on the autonomy of faith-based organizations. Instead, it looks at the notable changes in the worldviews of the population since the 1960s referred to by authors such as Glendon and Benson. Although the impact of the cultural and social revolution may not immediately have been equally clear in Western jurisdictions, it is plausible that these by now will start to manifest themselves in the case law as well. It seems likely that once the worldviews of the population have begun to change, it is only a matter of time before the effects also become noticeable in parliaments, and thus legislation. At that point, it becomes possible to look towards the state and courts to reinforce a particular trend. However, this trend was first set in motion by the population. Thus, this second type of explanation to a certain extent comprises the first one.

According to Michael Paulsen, a leading scholar of constitutional interpretation, "the fundamental liberal paradigm of constitutional religious liberty is that the state recognizes and protects religious liberty as a natural right, out of an essentially religious acknowledgement that God's authority categorically prevails over the state's" (2013: 1170). He contrasts the liberal paradigm of religious freedom with "the 'modern' view of rational skepticism":

> If the liberal view is, as I think, the original American constitutional view embodied in the First Amendment's Religion Clauses, the modern view is the late-twentieth century and early twenty-first century dominant American cultural understanding of religious freedom, and the one that increasingly has come to be embodied in Supreme Court decisions interpreting the Religion Clauses. "Religious freedom" is not about the priority of God's claims over Man's. Religious freedom is, rather, society's and the state's gently condescending indulgence of the fact that certain benighted people continue to take the notion of religion seriously and that it is not very nice, or very important, for the state to suppress such views. To be sure, the First Amendment contains distinct religious freedom provisions that appear to have treated *religious* freedom in particular as its own kind of special right, but the modern attitude is almost one of viewing the First Amendment's protection of religion as akin to "historic preservation" of something quaint. (1171)

France and several other European democracies even appear to represent a post-modern view—that is:

> that religious truth does not exist and that it is affirmatively harmful to secular society to permit the free exercise of such views. . . . The consequence of this

> view is an "establishment" of sorts, not of religion, but of secularism—a thoroughly secular state, educational establishment, cultural identity, and system of laws. The free exercise of religion never requires an exemption or immunity from any such law. There may be no "free exercise" at variance with the rules of the secular establishment.
>
> (1178–9)

This view resembles the pre-liberal stance of religious intolerance out of the conviction that religious truth exists.

Seen from the modern and post-modern perspectives identified by Paulsen:

> [R]eligious institutions present a determined challenge to the atomizing and detraditionalizing tendencies of the liberal secular order. . . . Religious institutions are the primary bearers of moral tradition and practice. In this respect, they are something of an anomaly within a flattened secular order divested of deep moral meaning. Indeed, they might be seen to embody a distinctive threat to the secular order. . . . They embody strong normative accounts of the world, precisely the sort of beliefs that are anathema to the late modern secular order. It is unsurprising, in light of this, that institutions have become the central battleground in law and religion disputes.
>
> (Calo 2014: 15–16)

There is thus an apparent parallel between developments that have taken place in the Netherlands since the 1960s, and were set out in a previous section, and developments in other Western countries such as the United States. Although in several cultural and other respects the United States is traditionally in the lead, and other Western countries including the Netherlands follow after a while, the process of secularization is one example where the Netherlands has turned out to be years ahead. Just as the Netherlands was a relatively pluriform society for the better part of the twentieth century, the country has now all of a sudden become relatively secularized. The degree to which this has already affected the internal autonomy of faith-based organizations must, as we have seen, not be exaggerated. Yet the question is whether the resurgence of Enlightenment liberalism is an example that will in due course be followed by the United States.

There is some reason to believe that this will not happen immediately. One reason for this is that the secularization process still seems to be at an early stage in the United States. With the Christian part of the population still at 70.6 per cent (Pew Research Center 2015), this marks a clear difference with the Netherlands, where the percentage has dropped below 50 or even, according to some surveys, to around 20. To the extent that the United States is rather pluralizing than secularizing, the country could even find itself at the point where the Netherlands was in the second half of the nineteenth century (Harinck 2016: 62). This could at least in part explain the relative popularity of neo-Calvinism in the United States (e.g. Oppenheimer 2014), as Kuyper developed his idea of a principled pluralism at exactly that point in Dutch political history.

It is also conceivable that the secularization process will take place as rapidly in the United States as it has done in the Netherlands, in which case the two countries might sooner rather than later find themselves in comparable situations. At first, it was believed that the United States constituted the exception to the rule that all developed societies would sooner or later secularize. This was the secularization theory as it had developed within the social sciences. Then, when the secularization theory came under increasing scrutiny, the question was asked whether Europe was indeed the exception to the rule that religion had continued to play a public role globally, and that we had even witnessed an increase in the salience of religion in both international and national politics (e.g. Broughton and Ten Napel 2000). Now, a partial return to the secularization theory may be justified, to the extent that both Europe and North America are becoming increasingly secularized after all. The idea that, for example, European countries and Canada are transforming into postsecular countries could turn out to have been not much more than a form of wishful thinking by religiously or spiritually inclined scholars, although it may still be too early to tell.

Hobby Lobby

The second explanation, as put forward by Glendon, Benson, and others, can be elaborated upon a little bit further. For one thing, as we have argued already with respect to the Netherlands, it is obviously too simple to present the 1960s as the only decade of any significance in this regard. As has rightly been argued (see e.g. Brooks 2015), a cultural and social revolution does not normally come out of the blue and, in the case of the most recent one in the West, it had probably been in the making since at least the Second World War.

Another observation is that although the cultural and social revolution may therefore in reality have been a matter of decades, it was not until rather recently that the implications for religious freedom have started to become apparent. In this context it is necessary, in addition to the three recent cases discussed earlier, to refer to a fourth one: the so-called *Hobby Lobby* case (134 S. Ct. 2751 (2014)). The reason for this lies in the fact that, as Horwitz has argued in an already famous phrase (2014), at least in the United States a kind of "*Hobby Lobby* moment" can be discerned. The *Hobby Lobby* case concerned a private company which wanted an exemption from the obligations under the health care mandate. In a controversial ruling the U.S. Supreme Court appeared willing to grant this exemption, be it with the smallest possible majority (5:4). The majority based its decision on the fact that a private company such as *Hobby Lobby* could also exercise the right to freedom of religion or belief, among other things.

The degree of controversy surrounding this ruling reached an even higher level than in other religion cases. In his article on the case Horwitz rightly contends that this level of controversy can scarcely be explained by the legal aspects of the ruling alone. In a sense it concerned a narrow ruling, with a limited applicability outside the case at hand. There has to be another factor at work: what he refers to as "The *Hobby Lobby* Moment" (2014; see also Levin 2014; Schwartzman, Flanders, and Robinson 2016).

What Horwitz was hinting at in his article has also been captured by *The New York Times* Op-Ed columnist Ross Douthat in an article entitled "The Culture War's Sore Winners" (2014). As this title suggests, Douthat starts from the idea that by now it has become clear that the culture war between traditionalist and progressive values has been won, by the progressive Left, that is. This is only fair, as one of the two camps eventually had to win, and if this is the direction American society turns out to be moving in, then at least for the time being this outcome is inescapable.

However, there is at least one reason why the victory of the Left cannot be welcomed as wholeheartedly as might have been the case otherwise. This is that the progressive forces in society are gradually revealing themselves as "sore winners." Even though their victory is already a rather convincing one, they still appear to want to attain more, to almost completely crush whatever may have remained of their opponents.

These opponents can be largely identified as traditional religious associations, groups and institutions such as the Catholic Church. The fact of the matter is that although these associations, groups, and institutions may no longer dominate the culture as they did before the cultural revolution started, they have not completely disappeared either. As we have seen in the previous chapter, according to some authors we even live more in a postsecular age, where religious pluralism has increased but no linear process of secularization can be traced as had originally been expected.

As Douthat argues, sometimes the temporary winners of the culture war appear to have difficulty accepting this other fact of life. As a result, they are tempted to come down even further on these associations, groups, and institutions, hoping that sooner or later this may cause their complete collapse. He adds to this observation that others might regret this state of mind. These others, of whom Douthat himself is certainly one, would point to the fact that, particularly at a time of cultural change, one ought to think twice before doing away with any remaining islands of stability in the rising tides.

In another article, Douthat has summarized the above with the phrase "Making Religion the Problem" (2015). What makes the culture war's winners sore is that they are still not satisfied, and regularly appear to want to continue the war by declaring the loser of the culture war—religion—a problem itself. It sometimes seems as though a final victory for the Left is needed, which effectively erases the remaining religious associations, groups, and institutions from the surface of this earth.

As another observer puts it:

> [R]ooting religious autonomy in a liberal logic renders it susceptible to long-term erosion. Protecting religious autonomy so as to grant groups space to define their own form of moral order protects the very sorts of communities that are problematic within the modern secular order. The law will not long

> tolerate this contradiction and will move to circumscribe the scope of autonomy. The principle will endure but with a radically delimited scope. . . . This process will take time to fully work itself out. It will be slow and hesitant and uneven. It will unfold at a different pace in the United States and Europe. But it is a process well underway, even if the full drama is not yet manifest. We are now in medias res, and the legal situation projects a certain settledness. But undercurrents of deep change remain at work within law in ways subtle and pronounced. Law continues to shape secular order just as secular order continues to shape law.
>
> (Calo 2014: 16, 24)

In all its seeming simplicity, it appears as though this interpretation offered by Douthat and others actually contains a great deal of truth. This would imply that the United States is already closer to the current situation in the Netherlands than to where that country found itself in the late nineteenth century. Increasing pluralization of American society is certainly taking place, but within the context of a broader process of secularization. Neither Europe nor the United States is the exception anymore to a particular rule. Developments within both Europe and North America appear to be proving the secularization theory right after all. It is possible that secular majorities may arise across the West (see e.g. Sherwood 2016).

What must be added to this, however, is that even in this part of the world religion is not likely to disappear altogether. Also, the protection provided by fundamental rights such as the right to freedom of religion or belief, both in its individual and in its communal form, is not dependent on the adherents of a particular religion enjoying a majority or a minority status. This then finally raises the question of how to evaluate proposals regarding the right to freedom of religion or belief as set out in the introduction—for example, the idea to transform it into a general right to ethical integrity.

Evaluation

As stated in the introduction, some recent critics of the right to freedom of religion or belief argue that this right, as it is currently known, is largely of Christian origin and as a result biased against other religions. This criticism is difficult to assess directly on the basis of the three recent cases referred to above and *Hobby Lobby*, as all four concerned Christian organizations. It is, however, possible to note that "even" in the case of these Christian organizations certain inroads have become manifest in the internal autonomy of these organizations, although some critics would without doubt argue that these cases instead prove that communal religious freedom receives too much protection to the point that a jurisdictional approach to the right can be discerned (Cohen 2015).

Contrary to what legal and political theorist Jean L. Cohen believes, however,

> [t]he ministerial exception is constitutionally required, historically rooted, and essential to limited government and thus to political and religious

> freedom. . . . Although there are difficult questions to be asked and fine lines to be drawn, when it comes to interpreting the First Amendment's boundary between church and state, it cannot be the role of civil government to police the decisions of religious communities regarding who should be their leaders and teachers any more than the civil courts should review disputes over the meaning of religious doctrines.
>
> (Berg, Colby, Esbeck, and Garnett 2011: 190)

Or so at least it was argued earlier in this chapter, when we saw that, according to a more classical interpretation of liberalism, the current right to freedom of religion or belief has actually developed out of the pre-existing notion of the "freedom of the church."

What the inroads into the autonomy even of Christian organizations suggest is that a difference does not so much exist between the organizations of particular faiths, but that, on the contrary, the dividing line runs between religious associations, institutions and organizations of any faith and the secular society surrounding them. It can naturally be expected that the changing worldviews in society will sooner or later find their expression in the laws and case law of these same jurisdictions. In that case, Christian organizations will be affected as much as or even more—because of particular ressentiments—than Jewish, Muslim, and other faith-based organizations.

Yet it is crucial to understand—as was argued above—that these changes start from below. Thus, the existing laws and case law may serve as a barrier to the changing moods of the population, be it a partial one. It is submitted that this general hypothesis is supported by the situation surrounding communal religious freedom in Western countries. Generally speaking, the starting point in all three jurisdictions studied here (Canada, Europe, and the United States), as far as the laws and case law regarding the right to freedom of religion or belief are concerned, is (still) a full glass. To mention just one example, in the Loyola High School case referred to above the majority of the Supreme Court of Canada stated that "[r]eligious freedom under the *Charter* must . . . account for the socially embedded nature of religious belief, and the deep linkages between this belief and its manifestation through communal institutions and traditions" (para 60). The minority in the same case put it this way:

> The individual and collective aspects of freedom of religion are indissolubly intertwined. The freedom of religion of individuals cannot flourish without freedom of religion for the organizations through which those individuals express their religious practices and through which they transmit their faith.
>
> (para 94)

The same point can be demonstrated on the basis of the various national and international documents referred to in the rulings as well as by the precedents in the case law. These generally confirm the important role that the right to freedom of religion or belief has traditionally fulfilled in the different jurisdictions (see e.g.

Tahzib 1996; Evans 1997, re-issued 2008; Taylor 2005; Bielefeldt, Ghanea and Wiener 2016). Article 18 of the Universal Declaration of Human Rights (1948), for example, provides:

> Everyone has the right to freedom of thought, conscience and religion; this right includes freedom to change his religion or belief, and freedom, either alone or in community with others and in public or private, to manifest his religion or belief in teaching, practice, worship and observance.

The Concluding Document of the Vienna Meeting of the Conference on Security and Cooperation in Europe (CSCE), adopted on January 19, 1989, contains the following provision, which is also of interest because of the close connection it stipulates between the individual and the communal dimensions of religious freedom:

> (16) In order to ensure the freedom of the individual to profess and practise religion or belief, the participating States will, *inter alia*, . . .
>
> (16.4) respect the right of these religious communities to
>
> - establish and maintain freely accessible places of worship or assembly,
> - organize themselves according to their own hierarchical and institutional structure,
> - select, appoint and replace their personnel in accordance with their respective requirements and standards as well as with any freely accepted arrangement between them and their State,
> - solicit and receive voluntary financial and other contributions.

Finally, Article 6 of the UN Declaration on the Elimination of All Forms of Intolerance and of Discrimination Based on Religion or Belief of November 25, 1981 stipulates that the right to freedom of thought, conscience, religion, or belief, as it is called here,

> shall include, inter alia, the following freedoms:
>
> (a) To worship or assemble in connexion with a religion or belief, and to establish and maintain places for these purposes;
> (b) To establish and maintain appropriate charitable or humanitarian institutions; . . .
> (e) To teach a religion or belief in places suitable for these purposes; . . .
> (g) To train, appoint, elect or designate by succession appropriate leaders called for by the requirements and standards of any religion or belief.

Of course, it is only fair to note also that from the beginning constitutional law in general and case law in particular have obviously set limitations to religious freedom. It is difficult to conceive how this could possibly have been different, however, except if one was prepared to do away with states and with liberalism altogether.

What this also means is that one of the suggestions made by the new critics of religious freedom—that this right might just as well be abolished, or at least replaced by a more general right to ethical integrity (Laborde 2015)—is questionable at best. It is precisely the current right to freedom of religion or belief that in all four cases discussed earlier directly or indirectly sets limits on attempts to curtail the internal autonomy of religious organizations. Therefore, it is problematic to argue in the current circumstances that such changes in the national and international legal frameworks regarding religious freedom would remain without consequences for existing religious organizations (Tebbe 2014).

One final remark to be made here concerns the idea of a "multicultural democracy," as championed by the Supreme Court of Canada. Although often presented as a neutral model, in practice, as we have seen, it sometimes appears to contain at least an equally strong bias against religious associations, groups, and institutions as secularism, as is to a certain extent demonstrated by the case of Loyola High School. It could be argued therefore that although a conception of religious freedom as explored in this book may at first sight appear to be biased because of the social pluralist framework from which it is derived, paradoxically it might well turn out to be more tolerant towards other faiths than the secular model or a multicultural democracy. The very minimum that can be remarked is that such a multicultural model is not less neutral than the social pluralist framework of this book, because it is clearly rooted in a particular version of the liberal tradition as well. As the judgment in the case looked at here puts it: "Religious freedom must therefore be understood in the context of a secular, multicultural and democratic society with a strong interest in protecting dignity and diversity, promoting equality, and ensuring the vitality of a common belief in human rights" (para 47). Nor is it the case that the multicultural and social pluralist models are complete opposites, as important similarities between the two lines of thought also exist.

In sum, an evaluation of the case law that was presented above leads to the interim conclusion that the critical turn the debate on religious freedom has recently taken ought to be evaluated negatively. Rather, the cases point in the direction of a continuing relevance and value of the traditional formulations and interpretations of the right to freedom of religion or belief as can be found in existing (inter)national documents and subsequently also in the case law of different Western jurisdictions. This case law hardly represents a return to a truly jurisdictional approach to religious freedom. As the next chapter will argue, moreover, in a liberal democracy the state does not necessarily need to be the only source of sovereignty and multiple sources of sovereignty in society are perfectly compatible with the idea of constitutionalism.

Glendon would likely agree, given the fact that

> [her] work inside and outside of the legal academy has been driven by a set of simple propositions long honored in our history and traditions: each individual is a unique person; each person is endowed with dignity; human

> dignity is both the source and condition of liberty; men and women are society-oriented persons; all persons are entitled as a matter of necessity to all the social, economic, and cultural goods that human dignity requires; healthy mediating structures—seedbeds of virtue—are the true source of moral education and responsible citizenship; and, relatedly, human flourishing requires a buffer zone of protection against the impersonalism of the bureaucratic state and the social costs of unregulated market capitalism.
>
> (Kommers 1998: 1354)

"Not a bad formula, I would suggest, for the renewal of American constitutional law," the author of this characterization of Glendon's constitutionalism added, and the same might be said of the discipline of (comparative) constitutional law in general.

This quotation also makes clear what is at stake when our political order finds itself *in medias res*. Although there is clearly no reason whatsoever yet for alarm, not even from the point of view of social pluralist theory, there is something at stake in that there is a choice to be made. It is becoming clearer that changes are taking place in the worldviews of the population, even in a country such as the United States. Although, theoretically this does not affect church–state relations, in practice the kind of liberalism adhered to tends to change as a result. This also means that the relationship between faith-based organizations and the state has to be renegotiated. On the one hand these renegotiations form an ongoing process which is worth studying in an empirical manner. On the other hand, it is also an academic task to study these renegotiations in a comparative manner, in order to discern common patterns or differences. The comparison can be executed crossnationally or over time.

Although historians or sociologists may shy away from, in addition, adopting a more normative view on the matter, at least for constitutional lawyers more is at stake than meets the eye when faith-based organizations renegotiate their relations with the state. The constitutionalism of Glendon, for example, refers to such broad notions as human dignity, liberty, virtues, and, ultimately, human flourishing. According to her, healthy mediating structures are instrumental in achieving these formidable societal goods. To the extent that they succeed in actually realizing these goods, these mediating structures can be considered to be contributing to the common good even when each of them is acting only on behalf of particular religious and other groups in society. In order to be able to continue to make such contributions to the common good, faith-based organizations are dependent on the protection of their institutional religious autonomy.

Comparative constitutional law is a normative discipline in so far as some form of constitutionalism, liberal or illiberal, is often regarded as a contribution that public law can make to human flourishing. In many cases the importance of some kind of political legitimacy of these constitutional arrangements is also emphasized. Constitutional lawyers generally find it harder to recognize the role of mediating structures in society, as they are traditionally regarded as something that falls outside the scope of public law. What could minimally be observed, however, is that legal protection of institutional religious autonomy is required in order for faith-based organizations to be able to play their societal role, among other things. As a result, the renegotiations between faith-based organizations and the state are a matter of concern for constitutional lawyers as well. Religious freedom is more than an individual right, with a communal dimension as well. It has a potentially broader constitutional significance. This would only be different if constitutional lawyers were prepared to let go of the ideal of liberal democracy altogether.

Bibliography

Bachiochi, Erika (2016), "Secularism as Religion—Kirsanow and Eberstadt," *Mirror of Justice*, September 15.

Benson, Iain (2013a), "The Attack on Western Religions by Western Law: Re-Framing Pluralism, Liberalism and Diversity," *International Journal for Religious Freedom*, 6(1/2): 111–25.

Benson, Iain (2013b), *An Associational Framework for the Reconciliation of Competing Rights Claims Involving the Freedom of Religion* (University of Witwatersrand: Ph.D. Thesis).

Benson, Iain T. (2013c), "Law Deans, Legal Coercion and the Freedoms of Association and Religion in Canada," *The Advocate*, 71(5): 671–5.

Berg, Thomas C., Kimberlee Wood Colby, Carl H. Esbeck, and Richard W. Garnett (2011), "Religious Freedom, Church–State Separation, and the Ministerial Exception," *Northwestern University Law Review Colloquy*, 106 (December 22): 175–90.

Bielefeldt, Heiner, Nazila Ghanea, and Michael Wiener (2016), *Freedom of Religion or Belief* (Oxford: Oxford University Press).

Brennan, Patrick McKinley (2015), "An Essay on Christian Constitutionalism: Building in the Divine Style, for the Common Good(s)," *Rutgers Journal of Law and Religion*, 16(3): 478–540.

Brink, Jaco van den and Hans-Martien ten Napel (2013), "The Dutch Political Reformed Party (SGP) and Passive Female Suffrage: A Comparison of Three High Court Judgments from the Viewpoint of Democratic Theory," *Merkourios. Utrecht Journal of International and European Law*, 29(77): 29–41.

Brooks, David (2015), "When Cultures Shift," *The New York Times*, April 17.

Broughton, David and Hans-Martien ten Napel (2000), "Conclusion. European Exceptionalism?" in: David Broughton and Hans-Martien ten Napel (eds), *Religion and Mass Electoral Behaviour in Europe* (London and New York: Routledge) 198–209.

Calo, Zachary R. (2010), "Pluralism, Secularism and the European Court of Human Rights," *Journal of Law and Religion*, 26(1): 261–80.

Calo, Zachary R. (2014), "Constructing the Secular: Law and Religion Jurisprudence in Europe and the United States," EUI Working Paper RSCAS 2014/94.

Carlson-Thies, Stanley (2015), "The Sky isn't Falling: Religious Freedom is Context-Specific," available at www.irfalliance.org/the-sky-isnt-falling-religious-freedom-is-context-specific (accessed November 25, 2016).

Cohen, Jean L. (2015), "Freedom of Religion, Inc.: Whose Sovereignty?" *Netherlands Journal of Legal Philosophy*, 44(3): 169–210.

DeGirolami, Marc O. (2015), "Free Exercise by Moonlight," St. John's University School of Law Legal Studies Research Paper No. 15-2587216, March 30, available at http://papers.ssrn.com/sol3/papers.cfm?abstract id=2587216 (accessed November 25, 2016).

DeGirolami, Marc (2016), "The U.S. Commission on Abolishing Religious Freedom," Online Library of Law and Liberty, September 27, available at www.libertylawsite.org/2016/09/27/the-u-s-commission-on-abolishing-religious-freedom (accessed November 25, 2016).

Douthat, Ross (2014), "The Culture War's Sore Winners," *The New York Times*, July 1.

Douthat, Ross (2015), "Making Religion the Problem," *The New York Times*, April 2.

Eberstadt, Mary (2016), *It's Dangerous to Believe: Religious Freedom and Its Enemies* (New York, NY: HarperCollins).

Epstein, Richard (2016), "The Government's Civil Rights Bullies," *NYU Journal of Law & Liberty*, September 27.

Evans, Carolyn and Christopher A. Thomas (2006), "Church–State Relations in the European Court of Human Rights," *Brigham Young University Law Review*, 2006(3): 699–726.

Evans, Malcolm D. (1997, re-issued in 2008), *Religious Liberty and International Law in Europe* (Cambridge: Cambridge University Press).

Evans, Malcolm, Peter Petkoff, and Julian Rivers (eds) (2015), *The Changing Nature of Religious Rights under International Law* (Oxford: Oxford University Press).

Garnett, Richard W. (2012), "Religious Freedom and the Nondiscrimination Norm," in: Austin Sarat (ed.), *Legal Responses to Religious Practices in the United States. Accommodation and Its Limits* (Cambridge: Cambridge University Press) 194–227.

Glendon, Mary Ann (1991), *Rights Talk: The Impoverishment of Political Discourse* (New York, NY: The Free Press).

Glendon, Mary Ann (2012), "The Harold J. Berman Lecture. Religious Freedom—Second-Class Right?" *Emory Law Journal*, 61 (special issue): 971–990.

Glendon, Mary Ann (2015), "Religious Freedom: Yesterday, Today and Tomorrow," The 2015 Cardinal Egan Lecture, available at www.magnificat.com/foundation/pdf/M_A_Glendon_2015.pdf (accessed November 25, 2016).

Glendon, Mary Ann and Raul F. Yanes (1991), "Structural Free Exercise," *Michigan Law Review*, 90(3): 477–550.

Harinck, George (2016), *Varia Americana: In het spoor van Abraham Kuyper door de Verenigde Staten* (Amsterdam: Bert Bakker).

Hiemstra, John L. (2015), "A Calvinist Case for Tolerant Public Pluralism: The Religious Sources of Abraham Kuyper's Public Philosophy," *Religious Studies and Theology*, 34(1): 53–83.

Hirschl, Ran (2010), *Constitutional Theocracy* (Cambridge, MA: Harvard University Press).

Horwitz, Paul (2013), *First Amendment Institutions* (Cambridge, MA: Harvard University Press).

Horwitz, Paul (2014), "The Hobby Lobby Moment," *Harvard Law Review*, 128(1): 154–89.

Kennedy, James (2001), "Oude en nieuwe vormen van tolerantie in Nederland en Amerika: Tolerantie als ideologie maakt verdraagzaamheid kwetsbaar," in: Marcel ten Hooven (ed.), *De lege tolerantie: Over vrijheid en vrijblijvendheid in Nederland* (Amsterdam: Boom) 244–55.

Koffeman, L.J. and N.R. Koffeman (2008), "In dienst treden van de kerk; afstand doen van rechten?" (annotation on ECHR 23 September 2008, *Ahtinen v Finland*), *NJCM-Bulletin*, 34(3): 256–267.

Kommers, Donald P. (1998), "The Constitutionalism of Mary Ann Glendon," *Notre Dame Law Review*, 73(5): 1333–54.

Laborde, Cécile (2015), "Religion in the Law: The Disaggregation Approach," *Law and Philosophy*, 34(6): 581–600.

Langston, Chelsae (2015), "Reasons to Hope #Lovewins for Both Individuals and Religious Organizations," *Shared Justice*, July 8.

Langlaude-Doné, S. (2016), "Religious Organisations, Internal Autonomy and Other Religious Rights before the European Court of Human Rights and the OSCE," *Netherlands Quarterly of Human Rights*, 34(1): 8–40.

Levin, Yuval (2014), "Some Thoughts on Hobby Lobby," *National Review Online*, July 1.

Loof, Jan-Peter (2008), "Van praktische oplossing naar principiële stellingname: de CGB en de gewetensbezwaarde trouwambtenaar," in: J.P. Loof (ed.), *Juridische ruimte voor gewetensbezwaren?* (Leiden: Stichting NJCM-Boekerij) 95–114.

Mansvelt Beck, Floris (2015), *How We Do Things Here: Moral Communities, Integration, and Toleration in the Netherlands: Competing Interpretations of Liberalism in Parliamentary Practice, 2000–2013* (Leiden: Ph.D. Thesis).

Napel, Hans-Martien ten (2011) "'Finishing the Work Begun by the French Revolution': A Critical Analysis of the Dutch Supreme Court Judgment on the Political Reformed Party and Passive Female Suffrage," *European Public Law*, 17(1): 61–70.

Napel, Hans-Martien ten and Jaco van den Brink (2014), "The SGP Case: Did it Really (Re)Launch the Debate on Party Regulation in the Netherlands?" in: Ingrid van Biezen and Hans-Martien ten Napel (eds), *Regulating Political Parties. European Democracies in Comparative Perspective* (Leiden: Leiden University Press) 181–94.

Napel, Hans-Martien ten (2016), "Vrijheid van godsdienst als tweederangsrecht?" *Handelingen. Tijdschrift voor praktische theologie*, 43(1): 49–59.

Oppenheimer, Mark (2014), "Evangelicals Find Themselves in the Midst of a Calvinist Revival," *The New York Times*, January 3.

Paulsen, Michael Stokes (2013), "The Priority of God: A Theory of Religious Liberty," *Pepperdine Law Review*, 39(5): 1159–222.

Petito, Fabio, Daniel Philpott, Silvio Ferrari, and Judd Birdsall (2016), "FoRB—Recognising Our Differences Can Be Our Strength: Enhancing Transatlantic Cooperation on Promoting Freedom of Religion or Belief," Policy briefing, Summer.

Pew Research Center (2015), "America's Changing Religious Landscape: Christians Decline Sharply as Share of Population; Unaffiliated and Other Faiths Continue to Grow," May 12, available at www.pewforum.org/2015/05/12/americas-changing-religious-landscape (accessed November 25, 2016).

Reuter, Astrid (2009), "Changing the Boundaries of the Religious Field: Legal Conflicts over Religion as Struggles over Blurring Borders," *Journal of Religion in Europe*, 2(1): 1–20.

Rivers, Julian (2007), "Law, Religion and Gender Equality," *Ecclesiastical Law Journal*, 9(1): 24–52.
Rivers, Julian (2010), *The Law of Organized Religions: Between Establishment and Secularism* (Oxford: Oxford University Press).
Schall S.J., Rev. James V. (2012), "The Speed of Change in the Republic of Rights," *Crisis Magazine*, April 13.
Schauer, Frederick (1998), "Principles, Institutions, and the First Amendment," *Harvard Law Review*, 112(1): 84–120.
Schwartzman, Micah, Chad Flanders, and Zoë Robinson (eds) (2016), *The Rise of Corporate Religious Liberty* (Oxford: Oxford University Press).
Shah, Timothy, Thomas Farr, and Jack Friedman (eds) (2016), *Religious Freedom and Gay Rights. Emerging Conflicts in North America and Europe* (Oxford: Oxford University Press).
Sherwood, Harriet (2016), "People of No Religion Outnumber Christians in England and Wales—Study," *The Guardian*, May 23.
Tahzib, Bahiyyih G. (1996), *Freedom of Religion or Belief: Ensuring Effective International Legal Protection* (The Hague/Boston, MA/London: Martinus Nijhoff Publishers).
Taylor, Charles (2007), *A Secular Age* (Cambridge, MA: The Belknap Press of Harvard University Press).
Taylor, Paul M. (2005), *Freedom of Religion: UN and European Human Rights Law and Practice* (Cambridge: Cambridge University Press).
Tebbe, Nelson (2014), "The End of Religious Freedom: What is at Stake?" *Pepperdine Law Review*, 41(5): 963–82.
Trigg, Roger (2012), *Equality, Freedom, and Religion* (Oxford: Oxford University Press).
Tushnet, Mark (2015), "*Accommodation of Religion* Thirty Years On," *Harvard Journal of Law & Gender*, 38 (Winter): 1–33.
U.S. Commission on Civil Rights (2016), *Peaceful Coexistence: Reconciling Nondiscrimination Principles with Civil Liberties* (Washington, DC: U.S. Commission on Civil Rights).
Vorster, J.M. (2010), "Current Options for the Constitutional Implementation of Religious Freedom," in: A. van de Beek, E.A.J.G. Van der Borght, and B.P. Vermeulen (eds), *Freedom of Religion* (Leiden and Boston, MA: Brill).
Vyver, Johan D. van der (2012), "State Interference in the Internal Affairs of Religious Institutions," *Emory International Law Review*, 26(1): 1–9.

2 Social Pluralist Constitutionalism

Introduction

One of the reasons why it is appropriate to take the new critics of religious freedom seriously, as the current study aims to do, is that they see clearly how this right has historically been shaped by Western political thought in general and Christianity in particular. The discipline of constitutional law has changed considerably in recent years. It is starting, as Von Bogdandy has advocated, to become more comparative, interdisciplinary, and theoretical in character (2012). One aspect in which the discipline has been less successful is the identification and acknowledgment of some of the fundamental presuppositions on which even its central concepts such as constitutionalism and democracy ultimately rely.

Constitutionalism, on which the current chapter focuses, certainly qualifies as an "essentially contested concept" and is thus difficult to define. Former judge of the German federal court Dieter Grimm provides the following functional definition of the concept in a leading handbook of comparative constitutional law (2012: 104):

> (1) The constitution in the modern sense is a set of legal norms, not a philosophical construct. The norms emanate from a political decision rather than having their source in a pre-established truth.
> (2) The purpose of these norms is to regulate the establishment and the exercise of public power as opposed to a mere modification of a pre-existing public power. Regulation implies limitation.
> (3) The regulation is comprehensive in the sense that no pre- or extra-constitutional bearers of public power and no pre- or extra-constitutional means to exercise this power are recognized.
> (4) Constitutional law is higher law. It enjoys primacy of all other laws and legal acts emanating from government. Acts incompatible with the constitution cannot claim legal validity.
> (5) Constitutional law finds its origin with the people as the only legitimate source of power. The distinction between *pouvoir constituant* and *pouvoir constitué* is essential to the constitution.
>
> If all these elements are present, we speak of the *achievement* of constitutionalism.

This is, of course, a highly ideological definition of constitutionalism. For example, if it is necessary in order for a political order to be called constitutional that its norms do not have "their source in a pre-established truth," this means that no such thing as Islamic constitutionalism can exist (Quraishi-Landes 2015). This also connects with the fifth principle—that is, that the sovereignty of the people is the only source of legitimacy which can be recognized within constitutionalism. This principle does not only exclude Islamic constitutionalism, but also Jewish and indeed some forms of Christian constitutionalism (Friedell 2015; Brennan 2015).

It thus becomes clear that what Grimm is describing is not so much constitutionalism generally, but rather liberal constitutionalism. This is worthwhile attempting, even though certainly in the context of a handbook of comparative constitutional law it would have been useful to add that other forms of constitutionalism are also conceivable, even though he distinguishes between different types of constitutions. This is explicitly acknowledged in a recent editorial, which adds that the goal of the editorial is "somewhat disruptive" (Tushnet 2016: 1). Within the discipline of (comparative) constitutional law, it was until recently quite common to identify the concept of constitutionalism with liberal constitutionalism. Illiberal regimes were not considered worthy of the label constitutional at all. With the number of authoritarian regimes on the rise globally, and even within the West (Diamond, Plathner, and Walker 2016), it becomes almost inevitable to recognize that worldwide a variety of constitutionalisms can be distinguished.

Although it is naturally not the case that liberal and illiberal regimes can normatively be fully equated, it is also not possible to simply argue that liberal constitutionalism is "good" and that illiberal constitutionalism is "bad." Different types of constitutionalism are rooted in different religious and other worldviews of the population. It all depends on one's ultimate beliefs whether the one kind of constitutionalism is preferred over the other. As current developments within the European Union (EU) illustrate—for example, in Hungary and Poland—it is also possible for countries to move from one kind of constitutionalism in the direction of another. Both in academia and in practical politics, this sometimes seems to be little understood. The way forward is to acknowledge that liberal constitutionalism, like other forms of constitutionalism, relies on particular presuppositions.

As I already mentioned in the introductory chapter, my research interests in the field of Law and Religion acquired their current focus largely as a result of a stimulating conference on "Religion and Civil Society: The Changing Faces of 'Religion' and 'Secularity'" held at Harvard Law School in 2012. One of the reasons why this conference turned out to be so inspiring was precisely because for once it did not evade such questions. I remember that, just before I flew back, I bought a copy of one of the books that had been referred to in this context in Harvard Square: *Why We Should Call Ourselves Christians: The Religious Roots of Free Societies* by Italian philosopher and politician Marcello Pera. Pera is neither an atheist nor a believer. One of the central theses of his book is that "Christianity and liberals are *congeners.* If you remove faith in the former from the latter, then it too will disappear" (2008: 45).

In a similar vein, this chapter will argue that the extent to which protection by the right to religion or belief is (im)possible relies on the nature of constitutionalism, which in turn is dependent on the type of liberalism which prevails in a particular society at a particular point in time. All three—liberalism, constitutionalism, and religious freedom—are thoroughly interconnected. Finally, behind this threesome lie the pre-political moral foundations, religious and otherwise, on which a liberal constitutional order like any other political order ultimately rests (Jiménez Lobeira 2011).

Christianity and Liberalism

The fact that the discipline of constitutional law has thus far not been particularly successful in the identification and acknowledgment of some of the fundamental presuppositions on which its central concepts ultimately rely is all the more remarkable since not just constitutionalism and the right to freedom of religion or belief, but also liberalism in general, is indeed strongly linked to particular pre-political moral foundations. Thus, as constitutional law scholar Michael W. McConnell argued (2001), the history of liberalism goes back further than the Enlightenment of the late seventeenth and eighteenth centuries. It is probably accurate to regard the sixteenth-century Reformation as having given rise to classical liberalism, with its emphasis on the idea of individual conscience. To be sure, as political scientist Jacob T. Levy has argued (2015: 87),

> I do not think that it makes sense to talk about liberalism before about 1700, and I am quite sure that it doesn't make sense to talk about liberalism as such before the modern state took shape, even if we can sometimes identify one argument or another as more or less liberal.

Certainly, however, during the Enlightenment it became possible to build upon foundations such as the Reformation and to make significant further contributions. In the light of this history, it is problematic, however, to interpret liberalism as essentially the victory of reason over religion in politics.

McConnell has also elaborated upon the similarities between some of the core doctrines of liberalism and particular Christian theological principles, notably between the rejection of utopianism and the doctrine of original sin, between the notion of limited government and the idea of a separation of church and state, between the concept of rights and the notion of the primacy of conscience, and between the principle of equality and the idea of the priesthood of all believers. Of all these different connections, the second is the most directly relevant one here—that is, separation of church and state in the sense of there being *libertas ecclesiae* or the "freedom of the church." As McConnell puts it (2001: 9–10),

> In this view, religious freedom comes into being not as a result of ontological individualism but as a result of the jurisdictional separation between these two sets of authorities. . . .The two-kingdoms view is at the heart of our First Amendment.

He then continues (10):

> While theological in its origin, the two-kingdoms idea lent powerful support to a more general liberal theory of government. The separation of church from state is the most powerful possible refutation of the notion that the political sphere is omnicompetent—that it has rightful authority over all of life. If the state does not have power over the church, it follows that the power of the state is limited.

The term "church" in this context can, of course, be broadened up so as to also include faith-based organizations more generally.

Against this background, it becomes understandable that someone like constitutional law scholar Richard W. Garnett has defined "constitutionalism" in the classical liberal sense as "the enterprise of protecting human freedom and promoting the common good by categorizing, separating, structuring, and limiting power in entrenched and enforceable ways" (2009: 901). He added (903):

> Constitutionalism relies, both in theory and in fact, not only on the separation and limitation of the powers of the political authority, but also on the existence and the health of authorities and associations outside, and meaningfully independent of, the state.

What this does not intend to imply is that Christianity and liberalism are somehow inextricably linked to one another. Thus, as political scientist Robert P. Kraynak pointed out, "Christianity is not inherently a liberal or democratic religion, nor does it make the support of a political order its highest priority" (2001: xii). In fact, according to Kraynak, one "startling conclusion" of his book *Christian Faith and Modern Democracy* is precisely "that the Christian tradition has been rather illiberal and undemocratic for much of its history. The present democratic consensus is thus quite recent and, I might add, quite astonishing!" (3).

More specifically, Kraynak in this context refers to "the weaknesses and anxieties that underlie the liberal democracies of the modern Western world." Perhaps the central weakness is that it is not considered possible or even desirable to develop any meaningful sense of direction for liberal democracy:

> Surely it is a sign of confusion and loss of purpose when the most common argument that one hears today in defense of liberal democracy derives from moral relativism—from the denial of objective truth about good and evil

> which seems to suggest that liberal democracy is preferable because it permits any kind of behavior within the limits of the law.
>
> (10)

On the other hand, this agnosticism and skeptical relativism

> are actually a form of false modesty that disguise a rigid and stultifying dogmatism. . . . [T]he fact remains that modern liberal democracies have been shaped by philosophical doctrines in a way that previous regimes never were; and the decisive doctrine is the philosophy of liberalism.
>
> (201, 21)

As Kraynak points out, modern liberal democracy elevates "politics to a metaphysical, cosmological, or quasi-religious level. . . . Modern liberal democracy, therefore, is more than a political system: it is a philosophy of freedom and a theoretical doctrine of human dignity translated into practical action" (25). In particular, the modern welfare state as it has developed since the mid-twentieth century "is highly intrusive in the imposition of secular liberal values" (224). While liberalism pretends to be neutral, it is in fact a distinct ideology with a particular vision on what the good life comprises. Whatever one may otherwise think of (moral) autonomy, free market capitalism, or secular democracy, they are certainly not objective and unprejudiced (Rosenfeld 2014). Kraynak points out that this "secular humanism" is now widely promoted and inculcated in youngsters (2001: 124).

Interestingly, Kraynak criticizes not just democracy but also human rights. He even goes so far as to speak of "a deep resistance to the concept of human rights" that historically characterizes Christianity:

> As shocking as it may sound today, there are numerous and profound reasons why this is so. . . . Ultimately, of course, Christians cannot accept the premise of human autonomy or the natural freedom of the autonomous self that underlies most doctrines of rights.
>
> (153)

It is precisely this concept of autonomy that lies at the heart of Christianity's ambivalence towards human rights. A closer look at a key document of the Catholic Church, the *Compendium of the Social Doctrine of the Church* (2005), shows that the Vatican's recently more positive attitude towards democracy and human rights indeed remains conditional and by no means can be taken as an all-out acceptance of their liberal presuppositions (Carozza and Philpott 2012; Harinck and Ten Napel 2013; see, however, Moyn 2015).

The criticism voiced by Kraynak has recently taken on an increased salience in the form of the discussion about a so-called "benedict option" (Deneen 2014; Dreher 2015; Hanby 2015). The term "benedict option" refers to the phenomenon that, according to some Christian theologians and other thinkers, liberal democracy has developed in such a way that a withdrawal from society is the preferred alternative for Christians. The idea is that there is, or at least ought to be, a limit to reasonable adaptations that believers can be expected to make to the dominant culture. Christianity is believed to be under an obligation to act as a counterculture when appropriate, and in our time this means that it is necessary for it to distance itself from liberalism. By focusing primarily on their own church communities, and thus living a kind of monastic life, Christians can nevertheless attempt to influence society indirectly by offering a contrasting model of how we can live.

I should like to stress that, just as this book does not intend to polarize unnecessarily in the direction of the new critics of religious freedom, it does not want to suggest that authors subscribing to the idea of the benedict option do not have a point either. It is certainly the case that both liberal and evangelical Christian churches in, for example, the United States would do wisely to periodically ask themselves the question whether they have not conformed theologically too much to their environment. The same holds true for their social and political convictions.

On the other hand, it is also possible to discern a link between the new critics of religious freedom and theologians and others advocating the benedict option, in the sense that representatives of both groups sometimes appear to reject liberalism altogether. It is submitted here, however, that, despite criticisms such as those voiced by Kraynak, McConnell is still right in arguing that

> certain doctrines of mainstream Christianity point in the direction of liberalism, and that historically, liberalism was a product of those Christian impulses. It is, in short, no accident that liberalism arose when and where it did, in the lands of the Protestant Reformation.
>
> (2001: 6–7; cf. Shah and Hertzke 2016)

Hence, there also remains reason for Christianity to continue its constructive, yet critical, engagement with liberalism (Song 2006). In fact, this is precisely what the current study aims to do.

Before we elaborate further on the developments in liberalism that have taken place in recent decades, and their consequences for our understanding of constitutionalism, it is important to note that even the more classical type of liberal constitutionalism has not always been as accommodating of societal diversity as Garnett and others may have wished. As a result, the right to freedom of religion or belief in general and its associational and institutional dimensions in particular have to a certain extent been restricted from the beginning.

Constitutionalism and its Limited Accommodation of Diversity

Like liberalism, constitutionalism is, of course, hardly a new idea. On the contrary, it represents what has probably been the main contribution of constitutional law to legitimizing national political orders for nearly four centuries now. As such, it arguably started with the Dutch revolt against the Spanish of 1579 (Griffiths 1960), but certainly—and as it is more commonly noted—with the English Civil War (1642–1651) and the American and French revolutions of the late eighteenth century.

It is neither necessary nor possible to recapitulate that narrative here, which comprises basically the whole recent history of Western constitutional law (Van Caenegem 1995; Anastaplo 1999a, 1999b). For the purposes of this chapter, it suffices to highlight just three points concerning constitutionalism. Taking a closer look at the functional definition of constitutionalism offered by Grimm, what can be noticed in the first place is that the achievement of constitutionalism is presented as a radical break in human history. For him, the concept of constitutionalism originated in the seventeenth and eighteenth centuries. It is the direct result of the religious wars to which the Reformation gave rise, among other things. In order to put an end to the hostilities, it was thought necessary to henceforth concentrate all power in the state. The state had subsequently to be checked by constitutional principles, the sum of which make for constitutionalism as we still know it today (2012: 104; cf. Grimm 2009: 2371).

Second, what can be noticed is that in Grimm's definition of constitutionalism there appears to be hardly any room for the notion of a common or public good. On the contrary, "[b]ound was government in order to prevent it from pursuing goals other than protecting individual freedom and societal self-regulation" (2012: 117). This stands in sharp contrast to Garnett's definition, according to which constitutionalism in the classical liberal sense also aims at promoting the common good.

The third and final characteristic of Grimm's definition of liberalism is the strict separation it envisages between public and private power. In medieval times power had been dispersed. The rise of the nation state led to the privatization of civil society, however, which could no longer exercise what was now seen as exclusively public power:

> Public and private, still indistinguishable in the medieval world, became distinct spheres. The constitution did not question the concentration of public power in the hands of the state. Rather, it was this concentration that created the need for constitutionalism. The constitution's aim was to tame public power in the interest of individual freedom. The distinction between public and private was therefore constitutive for constitutionalism.
> (2012: 105)

The impression that it is essential to liberal constitutionalism that all public power be concentrated with the state is confirmed by a chapter on the concept of sovereignty in the same handbook of comparative constitutional law in which Grimm's contribution appears. Thus, the author of this article holds that state sovereignty means "that the state has the absolute power to make decisions on every aspect of human life," and "that this power is unlimited"

(Troper 2012: 354). Moreover, there is an "absence of any substantial limits to the power of the state" (355).

International lawyer Nico Krisch also brings home this same point, which is crucial for the argument of this chapter, clearly when he argues how constitutionalism, besides all other, better-known things,

> also encapsulates the very modern, Enlightenment idea of agency: it provides a form by which a polity can wrestle its affairs back from the forces of chance, history and power and remake, indeed refound, its institutions in a comprehensive way. Ideally, at the moment of constitution-making all traditional sites of public power come under scrutiny and are examined in the light of reason, and none of them can survive outside the constitutional framework.
>
> (2012: 207; see also 2010)

It is here that Krisch brings in Canadian political philosopher James Tully, however, who has argued that this very characteristic of constitutionalism that on the one hand explains part of its immense normative appeal through the ages in the West, potentially also causes severe difficulties on the other. The reason for this is that nation states, despite their undisputedly uniforming tendencies from at least the nineteenth century onwards, have in reality hardly ever turned into the kind of homogeneous societies that at least certain adherents of constitutionalism would have liked them to become. Much to the frustration of these theorists—and certain present-day practical politicians for that matter—cultural, religious, and political diversity has remained very much a fact of life in liberal democracies across the globe. In recent decades this diversity, if anything, seems to have increased even further. This is problematic in so far as modern constitutionalism, in embracing uniformity,

> fails to reflect the different customs and culturally grounded ideas of particular groups in society; and this even more so if these groups do not subscribe to the liberal vision of a "modern", free individual, able and willing to transcend her history and culture and ready to engage with all others in an unconditional deliberation over the course of the common polity
>
> (Krisch 2012: 212–3; see also Tully 1995: chapters 2 and 3)

Admittedly, in the course of the nineteenth and twentieth centuries constitutionalism has attempted to respond to the reality of persisting cultural, religious, and political diversity in society, among other things through consociationalism (Krisch 2012: 213–4; Choudhry 2008; Fleiner and Fleiner 2009). Consociationalism has been defined as bringing "together rival subgroups by including them in governing coalitions, granting the various groups mutual vetoes, ensuring proportional representation in elections, cabinets, civil service positions, and granting self-governance authority to segmented groups over such matters as education and culture" (Halberstam 2012: 603).

It is really only fair to say that it has sometimes succeeded in doing so, up to the point where it actually becomes difficult to distinguish between this type of accommodating, liberal constitutionalism and the "real existing" pluralism. This holds all the more true as a "pure" form of unfettered pluralism is difficult to imagine, and in practice pluralism therefore in turn encounters certain limits with a view to the minimum level of social cohesion required for nation states to hold together (Cliteur and Van den Eekhout 2001).

Elsewhere I have explored one particularly interesting illustration of such a more or less consociationalist approach—that is, the *Human Development Report 2004* published for the United Nations Development Programme (UNDP) (Ten Napel 2006; Ten Napel and Theissen 2009). As suggested already by the title of this section, however, this type of accommodation of diversity in constitutionalism is inherently limited by what Krisch rightly identifies as its central aim: "to create a comprehensive framework for all public power in a given polity under the rule of law" (2012: 217). It is not difficult to see why this trait of constitutionalism becomes more problematic in a postsecular age of arguably still further increasing diversity within nation states, and might sooner or later even threaten societal peace and stability, the very goals that most constitutional systems seek to achieve in the first place (219).

All this contrasts not just with certain forms of Jewish and Islamic constitutionalism but also with the notion of Christian constitutionalism as defended by law professor Patrick McKinley Brennan. Brennan admits that he has written his contribution from his personal perspective, which is that of a conservative Catholic, and that his opinions are not necessarily representative of the Christian tradition as a whole. Still, it is worthwhile to note how Brennan points out, first, that a Christian state will acknowledge the fact that only Christ is King and that therefore "no constitution . . . is truly the supreme law of any land" (2015: 502). Second, the same principle that Christ is King implies that worldly rulers, whether they have been elected or not, do not possess ultimate sovereignty: "[t]he earthly 'sovereign' is not truly sovereign" (502). A third characteristic of Brennan's Christian constitutionalism is that the state "will recognize the rights and vitality of the pluriform, flesh-and-blood associations in which men and women learn what nature, history, and the Church have to teach, and it will coordinate and respectfully harmonize the respective authorities embodied in such groups" (502). A fourth characteristic of a Christian state is that it will respect the so-called freedom of the church referred to earlier. Finally, it will try as much as possible to realize the common good, so as to make it possible for each person to achieve his or her "natural *summum bonum*" (502).

Brennan's version of Christian constitutionalism does not situate itself within the liberal tradition. Still, the contrast between Grimm's liberal constitutionalism and Brennan's Christian constitutionalism reminds one of the difference that is sometimes made between two kinds of liberalism, which was referred to in Chapter 1. It is possible to call the first kind of liberalism, to which Grimm's version of constitutionalism belongs, progressive and the second kind of liberalism, to which different kinds of religious constitutionalism will belong to the extent that they situate themselves within the liberal tradition at all, conservative (Levin 2012b). In the next section we will come back to this same distinction in partly different terms, and also elaborate a little further on it. The reason for this is that the distinction between the two kinds of liberalism appears to be of even increased salience at a time when, according to political theorist William A. Galston, (progressive) liberalism is tempted by a form of "civic totalism."

"Civic Totalism"

During a conference on "The Rule of Law with Chinese Characteristics in Transition" at the City University of Hong Kong, in 2013, I had the privilege of also briefly meeting with political theorist Kim Sungmoon. In a fascinating article, entitled "A pluralist reconstruction of Confucian democracy," Kim attempts "to revamp Confucian democracy, which is originally presented as the communitarian corrective and cultural alternative to liberal democracy, into a robust democratic political theory and practice that is plausible in the societal context of pluralism" (2012: 315).

The same source of inspiration that Kim uses to reconstruct Confucian democracy—that is, Galston's notion of liberal pluralism—can be used to critically appraise the current state of Western liberal democracy. As Kim notes, Galston's liberal pluralism "attempts the most sophisticated philosophical engagement with value pluralism by giving full attention to the intrinsic value of diversity and human plurality particularly in the modern democratic context, even though Galston's political pluralism is characteristically liberal" (317).

According to Galston, "[l]iberalism requires a robust though rebuttable presumption in favor of individuals and groups leading their lives as they see fit, within a broad range of legitimate variation, in accordance with their own understanding of what gives life meaning and value." He calls this presumption "the principle of expressive liberty," a principle which "implies a corresponding presumption (also rebuttable) against external interference with individual and group endeavors" (2005: 3).

Practically speaking, Galston's liberal pluralism has, as Kim rightly notes, two main consequences (2012: 321). The first is "multiple sovereignties"—that is, the notion that "our social life comprises multiple sources of authority and sovereignty—individuals, parents, associations, churches, and state institutions, among others—no one of which is dominant for all purposes and on all occasions" (Galston 2005: 36). Second, "public institutions must be cautious and restrained in their dealings with voluntary associations, and there is no presumption that a state may intervene in such associations just because they conduct their internal affairs in ways that diverge from general public principles" (9).

This kind of liberalism, called Reformation liberalism by Galston and the same as what was referred to as classical liberalism above, stresses diversity in the sense of "legitimate differences among individuals and groups over such matters as the nature of the good life, sources of moral authority, reason versus faith, and the like" (Galston 2002: 21; 2011). It differs from a type of liberalism that I referred to in Chapter 1 as Enlightenment liberalism, a term also used by Galston. Enlightenment liberalism stresses autonomy in the sense of "the commitment to sustained rational examination of self, others, and social practices" (2002: 21). This latter type of liberalism is tempted by a form of "civic totalism" that—as Galston puts it, following Stephen Macedo (2000)—"tacitly views public institutions as plenipotentiary and civil society as a political construction possessing only those liberties that the polity chooses to grant and modify or revoke at will" (2005: 23).

In the light of the principle of expressive liberty, the right to freedom of religion or belief is naturally of particular relevance. Kim rightly points out that, paradoxically, religious freedom is often "in practice grounded in the radical unavailability of freedom of choice for a person who is radically situated in a particular religious and/or cultural community as a member" (2012: 319). In the context of the current book this raises the question to what extent Western liberal democracy still manages to realize the principle of expressive liberty, also defined by Galston (2002: 28) as

> the absence of constraints, imposed by some individuals on others, that make it impossible (or significantly more difficult) for the affected individuals to live their lives in ways that express their deepest beliefs about what gives meaning or value to life.

As a political theorist, Kim does not answer in an empirical manner the question whether, just as by the ethically monistic character of certain theoretizations of Confucian democracy, expressive liberty is indeed threatened by a Western "civic totalism" as defined by Galston (Kim 2012: 320–1). The focus of his article is, moreover, on reconstructing Confucian democracy. Such a hypothesis would, however, fit in with the general framework of the current study. Since the cultural and social revolution of the 1960s, the worldviews of the population could indeed well be subject to change in the sense of classical or Reformation liberalism losing ground and Enlightenment liberalism (re)surging. As a result, contemporary liberalism, as, for example, McConnell also put it, runs the risk of degenerating from "a set of political arrangements by which persons of widely differing views can live together in relative harmony" into "a narrow and sectarian program enforcing its dogmas by force" (2000: 1259).

More specifically, McConnell has identified three developments which have contributed to a shift from classical or Reformation liberalism to Enlightenment liberalism in recent decades. The first of these developments is the change from so-called political liberalism to a more comprehensive type of liberalism. This change is marked by the fact that traditional principles of liberal government—notably neutrality, tolerance, and equality—started to be projected on to private persons and associations as well. A second relevant development concerns the extension of the regulatory jurisdiction of the state, which brings it more often into conflict with religious individuals and institutions. Finally, the notion of neutrality has become confused with secularism (2001: 17–24).

As a result, liberalism has undergone nothing less than a "regime change":

> The earlier liberal regime converged extensively with (because it was indebted to) a Christian conception of constitutionalism. In that regime, governments understood their role as the protection of the basic civil rights and freedom of its citizens, the provision of essential social welfare services for all those in need, and the widespread protection of freedom of association and self-government for the institutions of civil society. The new regime is taking upon itself a new mandate, one which is undermining some of those earlier commitments. It is attempting to refashion civil society associations in the image of the universal public principles applying to liberal governments.
> (Chaplin 2006; cf. Levin 2011, 2012a, 2012b; McClay 2012)

Illustrative of this development is that for certain scholars it has now become a question mark if, and to what extent, religion should be tolerated at all within a liberal democracy (Leiter 2013; Nehushtan 2015).

On the other hand, it should also be remembered at this point that the regime change that has arguably taken place within liberalism has not yet resulted in a similar shift in the case law regarding the right to freedom of religion or belief. Thus, in Chapter 1 we concluded that although the glass of communal religious freedom may have become half empty, there are simply no empirical grounds yet for any conclusions that the sky is falling. What the change from one kind of liberalism to another does make worthwhile doing, however, is to continue monitoring whether or not this will eventually result in further changes in legislation or case law. It is not self-evident that this will be the case, as in the meantime societal and other developments might take a different direction. The next section will argue that this is already happening, to the extent that the current trend towards transconstitutionalism mitigates any civic totalism that according to certain authors may have been discernible in recent times.

Transconstitutionalism

In a sense, the rise of transconstitutionalism could ease the problems that are potentially caused by a national state which is on its way to becoming omnipotent. The concept of transconstitutionalism is perhaps even more controversial and difficult to pin down than that of constitutionalism itself. What it refers to in a general sense, however, is that the notion of constitutionalism appears to become increasingly separated from its traditional nation-state context. What constitutional lawyers have therefore started to study instead, or at least in addition to conventional studies of constitutionalism, are processes of constitutionalization (Zumbansen 2012; Neves 2013). But the concept is also relevant, because it clearly demonstrates how both theoretically and in practice the doctrine of separation of powers is no longer restricted to state powers only. As we saw above, the separation of powers is a central element of the more general notion of constitutionalism as Garnett defines it. That is why our discussion of the concept of transconstitutionalism will be focused on this aspect in particular.

A useful starting point here is once again Krisch's work referred to above. For example, in a book chapter Krisch distinguishes between so-called constitutionalist and pluralist approaches to what he calls postnational order. From a public law point of view, we currently find ourselves in a time of transition, with all the conceptual confusion that normally comes with it (Cottier and Hertig 2003; Zumbansen 2012). Under the influence of processes such as Europeanization and internationalization, the centuries-old "Westphalian" system, characterized by its central position of the nation state, is grinding to a halt. However, we do not yet know what the future constitutional landscape is going to look like. It is also conceivable that the trend towards transconstitutionalism may be reversed, which as some would argue can already be witnessed in the EU, for example. Meanwhile, the present internationalized constitutional states and indeed the transnational order as a whole sometimes present a puzzle, in terms of democratic legitimacy generally and specifically also with regard to the doctrine of separation of powers (Krisch 2012: 203).

It is important to emphasize from the outset that a time of transition, such as the one we arguably find ourselves in from a public law point of view, is not necessarily one of decline and thus to be evaluated negatively. Although it is not true either that our constitutional future will necessarily only have good things in store for us, some of the ideas behind the traditional notion of the separation of powers, for example, might well turn out to be equally applicable in a post-Westphalian era. In fact, what can already be witnessed is that several rival paradigms present themselves as candidates to impact the current transnational constellation, notably constitutionalism and pluralism. Krisch (2012: 203–4) explains the difference between them:

> While constitutionalists, drawing on domestic inspirations, generally strive for a common frame to define both the substantive principles of the overall order and the relations between its different parts, pluralists prefer to see the postnational realm as characterised by heterarchy, by an interaction of different sub-orders that is not subject to common legal rules but takes a more open, political form.

Professor of Law, Politics, and International Studies Alec Stone Sweet (2013) has argued that, as is the case nationally with differences between an accommodating type of liberal constitutionalism and pluralism proper, this dichotomy is rather artificial in nature. Even if one disagrees with this criticism, if only because a considerable number of scholars still seem to actively aim at unity and centralization (Krisch 2013), the choice between these two paradigms is not a black-and-white one. In a way, it would be possible to argue that it is not even necessary to make a choice between the two paradigms at all. Thus, looking at the present-day, rather confusing, transnational state of affairs, one might, on the one hand, say that it is de facto a thoroughly pluralist constellation. On the other hand, theoretically one could carry on from there to plead, in a normative manner, for a more constitutionalist type of order in the future. A noteworthy recent example of such a line of thinking can be found in international lawyer Aoife O'Donoghue's work (2013, 2014). O'Donoghue took part in a book project on the separation of powers that attempts to rethink the classical doctrine in the light of the current transnational age (Ten Napel and Voermans 2015).

As transconstitutionalism is characterized by a mix of national, transnational, and international private and public powers rather than by public powers only, a principal question the development raises is, meanwhile, whether the central tenet of modern constitutionalism—that is, the sharp distinction between public and private—can be maintained. Thus, Taiwanese legal scholars Jiunn-Rong Yeh and Wen-Chen Chang conclude their article on the emergence of transconstitutionalism by observing that

> [l]ike any other constitutional community, a vibrant civil society coupled with a complex of powers and networks always serves as a genuine check on official powers. It is evident that the vibrant global civil society formed by transnational non-governmental organizations, private corporations or globalized citizens must shoulder the checks and balances on a vigorous and routine schedule.
>
> (2008: 123; cf. Storrar, Casarella, and Metzger 2011)

Professor of Transnational Law Peer Zumbansen similarly notes that the West has been characterized by "a pertinent obsession with the state" (2012: 79). Therefore, "[t]he 'emergence of private authority in global governance'—as expressed in areas such as trade agreements, rating agencies, product safety, standardization, or the lex mercatoria—constitutes a significant challenge for constitutional thought" (82–3). Transnational constitutionalism thus appears to be leading to a return of public power in private hands, in addition to the public power exercised by state bodies.

The same phenomenon can be witnessed in local governance, where so-called hybrid governance is on the rise. As a result, also here, public powers are increasingly exercised by forms other than the classic public administration at the municipal level. As in the international sphere, this obviously raises questions regarding the democratic legitimacy of local decision-making processes. According to at least one postdoctoral researcher, the way forward in this respect is to cross the boundaries of traditional administrative law, however: "To address the challenges, we need to reconsider the province of administrative law. It is crucial to: de-publicize its paradigm; stretch its boundaries to comprise not only private actors, but also different structures" (Colombo 2016).

Also more generally speaking, the advent of transconstitutionalism is changing the extent to which Grimm's version of constitutionalism prevails in the West. Thus, another characteristic of his definition was the idea that liberal constitutionalism had originated in the seventeenth and eighteenth century and constituted an entirely new development. Now that the nation state is eroding and transconstitutionalism appears to be on the rise, the general picture begins to look more like medieval times again, with its relative dispersion of power. This means that it may also be worthwhile once again to search for early forms of constitutionalism in that era, as well as in ancient Athens and Rome. As Levy (2015: 88) puts it:

> While liberal ideas did not and could not crystallize before the consolidation of the modern state, the intellectual materials from which they did so were older. The early modern state did not rupture intellectual history; it was analyzed and critiqued as it was taking shape, and those analyses and critiques drew on older ideas and institutions. If it is a mistake to treat an idea like "liberalism" as existing in every era, it is also a mistake to treat it as having no relevant prehistory.

Finally, the notion of a common or public good may be revitalized as well, because international organizations and non-governmental organizations are frequently started out of idealistic aspirations. This contrasts with the national context, in which constitutional law seems to have lost some of the idealistic fervor that still characterizes international law. However, the case for this argument admittedly seems less clear than the one for the other two characteristics of constitutionalism, notably the erosion of the dividing line between public and private power.

More generally, the sovereignty of the state appears to have come under pressure, both internally and externally. It is clearly not the case that states are disappearing from the international stage altogether, and there may even be a tendency to reaffirm traditional nationhood. States remain part of what is more like a network, and need to relate in a horizontal manner to, for example, non-governmental organizations. The hierarchical way both in which the national state was organized internally and which characterized the international order appears to belong to the past. Although among the general public, and in particular in populist circles, a return to the idea of sovereignty can be perceived, it is debatable how realistic this will be even in the case that transconstitutionalism as such will decline again.

It is submitted that the changes that transconstitutionalism nevertheless bring are a healthy correction of the way national constitutionalism has developed recently. This is the case because the kind of Enlightenment liberalism identified above lies at the root of the liberal individualist paradigm which we already encountered in Chapter 1. In addition to its obvious strong points, such as precisely its appropriate emphasis on the worth of the individual, the liberal individualist paradigm knows at least two disadvantages. The first disadvantage is that it has the potential to negatively affect the way in particular the associational and institutional dimensions of the right to freedom of religion or belief are interpreted and applied. This was illustrated in Chapter 1. Second, this type of liberalism can also give rise to exclusionism when it comes to the public square and parliamentary and public debates. This will be dealt with in Chapter 3.

In the current chapter the focus is on constitutionalism. More specifically with respect to constitutionalism, it can be observed that the liberal individualist paradigm paradoxically leads to a greater role of the state. This is illustrated by the concept of civic totalism. It is here that the importance of the erosion of the dividing line between public and private power becomes clear, as it leads to an increase in the checks and balances in society. Under Enlightenment liberalism these checks and balances are limited to the traditional state powers, the legislative, the executive and the judiciary. Transconstitutionalism, both theoretically and practically, makes it possible to add to these checks between state powers and non-state actors. We will explore this latter point a little further in the following section.

Pluralism and Checks and Balances

According to Krisch (2012: 235, 238),

> [t]he most common argument for a pluralist international order stems from an analogy with checks and balances in domestic constitutions. . . . [I]n both cases, no single site enjoys ultimate decision-making powers but has to face checks by others that, in some respects, may have equally strong claims to authority.

The principle of checks and balances was recently described by the former co-leader of the Center of Theological Inquiry's Working Group on Theology and International Law, legal and political philosopher Jeremy Waldron, as requiring "the ordinary concurrence of one governmental entity in the actions of another" (2013: 438), thereby still limiting it to the traditional state powers. Yet, although the principle may have developed in a national context, before it started to impact the international order as well, this does not mean that the developments taking place transnationally may not in turn influence domestic interpretations of the doctrine.

As Krisch explains, "pluralist approaches developed by political theorists for the domestic level, . . . typically start from some form of choice of the individuals involved. . . . Pluralist theories of the state have typically been grounded in the freedom of association" (2012: 240–1). Thus, for English pluralists such as Harold Laski (1893–1950), it was already the case that

> a political order based on voluntary associations appeared superior to a state-centred one because it promised individuals greater control of their own affairs. Because they originated in individual choice, such associations were also independent from the state in their basis of legitimacy and possessed non-derived powers.
>
> (240; cf. Hirst 1989)

These and similar arguments, which can also be found in the work of contemporary pluralist theorists such as Galston and Garnett, have not only acquired a renewed relevance in the transnational context, but may indeed also hold promise in relation to the principle of separation of powers within the domestic context as well. I am of course aware of the fact that the contrary view has also been expressed—that is, that even the *via media* of "constitutional pluralism" is "no better able to resolve the issues that sundered the earlier incarnation of pluralist thought" (Loughlin 2014: 11). Historically, however, the purpose of the doctrine of the separation of powers was to prevent tyranny. During the second half of the twentieth century the state grew much bigger. A type of separation of powers between only the state powers appears then no longer adequate.

Legal sociologist Gunther Teubner is one author who insists that it is indeed time to leave what he calls "the obstinate state-and-politics-centricity" of traditional constitutionalism behind us by extending the principle of separation of powers to also include non-state actors (2012: 3). As Teubner stresses (16), referring to a well-known essay by historian Reinhart Koselleck (2006),

> [t]he historical reality ought to be recognized that—as far back as the nation-state era—a more comprehensive societal constitution existed that governed not just state political activities, but also economic, social, and cultural institutions. Social, ecclesiastical, economic, and financial orders ought not to be treated merely as matters of simple legislation, but as problems of a genuine "societal constitution."

Teubner's own idea that the political constitution ought to also capture non-state sectors of society poses a certain risk, however, to the extent that it can be implemented at all on a structural basis in a well-functioning liberal democracy. It might be feared that such "societal constitutionalism" would have a negative impact on the autonomy of private associations, although Teubner certainly does not intend this, and on the contrary argues that so-called statist societal constitutionalism "will not work" (25). Given the already precarious situation in which these associations arguably find themselves (Benson 2013), this potential disadvantage weighs rather heavily. Historically speaking, this has paradoxically been precisely the reason why liberal constitutionalism limited itself to regulating the state and politics, thus achieving a separation of state and society (Teubner 2012: 15–16).

Perhaps a more promising direction is therefore indicated by, for example, law professor Abner S. Greene's notion of "permeable sovereignty," by which he means that "the sources of normative authority to which people turn are plural, and therefore we should see the state's sovereignty as permeable—full of holes, rather than full" (2012: 20). The principle of separation of powers in its classic form has long played a role in legitimizing the state. As Greene points out, however, today "[p]erhaps paradoxically, only by disclaiming plenary sovereignty, remaining unmasked as just one repository of the people's power, can the state defensibly claim—and perhaps gain—the authority it seeks" (253; cf. Clark 2013).

In his inspirational book *The Three Branches: A Comparative Model of Separation of Powers*, Professor of Public Law and Jurisprudence Christoph Möllers argues that it would be worthwhile to try to link the largely organizational principle of separation of powers to normative ideas again (2013: 3). In his case, these ideas concern individual freedom and collective self-determination (5). In the book Möllers furthermore limits himself once again to the three classical state powers that can claim a central role in "the *creation of law*" (81).

In light of the above, the question can be raised, however, whether, and to what extent, with a view to the realization of the ideals of individual freedom and collective self-determination within the internationalized constitutional state, more traditional notions of the division of powers need not be supplemented by the recognition that there are multiple sources of authority and sovereignty in society. Constitutional government (also) suggests a limited role of the state *vis-à-vis* the faith-based organizations that together constitute the "civil society." If all three or more public powers that are distinguished jointly intrude the autonomy that ought to characterize private associations from this perspective, a traditional interpretation of the doctrine of separation of powers no longer suffices to safeguard the freedom of the individual. As seen earlier in this chapter, according to at least some authors, we may already have reached that point. The very idea of a possible "civic totalism" gaining ground, no matter how exaggerated this may sound at first, points towards the system of separation of powers in place no longer being sufficient to actually prevent tyranny.

From a constitutional law point of view, it can in the twenty-first century—no less than in the days of Alexis de Tocqueville (1805–1859)—therefore be considered

> vital for the nation that there be checks on the government, because government is not always right—and may be seriously wrong. The needed creative alternatives exist in a thriving civil society, a culture with institutions that can dissent from the society's—and governments'—popular views. A thriving civil society is one with strong and independent organizations that can protect and promote views that are unpopular, but may turn out to be right. To keep a necessary check on government, society needs alternative moral voices and those voices will only exist if their institutional framework is protected.
>
> (Carlson-Thies 2010: 18)

Since the checks-and-balances principle forms part of the larger doctrine of separation of powers (Waldron 2013: 438), the notion of multiple sovereignties might clearly have a renewed relevance for the latter, in so far as it wishes to continue safeguarding our individual freedom and collective self-determination.

The good thing about world religions such as Christianity, Judaism, and Islam is that they naturally tend to generate such a civil society, because all three value the communal dimension of faith. In order for these religions to continue generating such a civil society, it is necessary that both the legislature and the courts continue to protect the associational and institutional dimensions of the right to freedom of religion or belief (Garnett 2013). Adherents to these religions ought not to necessarily have to subscribe to a monistic sovereignty conception, according to which state sovereignty is the only source of sovereignty in society:

> [I]n a genuinely pluralist democracy, the very reasons citizens understand and accept law are themselves contested—and reasonably so. It should be enough that we know that our neighbors accept the authority of law; we should not require that they accept it for the same reasons that we do.
>
> (Brink 2012)

At most, there exists a "practical priority of the secular legal order," not a doctrinal one (Bielefeldt 2007: 101). Occasionally, not even the law itself will have to be accepted, and room must be created by the state for conscientious objection and civil disobedience. This will be the case when other institutions, which also constitute sources of normative authority to which people turn in their pursuit of the good life, reach different conclusions than the state. Unanimous adherence to a monistic sovereignty conception can hardly have been what, for example, the American Founding Fathers or the drafters of the Universal Declaration of Human Rights had in mind either (Richard 2016; Loconte 2004).

Paradoxically, it is only when we allow the various faith traditions the space to develop their own connections with the liberal-democratic order that they can best succeed at sustaining that very order. As is all too well known,

> [a] state based on principles of freedom and democracy cannot properly claim to generate the values that citizens are called to share nor the attitudes that should support their participation in the life of the polis: for both of them the state can rely on civil society. Therefore the state's contribution to the common good is not in the field of creation, but in that of conservation and it performs this task by providing a legal framework where different projects of common good can peacefully coexist.
>
> (Ferrari 2011: 31)

Two final points need to be made. The first point is that frequent references were made above to the state. The notion of transconstitutionalism has arisen out of an alleged erosion of the traditional state. It creates more leeway for non-state actors in a way that can also be applied in the domestic context. For a proper functioning within the domestic context, states paradoxically remain essential, however. For this reason, it simply is not the case that the kind of constitutionalism inspired by social pluralist theory as laid out in this chapter, or Christianity in general for that matter (Biggar 2016), wishes to do away with the state. On the one hand, it does not want to idealize the state, certainly not in case it gradually becomes characterized by a civic totalism. On the other hand, the kind of associational pluralism that it favors and which will be set out further in Chapter 3 is at least in part dependent on the state facilitating it to a certain extent, as Professor of Law and Religion Silvio Ferrari rightly argues.

This ambivalence towards the national state is confirmed by the EU. On the one hand, the EU achieves greater cooperation and integration between states than had been the case in the past. On the other hand, the end of the European nation state is not in sight. Even if the EU were to become a full-blown federation, this would only result in a new, European state. Therefore, the importance of the concept of transconstitutionalism must not be exaggerated either. The phenomenon can serve as a useful correction to particular developments within liberalism as set out above. That is the point this chapter aims to make, among other things. It would be taking things a step too far to argue that henceforth we would only have to be concerned about processes of constitutionalization outside the traditional nation states, however. National constitutionalism will remain relevant for the foreseeable future as well, and rightly so. This is precisely the reason why this chapter was also, and even mainly, dedicated to questions surrounding precisely this more traditional type of constitutionalism.

The second point that deserves to be made is that it is possible to characterize the constitutionalism as advocated by the likes of Greene with the help of yet another constitutional concept. Reference was made above to such constitutional concepts as the separation of powers and checks and balances. Social pluralist constitutionalism also values federalism, however, but takes it "all the way down." As Halberstam (2012: 605) explains,

> following federalism all the way down suggests understanding many forms of private governance and perhaps even the autonomy rights of individuals as continuous with federal principles and federal design. As a matter of constitutional practice, protected spheres of private governance may come in disguise. Some free speech doctrines, for example, show evidence of constitutionally protected self-governance rights of social institutions. Political parties may be constitutionally protected, sometimes explicitly so. The family, too, is a constitutionally protected institution of collective self-governance. And even though traditional democratic theory tends to reject placing the individual on a continuum from small to large spheres of governance, it is not entirely implausible to understand individual rights as constitutionally protected spheres of governance as well—especially where an individual makes decisions that affect others.

The interesting thing about this social pluralist approach as I would be tempted to call it, even though in particular the principle of subsidiarity undeniably assumes a certain hierarchy of authorities, still according to Halberstam, is that it

> rejects the view that constitutional law is synonymous with a hierarchically ordered legal system. Instead, it recognizes that constitutional law can lead to a multiplicity of claims of authority without a single, final, legal authority, or to what Neil MacCormick first dubbed the idea of "constitutional pluralism". . . . [W]e can learn a good deal about global governance and perhaps even understand domestic constitutionalism better when considering

> that constitutionalism does not spell universal hierarchy and settlement. . . . [F]or federalism, the idea of pluralism and the unsettled nature of legal authority among different levels of governance is a coming home of sorts. After all, the Federalists created a new hybrid that mixed international and domestic forms of governance. And they created a hybrid that sought to complicate the question of final authority beyond what was conceived of as possible at the time.
>
> (606–7)

The reason I have taken quite some effort to situate social pluralist constitutionalism within the traditional vocabulary of comparative constitutional law is to point out that it does not mark a radical break with fundamental insights within the discipline. On the contrary, it can be relatively easily set out with the help of a few chapters in the *Oxford Handbook of Comparative Constitutional Law*. This also makes clear that such constitutionalism is not a remote ideal, but may instead be put into practice relatively easily, once there is the political will to do so. Still, the idea is innovative enough to require a reinterpretation of constitutional concepts such as sovereignty, separation of powers, and federalism. This, however, is in a sense the very purpose of the discipline of constitutional law. Constitutional concepts are not goals in themselves, which have to be realized even if the circumstances change. Constitutional concepts need to be constantly rethought in the light of changing circumstances, in order to make sure that the underlying values that they seek to protect remain intact.

The Common Good

There is a striking resemblance between Galston's theory of liberal pluralism on the one hand and what Kraynak has called "constitutional government under God" on the other (2001: 203–68). This comes as no surprise: after all, according to Galston, although himself a liberal, "[t]he most useful point of departure for the reconsideration of politics I am urging is found in the writings of the British political pluralists and thinkers working in the Calvinist tradition" (2005: 23; 2006: 819–20). For Kraynak, on his part, his "deepest inspiration" is

> the notion of "sphere sovereignty" developed by the Dutch Calvinist Abraham Kuyper and the Catholic doctrine of "subsidiarity," both of which try to articulate the appropriate associations for each level of political authority. When brought together into a coherent theory of two realms, the diverse spheres make up a hierarchy of being that is the metaphysical basis of Christian constitutionalism.
>
> (2001: 207)

Although such social pluralist constitutionalism is thus at least in part informed and inspired by mainstream Christian (Catholic, Protestant) social teaching and thought (cf. Chaplin 2005; Weinberger 2010: 304–8; Rosen 2014: 744–58), in a non-Western context and even for the West itself such theological foundations do not necessarily lead to a liberal democracy as the preferred system of government. As we saw, and Kraynak pointed out, Christianity as such is neither a liberal nor a democratic religion and can relate to a range of legal and political orders (2001: chapter 2). Thus, various authors referring to the term "Christian constitutionalism" sometimes have considerably more theocratic versions in mind (see e.g. Brennan 2015). And others, to the contrary, as we have seen consider withdrawing from society altogether by adhering to the benedict option.

Still, social pluralist constitutionalism can also be regarded as a major—though not exclusive—contribution of Christianity to Western political civilization. It mitigates Western monistic conceptions of political legitimacy in terms of popular sovereignty by adding a transcendental dimension to it. A well-known lemma on the concept of "political legitimacy" at one point asks the question what exactly it is that grounds its normativity (Peter 2010: section 4). It then concludes that since the seventeenth century, at least in the West, consent has replaced natural law and divine authority theories as the ultimate source of political legitimacy. As such, this constitutes an example of a monistic conception of political legitimacy. Yet, as the lemma rightly notes, non-monistic or mixed conceptions of political legitimacy are also feasible (cf. Domingo 2016). Tocqueville even believed that, ultimately, the success of secular checks and balances was dependent on the role of religion in creating spiritual ones (Kahan 2015).

The legitimization of Western liberal democracy is indeed not as strong as it may seem, as long as the sovereignty of the people on which its political legitimacy is ultimately based hinders instead of advances a true sort of value pluralism (Ten Napel, forthcoming). In this sense, not just a pluralist reconstruction of Confucian democracy may be needed, as Kim argues, but also a reconsideration of Western liberal democracy from the perspective of social pluralist constitutionalism. The idea of there being additional checks between state powers and non-state actors has traditionally been regarded as contributing to the notion of constitutionalism. It also has the potential to enhance liberal-democratic legitimacy, as the notion of civil society is strongly endorsed, not just by Christian but also by Jewish and Islamic constitutionalism.

In particular, the classical form of Islamic constitutionalism forms an interesting alternative to liberal constitutionalism as it has arguably developed in recent decades, and indeed to a certain extent an inspiration for the social pluralist model. This classical Islamic constitutionalism, which was referred to in the introductory chapter, is characterized by three pillars: "Government Action Must be Based on the Public Good," "A Diverse Realm of Religious Law Exists as a Voluntary Alternative to State Law," and "The Islamic Legitimacy of State Law is Evaluated by the Purposes (maqasid) of Sharia" (Quraishi-Landes 2015: 565–78).

These pillars are intended as a model for a constitutional system in Muslim-majority countries. The question is whether the principles can, with adaptations, not also serve as a basis for a reformed liberal type of constitutionalism. In particular, the legal pluralism that the second pillar implies has the potential of returning some of the space to be different to minorities, which in their own perception may have increasingly come to be oppressed by an Enlightenment liberal majority.

On the other hand, the common or public good can probably not be defined as "thickly" in a Western society as is possible in a Muslim-majority country. Islamic constitutionalism paradoxically resembles Enlightenment liberal constitutionalism in that both are absolute forms of constitutionalism, which hardly allow for dissent from the respective majority opinions.

It could be argued that the deep pluralism that characterizes current Western societies does not allow for the formulation of a common good at all (Inazu 2016). However, it is also possible to point out that some notion of the common or public good is necessary to hold Western societies together. Also, Christian, Jewish, and Islamic constitutionalism all stress the need for society to aim at a common or public good and can also contribute to formulating such a notion.

A relatively realistic solution of this dilemma would be the approach as set out by Catholic legal scholar Robert P. George, building on earlier work by Australian legal scholar and philosopher John Finnis. George refers in particular to Finnis' definition of the common good in his book *Natural Law and Natural Rights* (1980; 2nd edn 2011: 155) as

> a set of conditions which enables the members of a community to attain for themselves reasonable objectives, or to realize reasonably for themselves the value(s), for the sake of which they have reason to collaborate with each other (positively and/or negatively) in a community.

This at first sight is surely a complicated formulation. As George explains, however, what it means is that every community is likely to have a common good. Some of these common goods will be "intrinsic goods," such as in the case of the family or faith communities. In the case of the political community, however, it is rather an "instrumental good." What this implies, is that the task of the state is principally limited. In Catholic social doctrine this is called "subsidiarity." This principle reflects a particular vision of what human flourishing is about:

> Flourishing consists in *doing things*, not just in getting things, or having desirable or pleasant experiences, or having things done for you. . . . And so the common good is, as Finnis remarked, best conceived as a *set of conditions* for enabling members of a community to attain for themselves reasonable objectives or to realize reasonably for themselves the value(s) for the sake of which they have reason to collaborate with each other in a community. It is, in this sense, facilitative. It enables people to do things the doing of which advances their all-around or integral flourishing.
>
> (George 2013)

This "facilitative conception of the common good," as George calls it and which corresponds with Ferrari's conception referred to above, almost automatically leads to limited government. It is not so much the state that ought to pursue all kinds of substantive goals, but instead it ought to make it possible for faith-based organizations to do so. The role of these institutions of civil society thus takes on a broader constitutional significance. Not only are they a potentially even more important check on the government than, for example, the judiciary, but they also contribute to the transmitting of essential values to generations of new citizens. Such a transmitting of values is necessary in order to maintain limited government. Finally, these institutions contribute to the common good in a way in which the state is not able to. As a matter of fact,

> [t]he common good is not an abstraction or Platonic form hovering somewhere beyond the concrete well-being—the flourishing—of the flesh-and-blood persons constituting the community. It *is* the well-being of those persons and of the families and other associations of persons—Burke's "little platoons" of civil society—of which they are members.
>
> (George 2013)

In Conclusion

Western societies are increasingly characterized by pluralism, in the sense that more than in the past people with different religious and other backgrounds live together in one city or state. The way these societies attempt to maintain a stable government is with the help of the political philosophy of liberalism. This philosophy of government is subscribed to by most major political currents, from Left to Right. The exception to this rule is perhaps populism, because it puts the idea of the will of the people above that of inalienable rights of all citizens. One of these inalienable rights is the right to freedom of religion or belief.

This chapter has tried to make clear that the way this right to freedom of religion or belief is interpreted and applied is dependent on the type of liberalism that prevails at a particular time and place. As the political philosophy of liberalism is shared by virtually the whole political spectrum, from Left to Right, it is evident that the contents of liberalism can also change depending on the political preferences of the majority of the population. It makes a difference, for example, whether one regards religious freedom as a natural right or as a right that is created by the same liberal order within which it subsequently has to be interpreted and applied.

It was already submitted in Chapter 1 that, given the increasing pluralism in society, a kind of liberalism that tries to accommodate diversity may be best suited for contemporary purposes. Such a classical liberalism, or liberal pluralism as it has been referred to in this chapter, leads to social pluralist constitutionalism. Characteristic of this type of constitutionalism is that it regards the legal pluralism that has characterized the Western legal tradition since the notion of the "freedom of the church" was introduced in the early medieval Papal Revolution (Berman 1983) as essential to achieve proper freedom. This means that it creates the required space for the institutions of civil society to properly perform the constitutional role they have to play in any system of limited government. That way, these institutions can play a role in the more general separation of powers and checks and balances in the constitutional system, by creating a kind of federalism "all the way down," which allows for sovereignty to be shared by the state and civil society associations.

Bibliography

Anastaplo, George (ed.) (1999a), *Liberty, Equality, and Modern Constitutionalism*, Volume I, *From Socrates and Pericles to Thomas Jefferson* (Indianapolis, IN: Focus/Hackett Publishing Company).

Anastaplo, George (ed.) (1999b), *Liberty, Equality, and Modern Constitutionalism*, Volume II, *From George III to Hitler and Stalin* (Indianapolis, IN: Focus/Hackett Publishing Company).

Benson, Iain T. (2013), "The Attack on Western Religions by Western Law: Re-Framing Pluralism, Liberalism and Diversity," *International Journal of Religious Freedom*, 6(1/2): 111–25.

Berman, Harold J. (1983), *Law and Revolution: The Formation of the Western Legal Tradition* (Cambridge, MA: Harvard University Press).

Bielefeldt, Heiner (2007), "The Practical Priority of the Secular Legal Order: A Response to Javid Gadirov," in: M.L.P. Loenen and J.E. Goldschmidt (eds), *Religious Pluralism and Human Rights in Europe: Where to Draw the Line?* (Antwerpen/Oxford: Intersentia) 97–102.

Biggar, Nigel (2016), "The Nation State and the Case for Remaining in the EU," *Reimagining Europe*, June 13.

Bogdandy, Armin von (2012), "National Legal Scholarship in the European Legal Area," *International Journal of Constitutional Law*, 10(3): 614–26.

Brennan, Patrick McKinley (2015), "An Essay on Christian Constitutionalism: Building in the Divine Style, for the Common Good(s)," *Rutgers Journal of Law and Religion*, 16(3): 478–540.

Brink, Paul (2012), "Religious Freedom and Constitutional Democracy," *Respectful Conversation*, March 14, available at www.respectfulconversation.net/the-conversation/2012/3/14/religious-freedom-and-constitutional-democracy.html (accessed November 25, 2016).

Caenegem, R.C. van (1995), *An Historical Introduction to Western Constitutional Law* (Cambridge: Cambridge University Press).

Carlson-Thies, Stanley (2010), "Liberty or Liability: The Future of Institutional Religious Freedom," *Cardus*, December 22.

Carozza, Paolo G. and Daniel Philpott (2012), "The Catholic Church, Human Rights, and Democracy: Convergence and Conflict with the Modern State," *Logos: A Journal of Catholic Thought and Culture*, 15(3): 15–43.

Chaplin, Jonathan (2005), "Toward a Social Pluralist Theory of Institutional Rights," *Ave Maria Law Review*, 3(1): 147–70.

Chaplin, Jonathan (2006), "Living with Liberalism: Understanding Regimes of Tolerance," *Comment*, December 22.

Choudhry, Sujit (ed.) (2008), *Constitutional Design for Divided Societies: Integration or Accommodation?* (Oxford: Oxford University Press).

Clark, Elizabeth A. (2013), "Religions as Sovereigns: Why Religion is Special," Bepress online publication, February, available at https://works.bepress.com/elizabeth_clark/16 (accessed November 25, 2016).

Cliteur, P.B. and V. van den Eeckhout (eds) (2001), *Multiculturalisme, cultuurrelativisme en sociale cohesie* (Den Haag: Boom Juridische uitgevers).

Colombo, C.M. (2016), "Hybrid Forms of Local Governance and the Transformation of Administrative Law," PowerPoint Presentation during ICON-S Conference, Berlin, June 17–19.

Cottier, Thomas and Maya Hertig (2003), "The Prospects of 21st Century Constitutionalism," in: A. von Bogdandy and R. Wolfrun (eds), *Max Planck Yearbook of International Law*, 7: 261–328.

Deneen, Patrick J. (2014), "A Catholic Showdown Worth Watching," *The American Conservative*, February 6.

Diamond, Larry, Marc F. Plathner, and Christopher Walker (eds) (2016), *Authoritarianism Goes Global: The Challenge to Democracy* (Baltimore, MD: Johns Hopkins University Press).

Domingo, Rafael (2016), *God and the Secular Legal System* (Cambridge: Cambridge University Press).

Dreher, Rod (2015), "Benedict Option FAQ," *The American Conservative*, October 6.

Ferrari, Silvio (2011), "Religion and the Development of Civil Society," *International Journal for Religious Freedom*, 4(2): 29–36.

Finnis, John (1980; 2nd edn 2011), *Natural Law and Natural Rights* (Oxford: Oxford University Press).

Fleiner, Thomas and Lidija R. Basta Fleiner (2009), *Constitutional Democracy in a Multicultural and Globalised World* (Berlin/Heidelberg: Springer).

Friedell, Steven F. (2015), "A Jewish Constitution," *Rutgers Journal of Law and Religion*, 16(3): 541–52.

Galston, William A. (2002), *Liberal Pluralism: The Implications of Value Pluralism for Political Theory and Practice* (Cambridge: Cambridge University Press).

Galston, William A. (2005), *The Practice of Liberal Pluralism* (Cambridge: Cambridge University Press).

Galston, William A. (2006), "Families, Associations, and Political Pluralism," *Fordham Law Review*, 75(2): 815–31.

Galston, William A. (2011), "Pluralist Constitutionalism," *Social Philosophy and Policy*, 28(1): 228–41.

Garnett, Richard W. (2009), "Religious Freedom, Church Autonomy, and Constitutionalism," *Drake Law Review* 57(4): 901–11.

Garnett, Richard W. (2013), "'The Freedom of the Church': (Towards) an Exposition, Translation, and Defense," *Journal of Contemporary Legal Issues*, 21: 33–57.

George, Robert P. (2013), "Ruling to Serve: A Fundamental Argument for Limited Government," *First Things*, April.

Greene, Abner S. (2012), *Against Obligation. The Multiple Sources of Authority in a Liberal Democracy* (Cambridge, MA: Harvard University Press).

Griffiths, Gordon (1960), "The Revolutionary Character of the Revolt of the Netherlands," *Comparative Studies in Society and History*, 2(4): 452–73.

Grimm, Dieter (2009), "Conflicts between General Norms and Religious Norms," *Cardozo Law Review*, 30(6): 2369–82.

Grimm, Dieter (2012), "Types of Constitutions," in: Michel Rosenfeld and András Sajó (eds), *The Oxford Handbook of Comparative Constitutional Law* (Oxford: Oxford University Press) 98–132.

Halberstam, Daniel (2012), "Federalism: Theory, Policy, Law," in: Michel Rosenfeld and András Sajó (eds), *The Oxford Handbook of Comparative Constitutional Law* (Oxford: Oxford University Press) 576–608.

Hanby, Michael (2015), "The Civic Project of American Christianity: How the Public Significance of Christianity is Changing," *First Things*, February.

Harinck, George and Hans-Martien ten Napel (2013), "Democracy: Instrument for or Expression of a Christian Political Order?" in: *Journal of Inter-Religious Dialogue*, 11: 42–9.

Hirst, P.Q. (ed.) (1989), *The Pluralist Theory of the State* (London: Routledge).

Inazu, John D. (2016), *Confident Pluralism: Surviving and Thriving Through Deep Difference* (Chicago, IL, and London: University of Chicago Press).

Jiménez Lobeira, Pablo C. (2011), "Liberal Democracy: Culture Free? The Habermas–Ratzinger Debate and its Implications for Europe," *Australian and New Zealand Journal of European Studies*, 2(2)/3(1): 44–57.

Kahan, Alan S. (2015), *Tocqueville, Democracy, and Religion* (Oxford: Oxford University Press).

Kim, Sungmoon (2012), "A Pluralist Reconstruction of Confucian Democracy," *Dao*, 11(3): 315–36.

Koselleck, Reinhart (2006), "Begriffsgeschichtliche Probleme der Verfassungsgeschichtsschreibung," in: Reinhart Koselleck, *Begriffsgeschichten: Studien zur Semantik und Pragmatik der politischen und sozialen Sprache* (Frankfurt: Suhrkamp) 365–401.

Kraynak, Robert P. (2001), *Christian Faith and Modern Democracy* (Notre Dame, IN: University of Notre Dame Press).

Krisch, Nico (2010), *Beyond Constitutionalism: The Pluralist Structure of Postnational Law* (Oxford: Oxford University Press).

Krisch, Nico (2012), "The Case for Pluralism in Postnational Law," in: Gráinne de Búrca and J.H.H. Weiler (eds), *The Worlds of European Constitutionalism* (Cambridge: Cambridge University Press) 203–61.

Krisch, Nico (2013), "Constitutionalism and Pluralism: A Reply to Alec Stone Sweet," *International Journal of Constitutional Law*, 11: 501–5.

Leiter, Brian (2013), *Why Tolerate Religion?* (Princeton, NJ: Princeton University Press).

Levin, Yuval (2011), "What is Constitutional Conservatism?" *National Review*, November 28.

Levin, Yuval (2012a), "Religious Liberty and Civil Society," *National Review Online*, January 2012.

Levin, Yuval (2012b), "After Progressivism: A Response to Wilfred M. McClay," *First Things*, May.

Levy, Jacob T. (2015), *Rationalism, Pluralism, and Freedom* (Oxford: Oxford University Press).

Loconte, Joseph (2004), "Morality for Sale," *The New York Times*, April 1.

Loughlin, Martin (2014), "Constitutional Pluralism: An Oxymoron?" *Global Constitutionalism*, 3(1): 9–30.

McClay, Wilfred M. (2012), "Liberalism after Liberalism. How Can We Affirm Human Dignity When Liberalism No Longer Can?" *First Things*, May.

McConnell, Michael W. (2000), "Why is Religious Liberty the 'First Freedom'?" *Cardozo Law Review*, 21(4): 1243–65.

McConnell, Michael W. (2001), "Old Liberalism, New Liberalism, and People of Faith," in: Michael W. McConnell, Robert F. Cochran, Jr., and Angela C.

Carmella (eds), *Christian Perspectives of Legal Thought* (New Haven, CT: Yale University Press, 2001) 5–24.

Macedo, Stephen (2000), *Diversity and Distrust: Civic Education in a Multicultural Democracy* (Cambridge, MA: Harvard University Press).

Möllers, Christoph (2013), *The Three Branches: A Comparative Model of Separation of Powers* (Oxford: Oxford University Press).

Moyn, Samuel (2015), *Christian Human Rights* (Philadelphia, PA: University of Pennsylvania Press).

Napel, Hans-Martien ten (2006), "The Concept of Multicultural Democracy: A Preliminary Christian-Philosophical Appraisal," *Philosophia Reformata*, 71(2): 145–53.

Napel, Hans-Martien ten (forthcoming), "Western 'Civic Totalism,' Sovereignty of the People and the Need for Limited Government," in: Cole Durham and Donlu Thayer (eds), *Pluralism, Expression, and Minorities* (Abingdon: Ashgate).

Napel, Hans-Martien Th.D. ten and Florian H. Karim Theissen (2009), "Taking Pluralism Seriously: The US and the EU as Multicultural Democracies?" in: Bart C. Labuschagne and Reinhard W. Sonnenschmidt (eds), *Religion, Politics and Law: Philosophical Reflections on the Sources of Normative Order in Society* (Leiden: Brill) 363–92.

Napel, Hans-Martien ten and Wim Voermans (eds) (2015), *The Powers That Be: Rethinking the Separation of Powers. A Leiden Response to Möllers* (Leiden: Leiden University Press).

Nehusthtan, Yossi (2015), *Intolerant Religion in a Tolerant-Liberal Democracy* (Oxford: Hart Publishing).

Neves, Marcello (2013), *Transconstitutionalism* (Oxford and Portland, OR: Hart Publishing).

O'Donoghue, Aoife (2013), "International Constitutionalism and the State," *International Journal of Constitutional Law*, 11(4): 1021–45.

O'Donoghue, Aoife (2014), *Constitutionalism in Global Constitutionalisation* (Cambridge: Cambridge University Press).

Pera, Marcello (2008), *Why We Should Call Ourselves Christians: The Religious Roots of Free Societies* (New York, NY, and London: Encounter Books).

Peter, Fabienne (2010), "Political Legitimacy," in: Edward N. Zalta (ed.), *The Stanford Encyclopedia of Philosophy* (Summer 2010 Edition), available at http://plato.stanford.edu/archives/sum2010/entries/legitimacy (accessed November 25, 2016).

Quraishi-Landes, Asifa (2015), "Islamic Constitutionalism: Not Secular, Not Theocratic, Not Impossible," *Rutgers Journal of Law and Religion*, 16(3): 553–79.

Richard, Carl J. (2016), *The Founders and the Bible* (London: Rowman & Littlefield Publishers).

Rosen, Mark (2014), "Religious Institutions, Liberal States, and the Political Architecture of Overlapping Spheres," *University of Illinois Law Review*, 2014(3): 737–803.

Rosenfeld, Michel (2014), "Recasting Secularism as One Conception of the Good Among Many in a Post-Secular Constitutional Polity," in: Susanne Mancini and Michel Rosenfeld (eds), *Constitutional Secularism in an Age of Religious Revival* (Oxford: Oxford University Press) 79–109.

Shah, Timothy Samuel and Allen D. Hertzke (eds) (2016), *Christianity and Freedom*, Volume 1, *Historical Perspectives*; Volume 2, *Contemporary Perspectives* (New York, NY: Cambridge University Press).

Song, Robert (2006), *Christianity and Liberal Society* (Oxford: Oxford University Press).

Stone Sweet, Alec (2013), "The Structure of Constitutional Pluralism: Review of Nico Krisch, *Beyond Constitutionalism: The Pluralist Structure of Post-National Law*," *International Journal of Constitutional Law*, 11(2): 491–500.

Storrar, William F., Peter J. Casarella, and Paul Louis Metzger (eds) (2011), *A World for All? Global Civil Society in Political Theory and Trinitarian Theology* (Grand Rapids, MI: William B. Eerdmans Publishing Company).

Teubner, Gunther (2012), *Constitutional Fragments: Societal Constitutionalism and Globalization* (Oxford: Oxford University Press).

Troper, Michel (2012), "Sovereignty," in: Michel Rosenfeld and András Sajó (eds), *The Oxford Handbook of Comparative Constitutional Law* (Oxford: Oxford University Press) 350–69.

Tully, James (1995), *Strange Multiplicity: Constitutionalism in an Age of Diversity* (Cambridge: Cambridge University Press).

Tushnet, Mark (2016), "Editorial: Varieties of Constitutionalism," *International Journal of Constitutional Law*, 14(1): 1–5.

Waldron, Jeremy (2013) "Separation of Powers in Thought and Practice," *Boston College Law Review*, 54(2): 433–68.

Weinberger, Lael Daniel (2010), "The Business Judgment Rule and Sphere Sovereignty," *Thomas M. Cooley Law Review*, 27(2): 279–319.

Yeh, Jiunn-Rong and Wen-Chen Chang (2008), "The Emergence of Transnational Constitutionalism: Its Features, Challenges and Solutions," *Penn State International Law Review*, 27(1): 89–124.

Zumbansen, Peer (2012), "Carving Out Typologies and Accounting for Differences Across Systems: Towards a Methodology of Transnational Constitutionalism," in: Michel Rosenfeld and András Sajó (eds), *The Oxford Handbook of Comparative Constitutional Law* (Oxford: Oxford University Press) 75–97.

3 Pluriform Democracy

Introduction

The story of democracy within the context of this book is essentially a rather tragic one. It is, of course, a well-known fact that the concept of democracy has had a flawed reputation for the better part of its history (Keane 2009). In the past the notion of a "mixed regime" was looked upon more favorably. Democracy was certainly a constituent part of such a regime, but not the only part. Since the democratic revolutions of the eighteenth century the association that we in the West have with the idea of democracy has gradually become more positive, although the American constitutional system, for example, was still very much designed according to the model of a mixed regime. And certainly the events that took place in Germany during the 1930s, which led to the Second World War, once again put the reputation of the concept of democracy under pressure.

Yet during the post-War period the consensus within Europe, for example, was that a combination of the concepts of constitutionalism and democracy represent the preferred form of government. This holds true not just for post-War Germany but also, since the fall of the Berlin Wall in 1989, for several Central and Eastern European countries. This holds equally true for the European Union itself, which not only prides itself on adhering to the broad principles of constitutionalism and democracy, but also demands of new members that they adhere to these principles. There is currently a lively debate on the question of what the European Union can, or should be able to, do when a state which is already a member implements measures that affect its democratic character or the rule of law within the Member State (Müller 2015). However, the very fact that this debate takes place is proof of the existence of a consensus that Member States ought to stick to the ideals of constitutionalism and democracy, even though interpretations may differ among the Member States as to what exactly the characteristics of a democratic constitutional state are.

It is possible that established democracies will have to adapt their conceptions of democracy slightly to the standards of the newer Central and Eastern European democracies, as the worldviews of the various populations tend to differ across the continent. The discipline of comparative constitutional law may be of help in this respect, as constitutionalism and democracy are more or less its central concepts, albeit not exclusively in a Western (European) sense. Of course, for a while it appeared to legal scholars as though there was no other type of democracy conceivable than the American or Western European versions, just as they were convinced that basically only one kind of constitutionalism could exist. The discipline of comparative constitutional law will, however, have to come to terms with the fact that the democratic ideal has not only developed over time, but can also differ geographically. Given the performance of American and Western European versions of democracy, there can hardly be any reason to still claim that this is the only, or the best, model of democracy.

Since 1974 there has been a so-called third wave of democratization, contributing to the idea that constitutional democracy might eventually become the preferable form of government globally as well. Certainly, countries such as the United States have attempted in the past to promote democracy around the globe and still do. The same scholars who criticize the promotion of religious freedom internationally are also likely to have reservations concerning attempts to spread democracy outside the West. For those for whom the notion of a democratic constitutional state represents an important means to further the ideal of allowing people to become fully human, there is not much that can be held against democracy promotion as such, though. Discussion is likely to focus rather on the preferred means of doing so, with military intervention as clearly the most controversial way to achieve the otherwise laudable goal of international democracy promotion.

Magazines like *The Economist*, in particular its Intelligence Unit, from 2006 onwards have regularly tried to measure the exact degree to which this development was visible. These statistics initially tended to confirm the educated guesses that observers had made regarding the spread of democracy, although even in 2006 there turned out to be only 28 “full democracies” globally (The Economist 2007). What was striking in this first edition of the democracy index was not just the relatively modest total of full democracies globally, but also the fact that these were heavily concentrated within the West in general and Northwestern Europe in particular. Thus, the countries heading the list were virtually all Scandinavian countries, with the Netherlands in between these as the third highest ranking country measured by the 60 indicators employed by *The Economist*. It is surprising how little (social) scientific effort appears to have been made to explain this phenomenon. Sometimes the difference in political culture between these historically largely Protestant countries has been referred to as opposed to the predominantly Catholic character of some Southern European countries. Other authors have pointed to the fact that many of the countries heading the list were constitutional monarchies, making their democratic constitutional systems resemble even more the ideal of a mixed regime. Yet the question is whether this is all there is to say about it.

At approximately the same time that *The Economist* started its biennial democracy index, however, the fortunes of democracy seemed to change once again. As a result, subsequent editions of the index indicated instead a decrease in the number of democracies around the globe. Illustrative of this trend is the title of the 25th anniversary issue of the *Journal of Democracy*, published in 2015: "Democracy in Decline?" The title of one of the contributions to this special issue, by a founding editor, is also telling: "Facing Up to the Democratic Recession" (Diamond 2015; cf. Freedom in the World 2015, 2016). This is obviously a long way from the idea that came up shortly after the fall of the Berlin Wall—that is, that the democratic constitutional state was the only viable form of government and that it would merely be a matter of time before it was introduced in almost all countries where democratic constitutionalism had not yet taken root (Fukuyama 1992). It is interesting to note that Diamond refers not only to the decrease in the number of democracies around the world, but also to the fact that democracy has come under pressure in the West itself.

Indeed, as other authors have argued, it is not an exaggeration to speak of a general "disconnect" between citizens and the political system in both Europe and the United States. To some, the idea that there is such a thing as a "democratic disconnect" will, at least for the time being, remain a premise. They will point to the fact that this disconnect cannot be proven scientifically—that is, empirically. Thus, political scientists have repeatedly indicated that, on the basis of their data, at least in the Netherlands no such thing as a gap between the citizens and the government can be ascertained (e.g. Van Gunsteren and Andeweg 1994). Ethicists, on the other hand, tend to take the public discourse as a starting point for their analyses, and evaluate it on the basis of their "careful and critical thinking about how we should live, as persons and communities, in ways that are good, just, and responsible" (Schweiker 2014: 34). On the basis of such an approach, there may well exist less doubt that Western democracies are in a state of crisis. In a sense, this approach could be called more subjective than the more empirical approaches. Yet it should be remarked that empirical approaches also appear to be subjective, to the extent that different questions and methodology can yield different outcomes. Thus, as we have seen, *The Economist*'s Intelligence Unit has for almost a decade now pointed towards a trend of a general weakening in democracy in the world, and that includes the West. By 2015, the Netherlands had dropped from third place in 2006 to tenth place in its ranking of democracies.

At the time the writing of this book was nearing completion, in the summer of 2016, the British had voted in a referendum to leave the European Union. Although at first sight the consequences appear to be the most serious for the United Kingdom itself, it is also the case that the European Union and its remaining Member States will be affected by the withdrawal. Indeed, what seems to be at stake is the entire political order that was established in the West after the Second World War. Globally, the liberal order is arguably on the verge of collapse (Walt 2016). Even before the unexpected outcome of the presidential election in the United States in November 2016, it had already proved to be one of the most remarkable campaigns in American electoral history. When the primary season started in 2015, nobody would have predicted that Donald Trump would become the official nominee of the Republican Party let alone the President. On the other side of the political spectrum there was widespread skepticism about the personal and other credentials of the Democratic candidate for the presidency as well. All this occurs at a point in time when the racial dividing line in American society has become more salient once again. Police officers come under attack, while terror attacks are on the rise in both Europe and the United States. As a result, in various European countries populist and right-wing parties are on the rise. It is difficult to conceive what else would need to happen in order to start hypothesizing about democracy and its discontents.

"Dysfunctional Democracy"

The interesting question is whether the democratic disconnect referred to above is temporary—there have been crises in the past—or has a more structural problem manifested itself? Of course, another question is what is causing the democratic disconnect, and indeed how it can be cured? It is once again surprising how relatively little these more fundamental questions are addressed in, for example, social scientific research. Discussion of the topic usually remains limited to what the statistics do or do not tell, and how this relates to earlier figures. Despite its state-of-the-art methodology, this can be considered a real drawback in this type of research.

Ethicist Robin Lovin did address the more fundamental questions during a lecture at the Library of Congress (2014a), when he held the Cary and Ann Maguire Chair in Ethics and American History. In this lecture, Lovin deplored the loss of a moral vocabulary in American politics, but his argument can probably be extended to Western politics in general. Lovin rightly pointed out that for Aristoteles the essence of politics was constituted by deliberation about the good life. In this sense it resembled the discipline of ethics. Sometime in history, Lovin believes, already with the advent of the modern state in the sixteenth and seventeenth centuries, politics lost this essentially ethical character:

> At the same time that modern politics was taking shape, Europe experienced the Protestant Reformation and the rise of the first colonial empires, so the kind of modern nation states that we take for granted today came into being at a time of intense political and religious conflict. Moral and religious convictions thus become politically problematic, and one of the first tasks of the modern state was to contain Aristotelian politics within the limits of order.
>
> (2014a: 6)

Certainly now that, in addition, market mechanisms have emerged as an alternative to political deliberation, political discourse is dominated by economic and security considerations. To Lovin, this causes the general dysfunction of democracy, and as is clear from his periodization it is indeed a structural problem. A "dysfunctional democracy" can provisionally be described as a democracy in which "the institutions of government are unable to provide long-term solutions to society's common problems" and there is a risk that it "may develop in ways that limit religious expression and action generally, or restrict them for particular groups" (Lovin 2014b: 6). The result is an alienation of the citizens from the political system, even if the turnout at elections remains stable or at least at an acceptable level.

The dysfunctional nature of Western democracies therefore in turn lies at the root of the legitimacy crisis of these systems. Constitutional democracy may still be considered to be a leading type of government, but it is severely handicapped in its capacity to influence Western societies and indeed the global order of states by the loss of moral vocabulary. In this context, St. Augustine (354–430) in book IV of *The City of God* already posed the question—still relevant today—in what respect does a state differ from a band of robbers if justice does not prevail? In our current age there is not even talk of justice anymore, as the focus in the political debate is on economic, security, and similar issues instead.

The relative lack of discourse on justice starts early on, as the topic paradoxically tends to be evaded in, for example, law school curricula. Because of positivistic tendencies, students are trained in applying the law as it stands to particular cases. The question of whether the positive law itself is legitimate is seldom raised. The assumption is that as long as the legality of the law is assured, the law will be legitimate as well. The way in which law has come about does not constitute a guarantee for it being just law, however. Questions like this are often left for legal philosophy departments to answer, which they do, but in a way that is not always connected to positive law and legal practice. In a similar vein, it is sometimes argued that there is a need for a new political science (Brooks 2016b), in which political theory becomes more integrated in the more empirical approaches that are currently dominant. An interesting example of such a collaboration is an article entitled "The Danger of Deconsolidation: The Democratic Disconnect." In this article a principal investigator for the World Values Survey and fellow of the Laboratory for Comparative Social Research, in collaboration with a political theorist, and drawing on data from Waves 3 through 6 of the World Values Surveys (1995–2014), reports results that the authors find "deeply concerning":

> Citizens in a number of supposedly consolidated democracies in North America and Western Europe have not only grown more critical of their political leaders. Rather, they have also become more cynical about the value of democracy as a political system, less hopeful that anything they do might influence public policy, and more willing to express support for authoritarian alternatives. The crisis of democratic legitimacy extends across a much wider set of indicators than previously appreciated.
>
> (Foa and Mounk 2016: 7)

Contemporary novelist Marilynne Robinson sees an equally deep crisis in democracy (2015a). To her, democracy is rooted in a strong sense of humanism that sees the other as different but also as someone to be respected. What is currently witnessed is that, because of the erosion of this humanism, different factions in society regard each other more as enemies whose right to coexist as equal members of the same society is called into question. Obviously, this does not contribute to the ethical character of politics and instead turns it into a war of some groups against other groups. Or perhaps the vocabulary of enemies and war is not the most suitable, and it is rather the case that there is a widespread fear. Citizens increasingly fear one another, which—if not managed properly—can easily turn into hostilities and worse.

Social scientists could, of course, easily question observations such as these. After all, novelists write fiction, and fiction is not what academic work is or should be about. Still, as many would admit, novelists and other writers of fiction have occasionally if not regularly been able to trace particular developments that at the time were still taking place under the surface. Although scientists consequently still had difficulty identifying them, these developments were usually no less real. It certainly holds true for the topic of this study, that both legal scholars and political scientists, no matter how rigorous their research of citizens' attitudes to politics or the case law may be, still run the risk of failing to see the bigger picture that sometimes practitioners are also better at sensing. Robinson, of course, has the additional advantage of combining work that is fiction with more academic essays (2015b).

If a leading idea that sustains democracy can still be identified, then it would be liberalism. However, as liberalism principally strives to protect the human autonomy against external intervention, it runs the risk of giving rise to a "spiritually vacant state: the privatization of ultimate belief" (Koyzis 2003: 65). Again, like the emergence of the modern state in the sixteenth and seventeenth centuries (Lovin) or the more recent decline of a strong sense of humanism (Robinson), the potentially one-sided character of liberalism points towards a key democratic deficit: the fact that as a result of the loss of moral vocabulary, politics no longer resembles what it was originally supposed to be about—a meaningful deliberation about different conceptions of the good.

It is submitted that the core problem is not so much the combination of liberalism and democracy as such. Admittedly, the tragedy of liberal democracy is that by itself it is unable to formulate an answer to the question of how justice can be defined. Democracy is largely a procedure for decision-making and not an ideology, with relativism probably coming closest if one nevertheless had to identify such an ideology. Within liberalism the neutrality of the state is one of the central principles. Taken together this can result in what can be called an impoverishment of the political debate, with a disproportionate emphasis on the economy and security, for example.

Strictly speaking, liberalism cannot be blamed for the fact that the vacuum has not been filled, since it provides space for different worldviews to do so. To the extent that a particular type of liberalism—that is, Enlightenment liberalism—currently fills the vacuum, it can even be argued that liberalism solves the problem it has created in the first place. That this is perhaps not the most fortunate manner in which to solve the problem, as pointed out in Chapter 2, is a different matter.

In its broadest terms, a better solution would be the return to an Aristotelian concept of politics. This is characterized by the idea that politics is all about the common good. Given the fact that different concepts of the common good do exist in most societies today, politics is then all about encouraging an informed and substantive discussion on which proposed policy alternative for a particular problem is preferable from the point of view of the common good. In terms of the three most common varieties of constitutional democracies that can be distinguished, direct democracy, representative democracy, and deliberative democracy (Frankenberg 2012: 252–6), this comes down to an appeal to strengthen the deliberative nature of representative democracy. It should be noted, however, that if more elements of direct democracy are introduced, the same applies to the deliberative nature of that variety of constitutional democracy. As such, a greater emphasis on elements of direct democracy is not incompatible with an appeal to strengthen the deliberative nature of politics.

In such an Aristotelian notion of politics, hardly any difference exists between politics and ethics, because politics is all about a choice between various conceptions of the good. As a result, the various ethical and religious convictions of the citizens can, and must, be brought to the fore (Gamwell 1995; Weithman 2006; McGraw 2010). As such, this concept of politics stands in marked contrast to a Rawlsian concept of politics, to which we will now turn. A difference with most theories of deliberative democracy is that it is not imperative that a consensus be reached. As a result, participants in the political debate are not under an obligation to subscribe to arguments of their opponents, unless they wish to do so for substantive reasons. To the extent that within deliberative theory the emphasis today is more on compromise than consensus (Gutmann and Thompson 2012), the difference nearly disappears.

Public Reason

The American political philosopher John Rawls (1921–2002) must first be credited for revitalizing legal and political philosophy, starting with his book *A Theory of Justice* (1971). His later works—such as *Political Liberalism* (1993) in general, and his specific article on the concept of public reason in particular (1997)—make for a fascinating read. Rawls has obviously been deeply engaged with one of the most fundamental questions in legal philosophy—that is, how is it possible to stay together as a political community despite the existence of radically different comprehensive doctrines in society? This is becoming even clearer now that new manuscripts have been published, both from the start and from the end of Rawls's career. Obviously, the thought of a political philosopher can never be fully comprehended without knowledge of his or her biography, and this certainly also applies to Rawls. The relationship between Rawls and religion is a particularly fascinating topic, which has been explored in a recent volume (Bailey and Gentile 2014). Rawls had certainly also become more open towards the role of religion in a liberal democracy in the course of his career (Latterell and Witte 2015; see also Vallier 2014).

Having said that, the answer that Rawls gives to these questions still deeply affects the character of the political debate (R. Smith 2016a, 2016b). What

Rawls argues in his article specifically on the concept of public reason (1997) is that a distinction ought to be made between what he calls the "background culture" and the political domain. Within civil society, so-called comprehensive doctrines or worldviews can be referred to. Once a minority enters the public domain, however, it is under an obligation to stick to the notion of public reason, meaning that it can only use arguments that are intelligible for all other participants in the political debate, at least where fundamental political issues are concerned.

It is not just a matter of terminology, however. The concept of public reason also implies that the political decisions that are eventually taken need to be in conformity with what the lowest common denominator can still adhere to. What this implies is that the political vocabulary applied has to meet certain criteria, but also that the room for political decision-making itself becomes severely restricted. This is even more the case, as Rawls applies this substantial limitation with the help of the concept of public reason not just to the political domain but also to the "background culture." In other words, the different minorities in society are free to invoke their own vocabulary in their societal organizations, but can only to a certain extent also act upon these convictions.

It is worth mentioning here that Rawls does not single out religious convictions in this context. On the contrary, he makes quite some effort to make clear that the idea of public reason applies to non-religious comprehensive doctrines as well. Thus, as Rawls points out, secularism would not be able to impose its leading ideas on a society that also comprises religious groups either, because it is nothing more or nothing less than just another concept of the good among many (cf. Rosenfeld 2014). In practice, however, it may well be the case that religious convictions are more affected by the constraints that public reason imposes upon political debate than secular convictions. Certainly in our current age, and in the West, religious vocabulary and ideas will more readily be regarded as "irrational" and therefore invalid than secular discourse and ideas.

One other point to be made is that in a sense Rawls's work took on an entirely new relevance after his death. Looking back, it seems difficult to believe that Rawls originally was apparently so concerned about the effect that comprehensive doctrines might have in society, if not constrained by the demands of a public reason. After 9/11, of course, the resurgence of religion in world politics generally, and Western societies in particular, has made the problem that Rawls tries to address even more pertinent. In our age of religious extremism, and even violence, it is simply difficult to deny that there ought to be certain limitations on both the political vocabulary invoked and the political decisions made—that is, given that one would want to maintain the broadly liberal democratic character of our societies.

We will come back to this substantial dimension later on in this chapter. For now it suffices to conclude that the application of the concept of public reason in the political debate logically impoverishes the nature of that debate even further (Stout 2005: chapter 3; Habermas 2006; S.D. Smith 2010). It may be the case that it cannot completely be reduced to the elements that Lovin refers to—that is, economics and security. Yet it is also clear that many of the potentially rich moral vocabularies that could theoretically be put forward by the different minorities in today's society will not stand the test of public reason. This means that adhering to public reason in the political sphere represents the middle ground between a nearly total loss of moral vocabulary that can arguably be identified today on the one hand, and the kind of potentially rich moral arguments that could be made if minorities were free to make references to their deepest religious and non-religious convictions on the other hand (Chaplin 2012).

Rawlsians tend to regard their solution to perceived problems with differences in society as a means of enhancing political legitimacy. They believe that by restricting these differences largely to the private sphere, the remaining diversity in the public sphere will become manageable. An Aristotelian conception of politics, however, sees the referral of citizens' deepest convictions to the private sphere as precisely the problem in terms of legitimation. It is here that the alienation of citizens from the political order originates, as these citizens are urged to separate their deepest political convictions from the actual political decision-making. Taking the heart out of politics, also in this way, can hardly serve as a means to enhance the legitimacy of the political order, in this view.

As a result, the concept of public reason makes it even more difficult to find a solution for the problem identified by Lovin: the dysfunctionality of our current democracies as a result of the loss of moral vocabulary. That is, as long as the idea of public reason remains as influential as it has been in recent decades, both in philosophy and in practical politics. Fortunately, however, there are signs that the popularity of this notion is in fact declining (see e.g. Sen 2009). For the time being, however, it is important to be aware of the enduring dominance of Rawlsian thought, especially in the Anglo-Saxon world (R. Smith 2016a). Thus, the idea of public reason has also been a recurring theme in the discussions held during the inquiry on "Law and Religious Freedom" at Princeton.

At the same time, what puts the dominance of the idea of public reason somewhat in perspective is Lovin's historical argument about the effects of the rise of the modern state on political discourse in society. Of course, some would be tempted to argue that the conflictful conditions under which the modern state arose, and which made it necessary to restrict the nature of political argument, have by and large lasted until the present day or at least returned after 2001. Compared with that factor, the potential impact of Rawls's concept of public reason should not be exaggerated. Whether Rawls has made his influence on political debate felt or not, the current study proposes to take into account the limitations imposed on political discourse by a Lockean type of constitutional democracy, in which the task of government is inherently limited. In fact, it embraces this perspective to the extent that it emphasizes the important, subsidiary role of civil society in the polity. However, as the government even under such conditions still has a contribution of its own to make towards the realization of justice in society, it is important for its legitimacy that the contents and scale of this contribution be discussed from the points of view of all the different comprehensive doctrines represented in society.

Equal Political Voice Liberalism

Considerably lesser known, yet a main alternative to Rawls's public reason liberalism, is American political philosopher Nicholas Wolterstorff's equal political voice liberalism. In his book *Understanding Liberal Democracy* Wolterstorff argues that liberal democracy is characterized by an "equal right to full political voice within constitutional limits" (2012: 125). As the label already suggests, this type of liberalism emphasizes the fact that all citizens in a polity ought to have an equal voice. For Wolterstorff, this implies that there ought to be no restrictions as far as the type of political arguments that can be put forward are concerned. Although, like Rawls, he refers to the need to maintain a degree of civility in public discourse, this does not mean that citizens ought to comply with the demands of public reason. Even if the notion of public reason is not adhered to, it ought to be possible to conduct a political debate in a civilized manner.

The way this can be realized is further clarified by the notion of "moral engagement" that plays a crucial role in Wolterstorff's thought (138). He believes that the essence of liberal democracy is that citizens display a kind of moral engagement, by which he means that one ought to be willing to listen to the arguments that are put forward by other citizens, to reconsider one's own position if necessary, and to subsequently accept a majority decision where it has not turned out to be possible to reach full agreement. Rawls would aim at such full agreement with the help of his concept of public reason, and those who are not able to subscribe to the decisions made are in that case simply removed from the "legitimation pool" of citizens for whom the laws are supposed to be democratically legitimate (Wolterstorff 2012: 81). Wolterstorff, on the other hand, is willing to admit the fact that in a plural society it is inevitable that not every decision will be accepted by all the citizens. It is precisely his ideal of "moral engagement" that will nevertheless hold the polity together.

Obviously, the notions of civility and moral engagement are only able to do the work up to a certain point. Therefore, yet another important notion in Wolterstorff's equal political voice liberalism is that certain constitutional limits ought to be in place (133). The difference with Rawls is that in his case the limits are set by the concept of public reason. In the case of Wolterstorff, the constitutional limits consist of the classical rights of freedom of religion, expression, assembly and association, and so on. Although these rights set limits to the political debate, this is clearly necessary with a view to guaranteeing equal political voice. On the whole, these limits will not go as far as those imposed by the concept of public reason, however, as the latter concept is in a sense an additional limit imposed upon the political debate.

Thus, we have seen that Wolterstorff agrees with Rawls that it could theoretically be difficult to reach political consensus in a plural society, but that he does not believe it necessary to impose limits related to Rawls's idea of public reason upon the political debate. Wolterstorff identifies a different challenge regarding his democracy conception, however. He rightly notes that his ideal of an equal political voice liberalism is dependent on there being vital moral or religious communities in society that nourish the kind of convictions put forward by citizens and their political representatives (141). Should these convictions not be adapted and further developed on a continuous basis, then the risk is that the political debate will suffer and the moral engagement in society will decline, if only because there are no longer any substantial ideas with which to engage.

As Wolterstorff acknowledges, this can in fact be witnessed in the United States today (142). When politics is reduced to mere power politics, the legitimacy of the political order is put at risk, however. When citizens no longer morally engage with other citizens and their convictions, indifference takes root and political stability is no longer guaranteed. It is true that the same risk applies to public reason liberalism. As Wolterstorff argues, the number of people excluded from the legitimation pool could be much more substantial than Rawls assumes, in which case legitimate law could ultimately become a far-fetched ideal as well (120). However, whereas in the case of Rawls this effect is more or less artificially created in the statal sphere, and could thus be corrected, the chances of success of Wolterstorff's equal political voice liberalism are ultimately dependent on (civil) society and lie therefore outside the competence of the state. All the state can do is to facilitate the adaptation and development of the convictions by moral and religious communities by guaranteeing the freedoms of religion, expression, and assembly and association (Inazu 2012).

But what is the proper way for the state to facilitate civil society associations in a democratic constitutional state? Three concrete suggestions for constitutional commitments have been made in this respect by professor of law and religion John D. Inazu. First of all, there is "the Voluntary Groups Requirement": "Government officials should not interfere with the membership, leadership, or internal practices of a voluntary group absent a clearly articulated and precisely defined compelling interest" (2016: 48). Second, the "Public Forum Requirement" holds that

> [g]overnment should honor its commitment to ensure public forums for the voicing of dissent and discontent. Expressive restrictions in these forums should only be justified by compelling government interests. Private public forums that effectively supplant these government-sponsored forums should in some cases be held to similar standards.
>
> (64–5)

Third, Inazu mentions the "Public Funding Requirement": "When the government offers generally available resources (financial and otherwise) to facilitate a diversity of viewpoints and ideas, it should not limit those resources based on its own orthodoxy" (79).

Another characteristic of the solution to the problem proposed by Wolterstorff is thus that it broadens the notion of politics. In much contemporary legal and political science literature, the concept of politics is implicitly or explicitly supposed to be confined to the electoral process, political parties, legislatures, and executives. Although these directly political institutions are obviously relevant and to be held in high esteem, from a social-pluralist perspective these are not the only, and probably not even the primary, institutions to look to for the sake of the advancement of human development. Basically, all societal institutions, beginning with the family, are instrumental to this end. In fact, when these institutions erode, too much pressure is put on the directly political institutions, which can only lead to disappointment since they cannot possibly make up for societal defects (Brooks 2016a; Putnam 1994). As law professor Timothy Hall (1992: 110–2) has put it:

> First, religious groups in general continue to provide the associational structures necessary for training in the idea of the common good. Civic virtue, at the most fundamental level, lies in the disposition of individuals to attend to something other than pure self-interest, to be responsive to and responsible for the needs of other members of a community. Religious groups, in the form of voluntary associations, create a context in which individuals become sharers of a common life, and thus have occasion to acquire an other-regarding disposition.
>
> Second, religious groups have traditionally preserved didactic resources for discourse concerning the common good. The major religions, for example, have each emphasized perspectives that temper, at least to some degree, the purely selfish impulses that war against a concept of the public good. These didactic resources are available for use, and have in fact been used, in specific discourses about the public good, such as the discourse connected with the civil rights movement. . . .
>
> Third, religious groups in American society have provided visionary resources for debate concerning and for pursuit of the public good. Even if religious believers, on average, cannot claim any greater level of virtue than nonbelievers, one might nevertheless conclude that religions preserve aspirations to virtue that are socially important. Furthermore, one might also conclude that religions, at least on occasion, produce individual exemplars of virtue. . . . Thus, as keepers of a vision of virtuous life and incubators of occasional exemplars of virtue, religious groups remain a powerful force in creating a climate in which civic virtue can survive.

Pluriform Democracy

Wolterstorff is a philosopher of Christian, and more specifically Reformed, conviction. As such, his work clearly resembles earlier Reformed contributions on the topic. Particularly, this concerns the approach of principled public pluralism that neo-Calvinists such as statesman and theologian Abraham Kuyper (1837–1920) and the legal philosopher Herman Dooyeweerd (1894–1977) developed during the nineteenth and twentieth centuries (Skillen 1974; Lugo 2000; Chaplin 2016b). Some ten years ago, I presented a paper on this topic at the International Symposium of the Association for Reformational Philosophy, held in Hoeven, the

Netherlands (Ten Napel 2006). As I set out on that occasion, according to the approach of principled public pluralism, states are not considered to be entirely sovereign, as ultimate sovereignty resides in God alone. As such, this approach is a clear illustration of the kind of reasoning that Cohen wishes to do away with, as she is convinced that in a liberal democracy the state ought to enjoy a monopoly on sovereignty. One can also see what potentially can get lost if one insists on the principle of absolute state sovereignty. To the adherents of this approach, it is precisely the fact that modern states are not fully sovereign which puts them under an obligation to pursue justice. In order to avoid the impression that earthly authorities would be able to achieve anything close to biblical justice, the term public justice is used instead. In addition to some form of democratic constitutionalism, such public justice requires at least two types of pluralism: associational and directional pluralism (Mouw and Griffioen 1993: 16).

Associational pluralism refers to the idea that God has created society with the potential to unfold into a number of different spheres, such as the family, education, business, the arts, and government. Since government constitutes only one of these spheres, it is under an obligation to recognize and uphold the autonomy and freedom of civil society which has responsibilities of its own. Directional pluralism implies that although the church as an institution is also confined to its own sphere, religion does not constitute a separate sphere. Instead, it has a bearing on all aspects of life. However, since ultimate sovereignty resides in God alone, society should be governed neither by a particular religion, such as Christianity, Judaism, or Islam, nor by some other worldview, such as secularism. Instead, a government should uphold the right of all people who live within its territory to be free to practice their various religious or non-religious faiths in both private and public life.

As I set out on the same occasion, the rise of pluriform democracy in the Netherlands in the early twentieth century is to a considerable extent rooted in precisely this well-worked-out theory of Reformed origin. In 1917, under pressure from a political alliance of orthodox Protestants and Roman Catholics, principled public pluralism was introduced, making the Netherlands a confessionally neutral state, asserting as much as possible equal respect and principled distance to all religious and non-religious worldviews in society and their affiliated organizations. As the American political scientist Stanley Carlson-Thies (1993: iv–v) has rightly pointed out,

> [t]he four subcultures which took shape in the latter decades of the nineteenth century [Orthodox Protestants, Roman Catholics, Liberals and Socialists] did not pose a deadly challenge to democratic governance, as assumed by consociational theory. The challenge was instead to state policies inhospitable to the diversity of ways of life embodied in the subcultures. The prevailing liberal model tolerated, but privatized, differences. But Catholics and orthodox Protestants insisted that their religious beliefs should guide also their public activities and institutions. . . . Segmentation . . . necessitated the transformation of state policies and structures. The Netherlands became

> not a consociational democracy but a pluriform democracy—a democracy in which subculturally-rooted differences are affirmatively accommodated by the state.

It is in this sense that the term "pluriform democracy" is used here.

As I noted even before the International Symposium of the Association for Reformational Philosophy, because of the shifting worldview beliefs in society, from the 1960s onwards a new paradigm shift with regard to church–state relations in the Netherlands gradually took place (Ten Napel 2000). Although this obviously was not certain from the beginning, and even now remains partly uncertain, this most recent shift might bring with it the end of pluriformity. In that case, in essence, the shift would involve a return to the more Enlightenment liberal type architecture of the state of the nineteenth century, at a moment in time when society, because of both secularization and immigration, is becoming more plural than it already was. The pace of change has for a while been slow, because the social pluralist theories of society of Reformed and Catholic origin "have become part of the Dutch mindset on issues of church and state" (Monsma and Soper 1997: 58). Yet the change is unmistakable, as demonstrated, for example, by the now almost total demise of the formerly pluralist broadcasting system (Hiemstra 1997; see also Maussen 2013; Kennedy 2013).

Since 2002, moreover, under the influence of additional factors such as the fear of religious extremism and violence, the pace of change has accelerated. Still, ten years later three German researchers concluded, on the basis of an analysis of legal and parliamentary debates on issues such as gender equality, integration, ritual slaughtering, and same-sex marriage since the murder of Theo van Gogh (2004), that

> [w]hile there are substantive shifts in Dutch secular order, it is certainly too early to say conclusively whether they constitute a critical juncture that will lead into a finally dominant type of progressive secularity. At the moment, there are still forces, which balance the thrusts of progressive secularism.
>
> (Schuh, Burchardt, Wohlrab-Sahr 2012)

This is precisely the reason why an ongoing research project subsidized by the Dutch Organization for Scientific Research is investigating changing church–state relations in the Netherlands since the 1960s.

The current study does not provide new empirical insights in this subject matter, but rather attempts to develop a theoretical perspective with the help of which developments in the relationship between faith-based organizations and the state can be interpreted. It does so by adopting a broad comparative perspective, in which the Netherlands as a case study forms only one, and—although regularly referred to—in a sense a relatively minor, component. The reason for this is that the Netherlands may have been a special case during the first part of the twentieth century, when it was the pluriform democracy that Carlson-Thies and others have described. It may also still have been a special case during the 1960s, in the sense that the cultural revolution has probably had a relatively strong impact, precisely because the country had known such well-organized faith and other communities in the previous decades. The developments that have taken place since the 1960s, however, are less specific to the Netherlands. More and more, the country has become a "normal" Western country, which, like other countries, is secularizing. The only distinctive feature of the Netherlands may still be that it is well ahead of other countries in this respect, notably the United States. As such, it still represents an interesting case internationally, despite its small size. There appear to be fewer and fewer reasons to try to explain the developments from a uniquely Dutch cultural and historical perspective. It is thus at least in part a conscious choice for the current study, although also a part of the project specifically concerned with the Netherlands, to look for additional clues in the developments in both Europe as a whole and North America.

Notwithstanding the fact that Wolterstorff happens to be a philosopher of Reformed conviction, however, it is not just from a Christian perspective that one can reach the insight that equal political voice liberalism is a potentially worthwhile alternative to Rawlsian public reason liberalism, but also, for example, from a Jewish point of view (Novak 2005; Goodman 2014). Many theories of civil society are also secular in character, and thus the insight can perhaps best be regarded as a feature of mainstream conservatism (Levin 2014). What the different theories about politics that embrace equal political voice liberalism have in common is that they presuppose a measure of associative pluralism or, as Lovin calls it, institutional pluralism (2014b: 6). As a result, according to these theories a "resurrection of democracy" (Bretherton 2015) is not feasible along these lines without generous protection of the more communal dimensions of religions as well, such as churches, synagogues, and mosques. It is precisely within such faith and other communities that mature visions of the good life can develop, which simultaneously contribute to the notion of the common good.

Had it been the case that principled public pluralism was an approach that was so influenced by Christian theology that it could reasonably only be expected to be acceptable to practicing Christians, there would perhaps not have been much reason to deal with it in this study. Interestingly, however, the approach is both informed by Christian theology and sufficiently general in its concrete application that it has a potentially broader appeal and in fact fits in with approaches developed within other religious and non-religious traditions (see e.g. Bader 2007). In such a case, from an academic point of view it is fair to simultaneously make explicit the more specific theological roots of principled public pluralism and emphasize the remarkable similarities with insights from different sources.

Multicultural Democracy

One reason why equal political voice liberalism has a broader appeal, is that the same theoretical argument that in the past has been made with regard to the Netherlands can be made more generally and for the situation in which many Western countries find themselves currently. Thus, as a leading author on consociational democracy in the Netherlands has observed, "[m]ost experts on divided societies and constitutional engineering broadly agree that deep societal divisions pose a grave problem for democracy, and that it is therefore generally more difficult to establish and maintain democratic government in divided than in homogeneous countries" (Lijphart 2004: 96–7). If this is true, it does not bode well for the future of democracy, since to a certain extent all countries are multicultural societies today. Because of the migration crisis, this appears to be the case even more so today (Porter 2015).

In fact, the increasing societal divisions may well be behind the declining prospects for democracy discussed earlier. If a country has to be homogeneous in order to be able to enjoy a stable democracy, then the future of democracy looks gloomy indeed. Still, although the assumption may be justified empirically (see, however, Hanson 2016), there is something deeply unsatisfactory about the idea that in a heterogeneous society no proper democratic decision-making is possible. The fact that this idea is unsatisfactory at a theoretical level has to do with the contribution that political participation can make to becoming fully human. It is, contrary to what some theorists of democracy have proposed, certainly not the case that political participation is a precondition for human flourishing. Still, being able to participate in political decision-making when and to the extent that one desires is certainly a contributing factor to human development. This is why the current chapter aims at identifying a way of furthering democracy even in the context of today's divided Western societies.

Fortunately, therefore, the Human Development Report 2004, for example, published for the United Nations Development Programme (UNDP)—after having carefully examined it with the help of a global team of contributors—rejects the claim that deep societal divisions necessarily pose a grave problem for democratic government. According to the Report, cultural differences can indeed lead to social and political conflict, but only if the state does not recognize and accommodate the various ethnicities, religions, languages, and values in a particular country. Active multicultural policies are required to achieve this and to thereby make democracy viable in divided societies—that is, "policies that explicitly recognize cultural differences" (2004: 2). More specifically, according to the Human Development Report, multicultural policies are required in the following five fields: political participation, access to justice, language, socio-economic policies, and, last but not least, religion. I will limit myself to religion here, as this is even more directly relevant to the approaches of public reason liberalism and equal political voice liberalism than the exact institutional arrangements for political participation such as the electoral system.

In what follows, I will first of all briefly summarize, as I first did ten years ago, what the report has to say about this. Next I will offer some new reflections on the compatibility of the report with the approach of principled public pluralism, and indeed on the approach of principled public pluralism itself, that highlight the development of my own thinking on the topic. It is only fair to say that in writing down these thoughts I have benefitted greatly from the publication of Inazu's book on *Confident Pluralism* (2016), referred to above, and some of the comments that followed after its publication. According to Inazu's definition, such confident pluralism "allows genuine difference to coexist without suppressing or minimizing our firmly held convictions. We can embrace pluralism precisely because we are confident in our own beliefs, and in the groups and institutions that sustain them" (7). Both the book and some of the responses to the book have helped me to develop my thoughts on the topic, a process that had already been underway for quite some time, also during my stay at Princeton.

Because religion is of profound importance to one's identity, from the point of view of cultural liberty, guaranteeing religious freedom in the best possible way is of foremost importance. The Human Development Report 2004 distinguishes between secular and non-secular states. Non-secular states come in three varieties. First of all, a non-secular state can be a theocracy, governed as it were by divine law. An example of such a state is provided by the Islamic Republic of Iran since 1979. Second, a non-secular state can have an established religion—that is, a formal alliance between a particular religion and the government. Examples include Buddhism in Bhuta, Hinduism in Nepal, Islam in Bangladesh, and Roman Catholicism in Bolivia. Third, a non-secular state can have an established church or religion, but nonetheless recognize and even financially support more than one religion. Examples of such states include various Scandinavian countries and the United Kingdom. None of these three types of non-secular states stands out from the point of view of ensuring religious freedom, although in practice the third type without doubt performs better than the first two. Generally speaking, however, a secular state is to be preferred, according to the report.

Contrary to what is usually assumed, secular states come in at least three different varieties as well. To begin with, there are anti-religious states, which exclude religion from their own affairs but do not hesitate to interfere in the affairs of religion. Examples include Communist regimes in China and, formerly, in the Soviet Union and Eastern Europe. An interesting question is whether and to what extent contemporary Russia actually performs any better in this respect, although of course important ties exist between the Russian Orthodox Church and the state. The country thus illustrates nicely how states can in practice navigate between two entirely different systems of church–state relations, in the case of Russia between the model of a non-secular state with a more or less established religion and an anti-religious state as far as various other Christian denominations and religions are concerned.

Second, a secular state can be neutral or laicist. Neutral states are characterized by a strict separation between church and state. The state should be neutral as far as religion is concerned and this neutrality is considered to be best achieved by stripping the public square of all religious elements. France since the Separation Law of 1905 is probably the best example of a country with this type of church–state relationship, given, for example, the recent attempts to impose burkini bans; some would argue that the United States since the Second World War also comes close. The question is, of course, whether such assertions are exaggerated, and even if one nevertheless wishes to make a comparison between France and the United States, it is imperative to bear in mind also the differences between the two countries dating back in part to the nature of the French and American revolutions. Turkey can probably better serve as an alternative example of a laicist state, although in recent years democratically elected governments have attempted to modify the laicist character of the Turkish state. This has resulted in a number of coup attempts by the army, most recently in 2016.

Third, there are secular states asserting equal respect and principled distance to all religious and secular worldviews in society and their affiliated organizations. This engagement may take the form of support for religions, such as public funding of religious schools, as long as this is done more or less even-handedly. The Report mentions the Indian Constitution as an example, but the Netherlands also fits in this category, as will be clear from the above. What is important to note at this moment is that also, according to UNDP, secularism apparently does not automatically imply the privatization of religion. In fact, in this third type of secular state the neutrality of the state may well be protected better than in so-called neutral or laicist secular states. Or, as the Report puts it (2004:8):

> What is important from the human development perspective is to expand human freedoms and human rights—and to recognize equality. Secular and democratic states are most likely to achieve these goals where the state provides reasonable accommodation of religious practices, where all religions have the same relation to the state and where the state protects human rights.

This position roughly corresponds to what the American historian Wilfred M. McClay argued in an essay entitled "Two Concepts of Secularism." According to McClay (2003: 46),

> [t]here is on the one hand, a way of understanding the secular idea as an opponent of established belief—including a *nonreligious* establishment—and a protector of the rights of free exercise and free association. On the other hand, one can understand the secular ideal as a proponent of established *unbelief* and a protector of individual expressive rights, a category that includes rights of religious expression.

The former view, which understands secularism as a freedom from establishmentarian imposition of any worldview on society, is a rather minimal understanding of secularism and can therefore be called negative or minimal secularism. The latter view, called positive or maximal secularism, is held by more militant secularists, who to a certain extent can be considered enemies of religion (with important exceptions, such as the Christian separationists):

> Such a regime seeks, under the guise of separating church and state, to exclude religious thought and discourse from any serious participation in public life, and to confine religious belief and practice, as much as possible, to the realm of private predilection and individual taste.
>
> (47–8)

In this terminology the Human Development Report 2004 prefers minimal secularism, as it envisages a place at the table for both religious and non-religious worldviews (cf. Bouchard and Taylor 2008: chapter VII; Taylor 2016). For the sake of clarity, it could also have avoided the term "secular" for this type of church–state relations and referred to "impartiality" of the state towards religions and beliefs instead (Chaplin 2016a; cf. Bader 2010).

In order for minimal secularism or impartiality to work, however, religious faiths must undergo a certain degree of adaptation in accommodating themselves to it. "They must," as McClay puts it, "learn their table manners, and learn how to behave around strangers" (2003: 52). Or, as another author puts it strikingly, religious faiths have to "translate their expectations of *universal affirmations of a particular truth* into *particular affirmations of a universal truth*" (Ferrari 2005). Interestingly enough, neo-Calvinists have been among the first to adapt to minimal secularism, as my discussion of the Reformed contribution to the issue of church and state in religiously plural societies in the past has demonstrated.

From Pluriform Democracy to Multicultural Democracy?

Given that virtually all countries have by now become more or less multicultural societies, both in the Netherlands and elsewhere proponents of the model of pluriform democracy will be confronted with the question of how it relates to the concept of multicultural democracy as advocated by the UNDP. As political scientist John Hiemstra has observed, the principle of *ecclesia reformata semper reformanda est* ("the reformed church is always reforming") "reflects the biblical belief that the Holy Spirit is always urging Christians to renewal, reform, liberation and greater maturity in our sinful and broken lives and societies" (2005: 199). Would not a new adaptation of Calvinism to modern circumstances, after the adjustment to minimal secularism, be therefore in the spirit of Kuyper?

This is obviously a difficult question. On the one hand, there appear to be considerable similarities between the two models, in the sense that the notion of pluriform democracy already covers at least one of the five dimensions of the concept of multicultural democracy—that is, religion. On the other hand, from a social pluralist perspective something is probably missing in the concept of multicultural democracy, in that it is too much involved with directional pluralism and too little with associational pluralism. What this demonstrates once more is that the latter doctrine, associational or institutional pluralism (Lovin), remains the most distinctive social pluralist contribution to the topic of church and state. Yet it should be noted that associational pluralism is not incompatible with the concept of multicultural democracy.

In the paper presented in 2006, I therefore argued that the notion of a multicultural ethos, which is required to build multicultural democracies, does not necessarily have to be approached critically. It seemed to me that there is a clear link with contributions from the circle of Reformational philosophy to the debate on public justice. As a matter of fact, protection of cultural diversity (or contextual pluralism) can—in the words of political scientist David Koyzis—be regarded as

> a crucial element in the state's calling to do public justice. . . . If contextual diversity is based on created human finitude, then the attempt to eliminate it is rooted in an overwhelming effort to deny such finitude and to claim the right to mould people in accordance with a single monistic vision of the world, which is nothing less than idolatrous.
>
> (2003: 207; cf. Mouw and Griffioen 1993: 18; Rivers 2001; Chaplin 2008; 2011b: 48–60)

The model of pluriform democracy indeed appeared to me to present a middle course between the rival models of the neutral or laicist state and unbounded multiculturalism (not distinguished as such in the Human Development Report 2004), but the differences with the limited kind of multiculturalism defended by the UNDP were considerably less clear (Ten Napel 2006).

I added, however, that further reflection on the concept of multicultural democracy from a social pluralist perspective appeared desirable. With a view to this further reflection, the potential of Catholic social doctrine appears to be of particular relevance. The *Compendium of the Social Doctrine of the Church*, compiled in the 1990s by an editorial committee under the chairmanship of Pope Benedict XVI, potentially provides the beginning of an answer to the question of what distinguishes pluriform democracy from even a limited multiculturalism. It "values" democracy (Pontifical Council for Justice and Peace 2005: para 406), adding immediately, however (para 407), that

> an authentic democracy is not merely the result of a formal observation of a set of rules but is the fruit of a convinced acceptance of the values that inspire democratic procedures: the dignity of every human person, the respect of human rights, commitment to the common good as the purpose and guiding criterion for political life. If there is no general consensus on these values, the deepest meaning of democracy is lost and its stability is compromised.

Yet the lack of such a consensus is exactly what is missing in modern-day democracies, due to ethical relativism. This obviously constitutes a serious threat, according to the Compendium, because "if there is no ultimate truth to guide and direct political action, then ideas and convictions can easily be manipulated for reasons of power. As history demonstrates, a democracy without values easily turns into open or thinly disguised totalitarianism" (para 407). Understandably, the Compendium then goes on to warn that a further marginalization of Christianity in the West "would not bode well for the future of society or for consensus among peoples; indeed, it would threaten the very spiritual and cultural foundations of civilization" (para 572; cf. Cartabia and Simoncini 2015).

Elsewhere I have argued how, compared with Catholic social teaching, neo-Calvinist thought on democracy in general and Dooyeweerd's views on democracy have remained relatively underdeveloped (Harinck and Ten Napel 2013: 44; Ten Napel 2014). Thus, specialist in Christian political thought, political theology, and public theology Jonathan Chaplin's aim in his study *Herman Dooyeweerd: Christian Philosopher of State and Society* is to demonstrate "how his work amounts to a striking and characteristically Protestant philosophy of social pluralism and civil society, comparable in range and depth to contributions emerging from twentieth-century Catholic social thinkers such as Jacques Maritain and Heinrich Rommen" (2011a: 1–2). It can be argued, however, that "the contrast between the impressive legacy of Thomistic thought and the paucity of Calvinist philosophizing" (29), by which Dooyeweerd had already been struck in 1925, still exists with respect to pressing questions of values and democracy already raised by Tocqueville. These questions include the following:

> [W]hat is needed, apart from freedom of speech and the right to vote, to hold democratic societies together? Is the rule of law enough, or do we need common values, ethics, mores? And what is the role of religion in all this; is it a help or a hindrance to liberal democracy?
>
> (Buruma 2010: 3; cf. Inazu 2016)

The details do not need to concern us here, however, as the difference between neo-Calvinist thought and Catholic social teaching should not be overestimated either (Schindler 2008). Thus, neither of the two would probably find it contradictory to at least partially embrace the notion of a pluralistic liberalism. After all, such liberalism is "about the protection of legitimate diversity" (Galston 2002: 23). One difference would still be the acknowledgment of a metaphysical dimension to the constitutional order, however, which, as we saw in Chapter 2, could contribute to keeping the secular checks and balances in place. Before concluding, I would like to return briefly to the specific question of why the acknowledgment of a metaphysical dimension to the constitutional order is relevant also from the perspective of the current chapter (see J.K.A. Smith 2016).

One question can be asked regarding the similarities between principled public pluralism and liberal pluralism: Is it really correct that the two are virtually the same in outcome or is it appropriate to continue to distinguish between the two? Or, to put it slightly differently: Is it the case that principled public pluralism leads to precisely the kind of so-called neutral state that liberal pluralism envisages, or is there something more to it? Conceptually, the key to answering this question lies in looking even more closely at the different kinds of pluralism that social pluralist theory distinguishes. Earlier on, we saw how social pluralism welcomes in particular associative pluralism. We also argued that it should be open to cultural or contextual pluralism as, like associative pluralism, cultural differences can be considered by believers to be part of God's creation. This is different with respect to directional pluralism. Directional pluralism is taken seriously by social pluralist theory, but at least its religious components are likely to regard it more as part of the Fall—that is, when sin entered the scene—than as part of God's creation.

To the extent that social pluralist theory acknowledges directional pluralism, this is because people have been created with a free will. It is incompatible, for example, with Christian theology to force someone to believe in the "true" God. This doctrine is what ultimately makes the right to freedom of religion or belief acceptable from a Christian point of view, and thus also what makes directional pluralism something to be dealt with in as respectful a manner as possible. However, this remains a second-best scenario, because directional pluralism as such is not something to be embraced, let alone celebrated. This is also why in social pluralist theory it is not the task of the state to affirm directional pluralism as such. One senses the difference here with a liberal approach as advocated in the Human Development Report 2004, when it urges the state to recognize and accommodate the various ethnicities, religions, languages, and values, and requires active multicultural policies to make democracy viable in divided societies.

Here we encounter a major paradox, however. In theory, it would be easier for liberal pluralism to embrace and celebrate cultural diversity, and to develop state policies to facilitate this. Social pluralist theory, on the other hand, can be expected to be more reserved with respect to directional pluralism, although it is principally willing to accommodate it because it is indirectly the result of human beings being created as independent agents. In practice, however, as we saw in Chapter 2, liberal pluralism is no longer the dominant strand of liberal theory. This raises the question of whether accommodation of diversity is a structural characteristic of liberalism after all. Social pluralism, on the contrary, can still be said to represent the mainstream of Christian political thought, although here too there is increasing competition between several strands of such thought.

For the time being, however, it would be safer to bet on social pluralism than on liberal pluralism when it comes to accommodating diversity. This implies, then, that social pluralism should not de-emphasize its differences with liberal pluralism, but rather present itself as a distinctive alternative. The distinctive element of social pluralism lies precisely in its ambivalent attitude towards directional pluralism. Precisely because it cannot unconditionally embrace or celebrate diversity, it will consciously respect directional pluralism all the more. Directional pluralism is seen as a result of the Fall, but God has made it possible for human beings not to choose life. Therefore, human beings cannot be rejected because they do not (yet) choose life, but instead have to be deeply respected in the choices they make as they have been created in a way that they can make these choices. It is this internal struggle when it comes to managing diversity that also leads to a limited, yet outspoken, role of the state in establishing justice for all.

This leads to a second difference between social pluralism and liberal pluralism. It is clear that for a plural society to take shape, the people living in it ought to possess the capabilities of living out their comprehensive doctrines in daily practice. Liberal pluralism takes this for granted, but has hardly any means to empower people to actually achieve this goal for themselves and for others. Social pluralism, on the other hand, has in theory many houses of worship and faith-based organizations available for the development of the necessary virtues to create a truly plural society, as well as to manage the resulting diversity (Chaplin 2011b: chapter 7).

This, of course, is the point where one has to realistically acknowledge the fact that because of secularization this is a rapidly diminishing advantage that social pluralism has over liberal pluralism. At least, however, there is the knowledge of how the foundations for a truly democratic society must be laid. Ironically, these are by and large the same foundations on which liberal pluralism has to rely to the extent that it is willing to acknowledge this dependence. It is here that the recent book on *Confident Pluralism* is important, as Inazu does not limit himself to the constitutional framework that is necessary to build and maintain a pluralist society. He also elaborates on the virtues—or aspirations as he calls them—that need to be present in order to live together within constitutional limits.

As we have seen earlier in this chapter, Wolterstorff himself is all too aware of this precondition for equal political voice liberalism to actually work. This is so crucial, however, that a political theory such as principled public pluralism cannot itself afford to ignore this dimension. This means that an even greater interdisciplinary effort is required to realize the kind of constitutional democracy that social pluralism envisages. The theory needs to engage anthropological and other insights, and, to the extent that it is willing to do so, the difference with liberal pluralism may increase.

The point of all this is not to claim any kind of superiority of social pluralist theory whatsoever. If anything, whoever is in favor of constitutional democracy would really have to wish for social pluralist theory not to hold true, as its tenets will be very difficult to implement. The point is rather to express surprise that the question is not more often asked whether social pluralist theory is on to something. Because to the extent that it is, and the current study believes this to be case, the future of constitutional democracy as we know it may well be at stake.

Perhaps it is taking this point a little too far; perhaps it is not. In any case, the question is whether an even deeper reason why such a dysfunction of politics can be discerned is the fact that Western societies are rapidly drifting away from their Christian roots. Could it be the case that, just as the new critics of religious freedom argue that the right to freedom of religion or belief is a Christian invention, democracy too can hardly survive in the form we have come to know it in the past two centuries without the continuing nutrition provided by not just its religious roots in general, but perhaps even its Christian or Judeo-Christian roots in particular (Pera 2008: 4; cf. Maritain 2011)?

In Conclusion

In his book *The Global Public Square: Religious Freedom and the Making of a World Safe for Diversity*, English author and social critic who moved to the United States in 1984 Os Guinness defines his model of a cosmopolitan public square as

> a vision of public life in which citizens of all faiths and none are free to enter and engage public life on the basis of their faith, as a matter of freedom of

> thought, conscience and free exercise, but within an agreed framework of what is understood and respected to be just and free for people of all other faiths too, and thus for the common good.
>
> (2013: 180–1)

Both the title of his book and this particular quotation from the book demonstrate the intimate link that exists between the ideal of equal political voice liberalism and the right to freedom of religion or belief. The fact that Guinness is an evangelical is not a coincidence either, in the sense that there is—as this chapter has illustrated—a close connection between, for example, Christianity on the one hand and equal political voice liberalism and the right to freedom of religion or belief on the other. Similar accounts on the role of faith in the public square can also be found in Europe, such as former Archbishop of Canterbury Rowan Williams's notion of an "argumentative democracy" (2012: 135).

Looked at from this perspective, there is reason for some concern regarding the secularization of Europe and the United States. Nearly all remaining full democracies in the world are situated in countries in North America and Northern and Western Europe with a Protestant background. Apparently, there is something in Christianity in general and Protestantism in particular that is conducive to a pluralistic liberal order (Woodberry 2012). This "something" could well be the idea that all human affairs, including politics, are to be conducted in the honor of God, to whom every human being is ultimately accountable (Kinneging 2015; see also Spruyt 2002; De Bruijne 2010). Or, as European lawyer Joseph Weiler (2006) has put it,

> the only guarantee of successful democracy is a habit of self-restraint: You have the power, but you don't exercise it to the full. . . . Our political culture is a culture of self-restraint in the exercise of power, which—as even an atheist or agnostic would acknowledge—we owe to the Judeo-Christian tradition.

As a result, it does not seem too far-fetched to expect that the decline of (mainstream) Protestantism, for example, will also affect the way democracy functions in the West.

Even if a democratic system remains in place, the nature of democratic decision-making might change. Paradoxically, the influence of Christianity on democracy might make it more pluralistic and tolerant than democracy would otherwise have been or will be. As the editor of *First Things* magazine R.R. Reno put it:

> Without a transcendent orientation, secular progressivism makes a god of politics. Christianity, by contrast, recognizes that politics, while important, is not ultimate. Jesus said, "My kingdom is not of this world." St. Augustine distinguished between the City of God and the city of man. For this reason, a Christian society can accommodate pluralism in a way that a supposedly neutral secularism can't. The social consensus in a Christian society need not be final, as it were. It can be penultimate, and thus more open.
>
> (Cited in Movsesian 2016)

At the same time, however, it is useful to bear in mind that "[a]ll the world's major religions today are involved in struggles over the twin tolerations"—that is, "the minimal boundaries of freedom of action that must somehow be crafted for political institutions *vis-à-vis* religious authorities, and for religious individuals and groups *vis-à-vis* political institutions" (Stepan 2000: 54, 37). Finally, it can only be hoped that many more people of good will, notably also the nones and the secular, will contribute to the maintenance of a viable constitutional democracy in the twenty-first century. The ideal of a society that allows all to become "fully human" is an ideal that, fortunately, cannot be exclusively claimed by any religious or non-religious tradition in particular.

Bibliography

Bader, Veit (2007), *Secularism or Democracy? Associational Governance of Religious Diversity* (Amsterdam: Amsterdam University Press).

Bader, Veit (2010), "Constitutionalizing Secularism, Alternative Secularisms or Liberal-Democratic Constitutionalism? A Critical Reading of Some Turkish, ECtHR and Indian Supreme Court Cases on 'Secularism'," *Utrecht Law Review*, 6(3): 8–35.

Bailey, Tom and Valentina Gentile (eds) (2014), *Rawls and Religion* (New York, NY: Columbia University Press).

Bouchard, Gérard and Charles Taylor (2008), *Building the Future: A Time for Reconciliation* (Québec: Commission de Consultation sur les Pratiques d'Accommodement Reliées aux Différences Culturelles).

Bretherton, Luke (2015), *Resurrecting Democracy: Faith, Citizenship, and the Politics of a Common Life* (Cambridge: Cambridge University Press).

Brooks, David (2016a), "How to Fix Politics," *The New York Times*, April 12.

Brooks, David (2016b), "Let's Have a Better Culture War," *The New York Times*, June 7.

Bruijne, Ad de (2010), "Democratie adieu," *Nederlands Dagblad*, 13 maart.

Buruma, Ian (2010), *Taming the Gods: Religion and Democracy on Three Continents* (Princeton, NJ: Princeton University Press).

Carlson-Thies, Stanley Warren (1993), *Democracy in the Netherlands: Consociational or Pluriform?* (University of Toronto: Ph.D. thesis).

Cartabia, Marta and Andrea Simoncini (eds) (2015), *Pope Benedict XVI's Legal Thought: A Dialogue on the Foundation of Law* (Cambridge: Cambridge University Press).

Chaplin, Jonathan (2008), "Beyond Multiculturalism—But to Where? Public Justice and Cultural Diversity," *Philosophia Reformata*, 73(2): 190–209.

Chaplin, Jonathan (2011a), *Herman Dooyeweerd: Christian Philosopher of State and Civil Society* (Notre Dame, IN: University of Notre Dame Press).

Chaplin, Jonathan (2011b), *Multiculturalism: A Christian Retrieval* (London: Theos).

Chaplin, Jonathan (2012), "Law, Religion and Public Reasoning," *Oxford Journal of Law and Religion* 1(2): 319–37.

Chaplin, Jonathan (2016a), "'Living with Difference': Time for a Constructive Christian Engagement," *Law and Religion UK*, January 20.

Chaplin, Jonathan (2016b), "Liberty, Laïcité, Pluralité: Towards a Theology of Principled Pluralism," *International Journal of Public Theology*, 10(3): 354–80.

Diamond, Larry (2015), "Facing Up to the Democratic Recession," *Journal of Democracy*, 26(1): 141–55.

Ferrari, Alessandro (2005), *Religions, Secularity and Democracy in Europe: For a New Kelsenian Pact*, Jean Monnet Working Paper 03/05 (New York, NY: NYU School of Law).

Foa, Roberto Stefan and Yascha Mounk (2016), "The Danger of Deconsolidation. The Democratic Disconnect," *Journal of Democracy*, 27(3): 5–17.

Frankenberg, Günter (2012), "Democracy," in: Michel Rosenfeld and András Sajó (eds), *The Oxford Handbook of Comparative Constitutional Law* (Oxford: Oxford University Press) 250–68.

Freedom in the World (2015), *Discarding Democracy: Return to the Iron Fist* (Washington, DC, and New York, NY: Freedom House).

Freedom in the World (2016), *Anxious Dictators, Wavering Democracies: Global Freedom under Pressure* (Washington, DC, and New York, NY: Freedom House).

Fukuyama, Francis (1992), *The End of History and the Last Man* (New York, NY: The Free Press).

Galston, William A. (2002), *Liberal Pluralism: The Implications of Value Pluralism for Political Theory and Practice* (Cambridge: Cambridge University Press).

Gamwell, Franklin I. (1995), *The Meaning of Religious Freedom. Modern Politics and the Democratic Resolution* (Albany, NY: State University of New York Press).

Goodman, Lenn E. (2014), *Religious Pluralism and Values in the Public Sphere* (Cambridge: Cambridge University Press).

Guinness, Os (2013), *The Global Public Square: Religious Freedom and the Making of a World Safe for Diversity* (Downers Grove, IL: Inter Varsity Press).

Gunsteren, Herman van and Rudy Andeweg (1994), *Het grote ongenoegen; over de kloof tussen burgers en politiek* (Bloemendaal: Aramith).

Gutmann, Amy and Dennis Thompson (2012), *The Spirit of Compromise: Why Governing Demands It and Campaigning Undermines It* (Princeton, NJ, and Oxford: Princeton University Press).

Habermas, Jürgen (2006), "Religion in the Public Sphere," *European Journal of Philosophy*, 14(1): 1–25.

Hall, Timothy L. (1992), "Religion and Civic Virtue: A Justification of Free Exercise," *Tulane Law Review*, 67(1): 87–134.

Hanson, R. Scott (2016), *City of Gods: Religious Freedom, Immigration, and Pluralism in Flushing, Queens* (Oxford: Oxford University Press).

Harinck, George and Hans-Martien ten Napel (2013), "Democracy: Instrument for or Expression of a Christian Political Order?" *Journal of Inter-Religious Studies*, 11: 42–9.

Hiemstra, John L. (1997), *Worldviews on the Air: The Struggle to Create a Pluralist Broadcasting System in the Netherlands* (Lanham, MD: University Press of America).

Hiemstra, John L. (2005), "Reconciling All Things to Himself: Reflections on the Kingdom of God, the Church and the State's Role in Plural Societies," in: *REC The Netherlands 2005 Agenda* (Madison, WI: Printing Plus) 171–212.

Human Development Report 2004, *Cultural Liberty in Today's Diverse World* (New York, NY: United Nations Development Programme).

Inazu, John D. (2012), *Liberty's Refuge: The Forgotten Freedom of Assembly* (New Haven, CT, and London: Yale University Press).

Inazu, John D. (2016), *Confident Pluralism: Surviving and Thriving Through Deep Difference* (Chicago, IL: University of Chicago Press).

Keane, John (2009), *The Life and Death of Democracy* (London/New York, NY: W.W. Norton and Company).
Kennedy, James (2013), "The Public Role of Religion in Europe Since the 1960s: The Dutch Case," *Schweizerische Zeitschrift für Religions- und Kulturgeschichte*, 107: 49–62.
Kinneging, Andreas (2015), "Ook Nederland kan ontaarden in een tirannie," *Nederlands Dagblad*, 2 oktober.
Koyzis, David T. (2003), *Political Visions and Illusions: A Survey and Christian Critique of Contemporary Ideologies* (Downers Grove, IL: InterVarsity Press).
Latterell, Justin J. and John Witte, Jr. (2015), "Law Religion, and Reason in a Constitutional Democracy: Goodman v. Rawls," *Political Theology*, 16(6): 543–59.
Levin, Yuval (2014), "Taking the Long Way: Disciplines of the Soul are the Basis of a Liberal Society," *First Things*, October.
Lijphart, Arend (2004), "Constitutional Design for Divided Societies," *Journal of Democracy*, 15(2): 96–109.
Lovin, Robin W. (2014a), "Ethics and Politics: Restoring a Moral Vocabulary," Maguire Lecture, Kluge Center, The Library of Congress, January 23.
Lovin, Robin W. (2014b), "Religious Freedom and Dysfunctional Democracy," CTI Colloquium, September 30.
Lugo, Luis E. (ed.) (2000), *Religion, Pluralism, and Public Life: Abraham Kuyper's Legacy for the Twenty-First Century* (Grand Rapids, MI: Eerdmans).
McClay, Wilfred M. (2003), "Two Concepts of Secularism," in: Hugh Heclo and Wilfred M. McClay (eds), *Religion Returns to the Public Square. Faith and Policy in America* (Baltimore, MD, and London: Johns Hopkins University Press) 31–61.
McGraw, Bryan T. (2010), *Faith in Politics. Religion and Liberal Democracy* (Cambridge: Cambridge University Press).
Maritain, Jacques (2011), *Christianity and Democracy and The Rights of Man and the Natural Law* (San Francisco, CA: Ignatius Press).
Maussen, Marcel (2013), "Religious Governance in the Netherlands: Associative Freedoms and Non Discrimination After 'Pillarization': The Example of Faith-Based Schools," RECODE Working Paper Series, Online Working Paper No. 14.
Monsma, Stephen V. and J. Christopher Soper (1997), *The Challenge of Pluralism. Church and State in Five Democracies* (Lanham, MD: Rowman & Littlefield).
Mouw, Richard and Sander Griffioen (1993), *Pluralisms and Horizons: An Essay in Christian Public Philosophy* (Grand Rapids, MI: Eerdmans).
Movsesian, Mark (2016), "Conversations: R.R. Reno," *Law and Religion Forum*, August 9.
Müller, Jan-Werner (2015), "Should the EU Protect Democracy and the Rule of Law within its Own Member States?" *European Law Journal*, 21(2) 141–60.
Napel, Hans-Martien ten (2000), *From Principled Pluralism to Strict Separation: The Changing Relationship between Church and State in the Netherlands*, Paper prepared for delivery at the 28th Annual ECPR Joint Sessions of Workshops, University of Copenhagen, Denmark, Institute of Political Science, April 14–19.
Napel, Hans-Martien ten (2006), "The Concept of Multicultural Democracy: A Preliminary Christian-Philosophical Appraisal," *Philosophia Reformata*, 71(2) 145–53.

Napel, Hans-Martien ten (2014), "Joseph H.H. Weiler's Approach to the Democratic Legitimacy of the European Union. Is There a Message for Neo-Calvinists?" *Journal of Markets and Morality*, 17(1) 125–41.

Novak, David (2005), *The Jewish Social Contract: An Essay in Political Theology* (Princeton, NJ: Princeton University Press).

Pera, Marcello (2008), *Why We Should Call Ourselves Christians: The Religious Roots of Free Societies* (New York, NY, and London: Encounter Books).

Pontifical Council for Justice and Peace (2005), *Compendium of the Social Doctrine of the Church* (Washington, DC: USCCB Publishing).

Porter, Eduardo (2015), "A Migration Juggernaut is Headed for Europe," *The New York Times*, September 15.

Putnam, Robert D. (1994), *Making Democracy Work: Civic Traditions in Modern Italy* (Princeton, NJ: Princeton University Press).

Rawls, John (1971), *A Theory of Justice* (Cambridge, MA: Harvard University Press).

Rawls, John (1993), *Political Liberalism* (New York, NY: Columbia University Press).

Rawls, John (1997), "The Concept of Public Reason Revisited," *The University of Chicago Law Review*, 64(3) 765–807.

Rivers, Julian (2001), "Multiculturalism," *Cambridge Papers*, 10(4): December.

Robinson, Marilynne (2015a), "Fear," *The New York Review of Books*, September 24.

Robinson, Marilynne (2015b), *The Givenness of Things: Essays* (New York, NY: Farrar, Straus and Giroux).

Rosenfeld, Michel (2014), "Recasting Secularism as One Conception of the Good Among Many in a Post-Secular Constitutional Polity," in: Susanna Mancini and Michel Rosenfeld (eds), *Constitutional Secularism in an Age of Religious Revival* (Oxford: Oxford University Press) 79–108.

Schindler, Jeanne Heffernan (ed.) (2008), *Christianity and Civil Society: Catholic and Neo-Calvinist Perspectives* (Lanham, MD: Lexington Books).

Schuh, Cora, Marian Burchardt and Monika Wohlrab-Sahr (2012), "Contested Secularities: Religious Minorities and Secular Progressivism in the Netherlands," *Journal of Religion in Europe*, 5(3): 349–83.

Schweiker, William (2014), "Monotheistic Faith and the Cosmopolitan Conscience," in: S. Ilesanmi, W. Lee and J. Parker (eds), *The Rule of Law and the Rule of God* (New York, NY: Palgrave MacMillan) 31–49.

Sen, Amartya (2009), *The Idea of Justice* (Cambridge, MA: Harvard University Press).

Skillen, James William (1974), *The Development of Calvinistic Political Theory in the Netherlands, with Special Reference to the Thought of Herman Dooyeweerd* (Duke University: Ph.D. Thesis).

Smith, James K.A. (2016), "Reforming Public Theology: Neocalvinism and Pluralism," Herman Bavinck Lecture, Theological University Kampen, June 27.

Smith, Randall (2016a), "Defeated by Assault: The Abiding Influence of John Rawls, Part One," *Public Discourse*, June 13.

Smith, Randall (2016b), "Neutered by Neutrality: The Abiding Influence of John Rawls, Part Two," *Public Discourse*, June 14.

Smith, Steven D. (2010), *The Disenchantment of Secular Discourse* (Cambridge, MA: Harvard University Press).

Spruyt, Bart Jan (2002), "Democratie binnen vaste grenzen. Rechtsfilosoof Kinneging bepleit terugkeer naar grote traditie van het natuurrecht," *Reformatorisch Dagblad*, april 10.

Stepan, Alfred C. (2000), "Religion, Democracy, and the 'Twin Tolerations.'" *Journal of Democracy*, 11(4): 37–57.

Stout, Jeffrey (2005), *Democracy and Tradition* (Princeton, NJ: Princeton University Press).

Taylor, Charles (2016), "Democracy and Its Exclusions: Political Identity and the Challenge of Secularism," *ABC Religion and Ethics*, April 5.

The Economist (2007), "Democracy Index. Liberty and Justice for Some," August 22, available at www.economist.com/node/8908438 (accessed November 28, 2016).

Vallier, Kevin (2014), *Liberal Politics and Public Faith: Beyond Separation* (London and New York, NY: Routledge).

Walt, Stephen M. (2016), "The Collapse of the Liberal World Order," ForeignPolicy.com, June 26, available at http://foreignpolicy.com/2016/06/26/the-collapse-of-the-liberal-world-order-european-union-brexit-donald-trump (accessed November 28, 2016).

Weiler, Joseph (2006) "The Only Guarantee of Successful Democracy is a Habit of Self-Restraint," Europe4Christ.net, Newsletter No. 10, available at www.europe4christ.net/index.php?id=137 (accessed November 28, 2016).

Weithman, Paul J. (2006), *Religion and the Obligations of Citizenship* (Cambridge: Cambridge University Press).

Williams, Rowan (2012), *Faith in the Public Square* (London: Bloomsbury Publishing).

Wolterstorff, Nicholas (2012), *Understanding Liberal Democracy: Essays in Political Philosophy* (Oxford: Oxford University Press).

Woodberry, Robert D. (2012), "The Missionary Roots of Liberal Democracy," *American Political Science Review*, 106(2): 244–74.

4 A Generous Conception of Religious Freedom

Introduction

Mary Ann Glendon and Raul F. Yanes have not just analysed the case law of the U.S. Supreme Court with respect to religious rights since the Second World War. In the article that we considered earlier, they also plead for an alternative, more holistic approach to religion cases which they baptize "structural free exercise." Glendon and Yanes define the term "structural" in this context as "the relations within and among texts, and between legal and social institutions" (1991: 537). Their approach thus attempts to take into account the role religion has played culturally and historically in the American democratic experiment. In doing so, it almost automatically comprises both the individual and the communal dimensions of religious freedom.

A more robust conception of religious freedom as defended by Glendon and Yanes is intimately connected with both the notion of social pluralist constitutionalism as set out in Chapter 2 and the (further) development towards a pluriform democracy as advocated in Chapter 3. As we have seen, the notion of social pluralist constitutionalism extends the doctrine of the separation of powers from the state authorities to non-state actors, among other things. In order to achieve this, however, citizens need to be free to organize themselves in faith-based organizations and these organizations in turn need to enjoy a certain measure of autonomy. Also, there can be no truly pluralistic public square without the participation of faith and other communities, with well-developed visions of what is deemed to be the good life, in the political and public debate.

At the time they wrote their article, Glendon and Yanes prophetically foresaw that the major challenge ahead would become "to accord as much scope as possible to the constitutional guarantee of free exercise in its personal, associational, and institutional dimensions, while respecting the freedom of conscience of nonbelievers and without preferring one religion to another" (549). Still, as the current chapter will argue, in order for the right to freedom of religion or belief to perform this essential function for democratic constitutionalism, no radically new theory of the right is needed. The reason for this is that, from the beginning, the importance of the communal dimensions of religious freedom has been recognized in the relevant case law and documents, in addition to the clearly also fundamental individual dimension of the right (Rivers 2010; Leigh 2012). It is submitted that, rather than doing away with the right to freedom of religion or belief in its current form, a both pragmatic and principled effort is needed to build on this valuable legacy (cf. DeGirolami 2013; Koppelman 2013). To the extent that the right maintains a distinctively Western, or even Christian, character as a result, there is no reason to be particularly concerned or even surprised about that. Democratic constitutionalism will necessarily always be value-laden, whether the type of constitutionalism in question is Christian, Jewish, Islamic, or secular in its origins.

Sphere Sovereignty

In the case of a social pluralist constitutionalism, it all starts, as we have seen in previous chapters, with the recognition that society does not consist of autonomous individuals and the state alone, but that families and other institutions play a major part as well and that human rights are thus in part also communal in nature (McCrudden 2012: 11; Calo 2015: 107; Monsma and Carlson-Thies 2015). This means that a social pluralist approach to religious freedom will make a plea against any "institutional blindness" that might characterize particular other approaches (Horwitz 2009: 85). Delineating the legitimate powers for societal institutions is deemed a crucial activity, also with a view to defining the limits of state sovereignty (cf. Galston 2005: 40–2; Galston 2006).

The sources of this alternative approach can, *inter alia*, be found in the Christian tradition (Skillen and McCarthy 1991: 137–41). Thus, in the Catholic line of thought, which views society as a hierarchically ordered unity of different types of institutions, the principle of subsidiarity has become a leading principle. This principle, which we already encountered in Chapter 2, means that every institution has the right to perform its proper tasks, and that higher institutions may not engage in activities that can be carried out just as well or better by lower institutions. Every lower institution must therefore have as much autonomy as possible.

In the Protestant tradition, a form of social pluralism has developed that has much in common with this Catholic line of thought described above. Of special importance are the Dutch thinkers Abraham Kuyper and Herman Dooyeweerd, who developed the principle of "sphere sovereignty." This principle, also known as associative or institutional pluralism, holds that every authority in every sphere of life "derives the power at its disposal, not as a grant from the state but as a direct gift from God" (Kuyper 2015: para 59). Thus, each and every social sphere needs to be sovereign with regard to its own internal affairs and the state as one of those institutions has to respect this sovereignty (Skillen and McCarthy 1991: 229–64; Kuyper 1994: 78–109). As such, the principle lies at the root of the approach of principled public pluralism set out in Chapter 3. Legal historian Mark De Wolfe Howe has also more generally described "the heart of the pluralistic thesis" as

> the conviction that government must recognize that it is not the sole possessor of sovereignty, and that private groups within the community are entitled to

> lead their own free lives and exercise within the area of their competence an authority so effective as to justify labeling it a sovereign authority. To make this assertion is to suggest that private groups have liberties similar to those of individuals and that those liberties, as such, are to be secured by law from governmental infringement.
>
> (1953: 91)

Van der Vyver (2001: 657) aptly sums up the implications of the principle of sphere sovereignty for the institutional dimension of the right to freedom of religion or belief as follows:

> The sphere sovereignty of a religious community denotes the inherent competence of members of a particular faith:
>
>> to establish institutions as a means of uniting their number and to facilitate the execution of their calling;
>>
>> to decide upon and organize the internal structures of such institutions;
>>
>> and to contrive and to proclaim rules of behaviour and exercise authority for the sake of order within their own ranks.
>>
>> Sphere sovereignty is thus a matter of existence, organization and power of social institutions.

Without doubt, certain differences have existed, and may well continue to exist, between the Catholic and Protestant lines of thought. Thus, in Kuyper's and certainly also Dooyeweerd's view, the state's task is more narrowly defined than in the Catholic tradition, since it is characterized by the ideal of public justice rather than the broader notion of the common good (Chaplin 2011: 225–41). However, of more relevance to the purposes of the present chapter is that the similarities of the two traditions together constitute a distinctive, Christian brand of pluralism from which guidance for the development of a distinctive religious freedom conception can also be, and has been, derived.

Thus, Garnett has argued that in applying the right to freedom of religion or belief, religious institutions as such must receive attention as right-bearers, because of their indispensable role in preserving religious freedom, as with the press and universities in preserving freedom of expression (2012, 2007, 2008). The long Western tradition of the independence of the church suggests that there is indeed reason to provide churches and other faith-based institutions with specific protection against state interference (Van der Vyver 2001: 652 ff.). At a point in time in which some refer to a "civic totalism" on the rise, specific attention given to religion continues to be justified. Should this no longer be the case, we run the risk that, as one author put it, "[i]n the name of 'human rights', the government will assume control of both the public and familial orders. No longer will we find any recognition of an order of truth that is independent of the state's own definition of itself" (Schall 2012).

What this quotation indicates is that once again the question of how absolute the sovereignty of the state must be considered to be lies at the centre of the debate. It is in many gradually secularizing Western societies simply difficult to imagine for state authorities that some citizens may still recognize other sovereignties in their personal and social lives besides that of the state. As a result, when they encounter such a citizen, they will at the very least try to regulate this person's acknowledgment of these other sovereigns. Thus, it is sometimes required of churches to register with the state before they are allowed to act as such in a particular country. Once registered, other restrictions may apply.

The right to freedom of religion or belief may be regarded to be intended precisely as a guarantee for both individual citizens and faith-based organizations against such notions of absolute state sovereignty. In the Catholic and Protestant versions of the theory, this is because these institutions of civil society are deemed to be part of a divine creation order. Other, not religiously inspired, adherents of social pluralist theory may refer to a different kind of historical perspective, according to which the modern state is only a recent phenomenon, which naturally has to respect what existed prior to its establishment. One way or another, religious freedom is a potentially disturbing and even threatening notion for all those worldly powers that wish to rule over citizens and their institutions rather than to serve them.

Additional Guidelines

From the principle of sphere sovereignty, which focuses specifically on the communal dimensions of the right to freedom of religion or belief, follow additional, more comprehensive, guidelines with respect to religious freedom. Thus, in a recent guidebook on *How to Think about Religious Freedom* by Theos, a UK think tank on religion and society, seven "unapologetically Christian" principles are distinguished which could guide our thinking about this right (Spencer 2014: 7; cf. Ahdar and Leigh 2005: 11–37). In the context of the current study, it would be more appropriate to call these social pluralist principles.

The first principle is that "spirituality" is key to human identity, and requires recognition and respect (14). This principle concerns the "keystone of Christian anthropology"—that is, that "[h]uman beings are made in the image of, and intended for relationship with, their creator." Not only is the Trinitarian God—Father, Son, and Holy Spirit—in whose image man is made "irreducibly relational" itself, but we are also invited to enter into that same relationship. From this notion that "human nature only finds its fulfilment in communion with God," it follows that the right to religious freedom has a special place in Christian legal thought:

> The *details* of religious freedom may not be qualitatively different from other freedoms, involving freedom of conscience, speech, association etc., but they are conceptually different, justified by different considerations, in particular a different understanding of what it means to be fully human.
>
> (15)

It is clear that this first principle is the most important principle regarding religious freedom. Although reference is made to anthropology, this principle also explains why there is a link between theology and the right to freedom of religion or belief. The notion that spirituality is a central dimension of human existence is what makes this human right the first freedom for those who subscribe to social pluralist theory. Thus, the reason is not a desire to play down the importance of other human rights. The reason is rather that in interpreting and applying these other rights, which are often also linked to the same Christian anthropology, it needs to be ascertained that every human being must remain able to maintain the relationship with his or her creator. It is only by entering into such a relationship that human beings can become fully human.

Obviously, this is not to say that human beings need to be forced into a relationship with their creator. Characteristic of a liberal democracy is that it is not considered legitimate for the government to force people to be free. To the extent that there is a link between Christianity and liberal democracy, one parallel is that according to Christian theology it is simply inconceivable that a person should involuntarily approach God. As a result, the right to freedom of religion or belief involves not only the fundamental right to engage in a living relationship with one's creator, but also the right not to. Moreover, although according to a Christian anthropology all people are considered essentially spiritual beings, the possibility is principally left open that some people will find other gods than the Christian one.

The first principle is also what makes the right to freedom of religion or belief controversial. Increasingly, it appears that at least in the West the notion that human beings are essentially spiritual beings becomes more difficult to comprehend. To the extent that one comes to live more within an "immanent frame," one will simply no longer see the added value and relevance of a human right based upon the assumption that a person ought to have the opportunity to enter into a relationship with her creator. What we see occurring here is that, although the right to freedom of religion or belief principally leaves room for people not to recognize the fact that they are made in the image of their creator, the reverse does not hold true. Sometimes those who do not see spirituality as central to their lives in any meaningful sense do not want to create space for those fellow citizens for whom this is the case to live according to their fundamental convictions in this respect.

Yet it is important to see that this certainly does not hold true for all people of no faith. Many of these people live according to deep ethical principles of their own, which imply that the fact that for other people spirituality is a key to their human identity needs to be recognized and respected. This should continue to permit a broad alliance with people of no faith who are in favor of a right to freedom of religion or belief. Obviously, this alliance also includes adherents of other faiths besides the Christian one. Here, in some cases, the difficulty may be that religions find it difficult to accept that people who adhere to a "false" religion ought to be as free to practice that religion as adherents to their own faith. At this point, it should be remembered that this was precisely the reason why until relatively recently the Catholic Church itself was opposed to the idea of religious freedom.

What the above implies is that the debate on the right to freedom of religion or belief ought to continue. Discussions must take place between religious people and people of no faith, just as there ought to remain exchanges between people of different faiths on this topic. There is no reason to assume, however, that in the twenty-first century the idea that a person is essentially a spiritual being ought to be abandoned. Not only would such an idea not be in accordance with the empirical fact that across the globe a clear majority of people are religious in one way or another, but it would also wrongly take for granted that people of no faith are not able or willing to acknowledge the fact that others are religious and ought to have the freedom to live out their beliefs in their daily lives. Nor would it be consistent with liberal democratic principles, as constitutionalism and democracy are based on the same social pluralist anthropology as the right to freedom of religion or belief.

The second social pluralist principle with respect to religious freedom distinguished in the guidebook is that "religious belief cannot be neatly detached from religious practice." Although it is currently sometimes argued that Western conceptions of religious freedom have a Christian or Protestant bias, in that they define religion essentially as belief and/or worship, the entire Old Testament is proof that such religious practice is not unknown to Christianity itself either. As the guidebook puts it,

> Recovering the irreducible materiality of spirituality is important, partly because it is true to the doctrine of creation and resurrection; partly because many of the legal issues in this area relate to "manifestations" of belief; and partly because it provides a framework by means of which other non-Christian religions can be engaged on their own terms, rather than imposing a more narrowly Protestant conception of "faith" on them.
>
> (Spencer 2014: 16)

It is indeed noteworthy, in the light of observations by the new critics of religious freedom, that this is the second basic principle. It is only fair that the guidebook emphasizes that within Christianity in general, and also within Protestantism in particular, religious doctrine and religious practice are intimately interconnected. Although for legal purposes it may be necessary to distinguish between beliefs and manifestation of beliefs, this is often not the case in the real lives of believers. Similarly, liberalism may find it helpful to separate the public sphere from the private sphere. It will not convince religious voices in society, however, whenever they feel the need to engage in the political debate. Life is whole, according to most Christian denominations, and there is no room for any kind of duality whatsoever. This includes the false duality which is sometimes suggested to exist between religions for which beliefs and practice are one and Christianity.

To be fully human is also a matter of being able to live one's life completely in conformity with one's identity. To the extent that the new critics of religious freedom are right in saying that the dividing line runs between Christianity and other religions, this should not be a problem to accept for those other religions. However, it is submitted here that no such contrast exists between other religions and Christianity. Nor should it be difficult for people of no faith to accept that it is a precondition for true freedom not to have to divide one's life into different compartments and only live according to one's fundamental convictions in certain of these compartments. Again, this is a principle that cannot be given up today, as the fact that it is a precondition for freedom also implies that it is a precondition for constitutionalism and democracy.

The third principle is that "religious freedom means freedom to adhere to, exercise and choose between all religions and none." This is a particularly interesting principle, in that it demonstrates why an historically Christian approach to religious freedom does not have to constitute a threat to other religions, but may instead give rise to a more generous conception and practice of religious freedom than, for example, certain secular notions of religious freedom. As the guidebook states,

> The point here is not to attempt to create that most chimerical of beasts, the neutral state, but rather to recognise that the principles of wider religious freedom are inherent within Christian thought. Put another way, if we are to adopt an authentically Christian approach to religious freedom, it must be one that is prepared to fight for the right to practice and manifest other religious commitments.
>
> (Spencer 2014: 17)

In part we already touched upon this point above. However, it is worth noting that contrary to what some would expect to be the case, secular notions of religious freedom are not necessarily more generous than a social pluralist one. Of course, if the new critics of religious freedom had their way, religious freedom would still remain protected to some extent. The question is, however, whether religious believers would be better off as a result. It sounds almost too good to be true to have all ethical convictions protected in an equal manner. To the extent that this ideal arises within the context of a secular worldview, it might well be the case that religious convictions would be regarded as unconventional and thus less worthy of protection than mainstream ones. Paradoxically, a right to freedom of religion or belief firmly rooted in a particular faith tradition may well yield more protection than an abstract legal provision not rooted in such a strongly held worldview.

A parallel can be drawn here with the ideal of the neutral or secular state. It is certainly the case that some erudite proponents of this concept do so with a view to protecting society as much as possible from religious extremism and violence. It is also the case, as we have seen in the previous chapter, that constitutional limits ought to be in place when embarking on the course of a true equal political voice liberalism. Yet it seems justified to question whether a neutral state advanced for these reasons would be as welcoming of the different faith traditions as, for example, a state based on a social pluralist type of constitutionalism. The difference appears to be that in the first case the role of religion is limited out of fear for its potentially harmful effects on society, whereas in the second case room is created for different religious and non-religious worldviews up to the point that certain well-defined constitutional limits are transgressed.

The fourth principle concerns the notion that "associational rights, beyond those of religious communities, are legitimate." This is, of course, the principle that most directly touches upon the notions of sphere sovereignty and subsidiarity discussed above, with their emphasis on "intrinsically legitimate institutions" other than the state. Interestingly, it focuses on the important role of civil society in general. In order to become fully human, man is arguably called not only to enter into a relationship with his creator, but also to love his neighbors. This points to

> a firm basis for the significance and dignity of associational activity in a range of forms that far exceeds the narrowly religious. Whether that is in teaching, healing, serving, working, trading or governing—much of which we would now term as characteristic of civil society—such corporate activity is legitimate, constructive and humanising.
>
> (Spencer 2014: 20)

It follows that "recognising the rights and responsibilities of these forms of association is also an important element in navigating the various claims pertaining to religious freedom" (20; cf. Benson 2013).

In this fourth principle lies the explanation for the fact that religion's socio-economic value in, for example, the United States was recently estimated at approximately $1.2 trillion, the equivalent of the world's fifteenth largest national economy and more than the annual revenues of Apple, Amazon, and Google together (Grim and Grim 2016). This is not to be turned into a caricature; the connection between religions and their potential social value remains "complex," to say the least (Berg 2016). However, it can serve to argue that a society can hardly afford to limit the range of societally relevant activities that believers wish to pursue. It is not just the case that within faith communities a democratic ethos can be developed that helps to sustain liberal democracy. It is also true that several faith and other communities help provide essential services in society that the state cannot provide as well. To the extent that human flourishing depends on these social activities and services, the right to freedom of religion or belief can be said to contribute not just to the liberal democratic character of a state, but also to the degree of human flourishing that is actually achieved within that state.

According to the fifth principle, "the family has its own right but is not sacred or inviolable." Although intrusions on family life do not (yet) play a major role in this book, with a view to possible further developments in constitutional law in the future it is good to note with respect to this prime example of a human association that "the fact that the judgement under which the family is placed in the gospels is the call of Christ strongly suggests that the bar for interference is set very high" (Spencer 2014: 22).

When speculating about future frontiers of constitutional law, it is sometimes argued that its reach might increasingly (have to) expand into what was previously regarded as the private domain of the family (e.g. Rubio-Marín 2015). It is true that this, again, is sometimes done out of a noble idealism. However, it is also the case that a state can easily become totalitarian when such boundaries are crossed by public authorities. It is a crucial corollary of the notion of sphere sovereignty that families function directly under a divine authority instead of under state authorities. It is a sign of the times that such ideas about the reach of public law are being advanced, and also a threat to the principle of limited government. The right to freedom of religion or belief, together with other classical rights, functions as a shield in this respect and can therefore in the light of developments such as these be considered more necessary in the twenty-first century rather than superfluous.

The sixth principle of religious freedom points out that "human dignity, as expressed in rights, is an authentic Christian principle." This is not to deny that in the history of Christianity it has been a controversial issue whether the concept of *human* rights could be accepted, and to a certain degree will always remain so. Still, there is at least some common ground to the extent that "the principle of inherent, equal and inalienable human dignity is central to the Christian tradition, and foundational to the idea of human rights" (Spencer 2014: 24; cf. Witte and Latterell 2015).

It is a topic of current debate how useful the potential role of the notion of human dignity is within national and international public law. Admittedly, it is a rather vague notion that, like, for example, the principle of subsidiarity, can easily be interpreted in numerous ways (Movsesian 2016). It is simply not the case that a plain reference to the notion of human dignity can resolve a legal case, as its definition will depend on the tradition from within which it is appealed to. Reservations with respect to the relevance of the concept of human dignity can also be too great. The argument that it cannot be considered as belonging to positive law becomes an excuse for avoiding arguably difficult subject matter.

Within the context of the current topic, it can be seen that a notion such as human dignity also has a good side. When it comes to religious freedom, it can serve as a conversation opener rather than a conversation stopper. When reflecting upon the question of what a generous religious freedom conception implies, the question of what is in the best interests of human dignity is something that the various religious and non-religious traditions can, almost without exception, relate to. The only condition is that one subscribes to some kind of notion of human dignity, but if this is not the case, one can hardly be in favor of human rights in general and the right to freedom of religion or belief in particular in the first place.

The seventh and final principle holds that "equality does not mean sameness or necessitate identical treatment." This, for example, applies to different religious groups, which—depending on their particular characteristics—do not necessarily always have to be treated in exactly the same manner. Also more generally speaking, however, "[d]ifferent things may legitimately be treated differently if there are sufficient and relevant grounds for doing so" (Spencer 2014: 27).

In our current age this principle obviously raises some sensitive issues. Across the West, Islamophobia is arguably on the rise. When present, Islamophobia may give rise to the idea of differential treatment between religions, notably between Christianity, Judaism, and Islam. If no two religions are entirely the same, why would they necessarily have to be treated equally in all respects? Obviously, a question like this easily raises suspicion. Too easily can it be used to discriminate against the adherents of a particular faith. Some would argue that Donald Trump went a long way towards this in the rhetoric he used during his campaign as a presidential candidate in 2016. For many people, including Americans, this has not been an inspiring example of a possible way forward. Yet the issue is too complex to simply leave it there.

Take, for example, the case of Eastern European countries. Orthodox churches there adhere to a theology that emphasizes the links between the historic faith and the nation (Burgess 2013). This makes it difficult to accept a status according to which Orthodoxy would be one among many different churches. Without doubt, a position like this has in part to do with a longing for political influence that makes Christians from other denominations sometimes wonder whether the embrace of church and state in certain instances does not become too tight. Yet, equally without doubt, it is also part of the particular theology of these churches. This raises the question whether for the sake of the right to freedom of religion or belief a church or religion should modify its basic tenets.

The answer to this question cannot be explored in full here. For the present purposes it suffices to conclude, however, that the principle of equality is not as straightforward to apply as it may seem at first sight, even within the context of religious freedom. This certainly holds true in a global context, to which point we will return later. It also holds true within the West, however. A social pluralist perspective will likely try to reconcile the entitlements that flow from a universal right with circumstances as they have historically developed in a particular country. This means, for example, that the Grand Chamber of the European Court of Human Rights when it ruled in favor of the crucifix in an Italian classroom may have been right (Ten Napel 2012). It is hardly a coincidence that the support for Italy before the Court came largely from Eastern European countries. At least part of the indignation in Western Europe, when the Court ruled the way it did, originated moreover in a specific view on the role of religion in the public domain that is not necessarily representative even of Western Christianity, or classical liberalism for that matter.

At the end of the section on principles of religious freedom, the paper notes how "[t]he freedom to speak, to assemble, to campaign and to co-operate is hard to sustain if the ultimate reasons for that speech, assembly and co-operation are denied." This does not imply that the right to religious freedom necessarily trumps other human rights at all times. Still, "the co-ordinating idea" to be used in applying the seven—admittedly contestable and non-exhaustive—principles of religious freedoms from the social pluralist perspective identified above should be that

> in the fluid balance of principles in which no one principle serves as an immutable centre of gravity for all the others, a proper recognition of the intrinsic nature of religious liberty must be allowed to take its full and proper place in discussions.
>
> (Spencer 2014: 30)

The notion of a "co-ordinating idea," self-evident as it may seem at first, actually makes a lot of sense. In analyses of the case law of the high courts in various Western jurisdictions, one can often observe how the courts try to find their way in what are sometimes extraordinarily difficult cases. A whole system is then developed with the help of which these cases can be decided in a consistent and systematic manner. These systems can get so elaborate and complex, however, that handbook-size treatises are needed to explain to outsiders what sometimes are still only the leading principles of such a body of jurisprudence. When the leading principles become too complicated, however, the risk is that the case law is no longer transparent and that parties find it increasingly difficult to predict what the outcome of their cases is going to be.

What is even more important is that the very notion of religious freedom becomes ever more complex to discern in the web of leading and subsidiary principles which are applied to cases (see e.g. Witte and Nichols 2016). As a result, although a case may have been decided in accordance with all the rules, the outcome can sometimes still be rather unsatisfactory. Of course, to some extent this risk applies to all fundamental rights. In the case of religious freedom, the risk is gradually becoming higher, as lawyers and courts become less familiar with what this right is about in the first place. When society secularizes, the legal profession is affected as well. In fact, the legal profession might find itself at the forefront of such a more general societal development. In a sense, this is a good thing, as the judiciary is supposed to be in touch with what is happening in society. Also, it is not to be expected that the legal profession will launch a coordinated attack on religious rights. Ignorance about what these rights are about, however, can also lead to suboptimal results for the parties in a particular case.

In such a situation it can help if a clear picture exists of what the notion of religious freedom was all about to begin with. When academic specialists in the field are not able to come up with much more than an overview of the existing case law as it stands, and the different principles and rules with the help of which these appear to have been decided, this will not be of much help. Legal scholars become in that case part of the system themselves, and the legal profession including academic commentators becomes increasingly isolated from the rest of society. If, instead, legal scholars succeed in reviewing and evaluating the case law in light of "the intrinsic nature of religious liberty," then they have added value compared with practicing lawyers. The calling of an academic lawyer is not to provide the positive law with an external legitimation, but rather to help keep the case law focused on the coordinating ideas of the various fundamental rights.

Obviously, even with the help of such a coordinating idea, the seven principles cannot be expected to solve every legal puzzle that may arise with respect to religious freedom. Still, it is remarkable how much light the principles are able to shed on some of the most salient issues that arise in religion cases today. This is confirmed by the second part of the guidebook on *How to Think about Religious Freedom* by Theos, in which a couple of those puzzles are presented.

Thus, a first question is whether "religious groups [should] be free to run according to their own rules." This is very much the central question of this book. One important remark is that, although the guidebook recognizes the potential for tension, "without group rights, *individual* rights become attenuated and vulnerable." There is also clearly a connection with the role of the state, in that "our natural human tendency to form groups means that their restriction, in the name of equality or of liberty, results in an invasive and hyperactive state, involving itself in areas where it has, at best, only a limited role" (Spencer 2014: 39). The guidebook stresses that

> the core of a liberal society is one that resists the temptation to implement whatever conception of morality is fashionable at the moment through law, or to construct and secure a morally-harmonious society. . . . The right for religious groups to self-organise is, thus, recognised in law, not simply for negative reasons—because a liberal society is under an obligation to do so—but for positive ones—because a liberal society is itself protected and sustained by the liberty of such groups.
>
> (40)

The guidebook therefore also expresses its concern about the recent tendency that individual rights appear to trump group rights in general, and that concern for equality outweighs concern for religious freedom in particular. There is a danger involved when the answer to the question whether religious groups are free to run according to their own rules changes from "yes but" to "no except." That danger is that it

> is liable not only to limit religious liberty in public life, licensing it just so long as it is sufficiently close to a liberal worldview not to disturb it, but also, in the long run, to hollow out the space between state and individual, as all substantive efforts at civil self-organisation are caught in a pincer movement between individuals' rights and the state that secures them.
>
> (43)

As the guidebook notes, adding a historical perspective on the same matter:

> The great leap forward in the English (latterly British) legal mind came with John Locke's enormously influential *Letter Concerning Toleration*, published

> in 1689. This argued convincingly, and from deep and explicit first (biblical) principles, that morality and legality were different things and to attempt to secure the former by means of the latter was a mistake. It would be a tragedy of the 21st century if an apparent concern for human liberty were to lead to the attempt to impose liberal morality through illiberal laws, thereby reversing the process initiated by Locke over 300 years ago.
>
> (43)

This is, of course, not surprisingly because of its social pluralist framework, very much part of the argument that this book tries to make as well.

A further question is "Should religious groups be free to operate their own legal systems?" Although this is in fact a subquestion of the question of how much autonomy religious groups ought to enjoy, it deserves to be treated separately due to the controversy surrounding it and the amount of attention it consequently attracts. The main point the guidebook makes in this context is that this question concerns "supplementary" or "minority" legal orders rather than "parallel" legal orders. As such, the concept is not limited to Islam, nor indeed to religious legal orders. Supplementary does not just mean that it does not involve an alternative legal order, but also that the choice for such an order must be voluntary—that is, not coercive. Even then, the supplementary legal order, in order to be eligible for recognition, ought not to be "demonstrably dehumanising."

Under these conditions, the notion of supplementary legal orders is not just acceptable, but might even prove to be vital from the point of view of religious liberty, including that of former majority religious groups such as Christianity:

> [I]t is possible that if the ethical foundations beneath family law do de-Christianise over coming years, Christians may seek to recognise a greater freedom for couples and families to enter into commitments and resolve disputes in a way that better reflects their own religious and ethical commitments. In this way, it is right that the desire among some religious minority communities to do this today is not simply dismissed out of hand but treated seriously, if qualifying criteria such as those outlined in [Archbishop] Williams' lecture can be met.
>
> (45; see Williams 2008)

In doing so, we will make sure "that the communal identity and rights that derive from our spiritual nature are not negated by obedience to government, any more than the rights and responsibilities of citizenship are negated by religious identity" (Spencer 2014: 46).

It is of vital importance to explore whether this social pluralist notion of legal pluralism is compatible with the kind of Islamic constitutionalism as referred to in the Introduction and in Chapter 2. It is clear that this will be a different dialogue to the one between advocates of the idea of a neutral or secular state and religious pluralists of Islamic inspiration. In the latter case, there can hardly be any meaningful dialogue, as the position of the advocates of the neutral or secular state is absolute. If state sovereignty is considered to be complete, then there will not even be room for subsidiary legal systems. The consequence of such a position is that legal pluralists of whatever kind will feel shut out of the existing liberal democratic order.

A dialogue between adherents of different types of strong and weak legal pluralism, on the contrary, is worthwhile. Such a dialogue will of course not be easy, as on both sides fundamental convictions and principles are involved. All those involved in this dialogue will likely feel that they are being taken seriously, however, no matter what the outcome of the discussion will be. It is only fair to admit that this second dialogue will also have its limitations. These limitations result from the notion of liberal democracy as defended in this book. There are forms of legal pluralism that are simply not compatible with such a liberal democratic order. Legal pluralism can never be coercive in nature, nor can it be dehumanizing, as the goal of liberal democracy is arguably to make it possible for citizens to become fully human. As this conception of what it means to be human takes the spiritual dimension of human beings seriously, however, there will nevertheless be more that Muslims, for example, will have in common with this state conception than with the one of a neutral and secular state.

Another pressing question is "[S]hould other beliefs be classed the same as religion?" What the guidebook suggests in this context is that it is important to stick to the idea that in order to qualify for protection under the right to freedom of religion, beliefs—and indeed practices—should not just be sufficiently genuine, cogent, serious and coherent, as the case law requires. The beliefs and practices also need to involve "*ultimate concerns.*" This way, the beliefs and practices will remain at least similar to religious beliefs. As the guidebook notes (49),

> It could be argued that the expansion of the belief category in recent jurisprudence merely reflects the fact that, in a less traditionally religious society such as ours, people's ultimate concerns are as, if not more, likely to be "secular" than spiritual. Nevertheless, even if it were the case, the danger is that incorporating such beliefs into the category of "religion and belief" threatens to broaden it to such an extent that it becomes unmanageable or meaningless.

Once again, although not that long ago such a point would have been rather self-evident, under the gradually secularizing circumstances in which the West finds itself it takes on an entirely new relevance. One could say that the very idea of there being a right to freedom of religion or belief depends on the possibility of distinguishing such religious and other beliefs. The traditional way to do so is to ask whether these beliefs involve answers to ultimate questions. For the better part of their history, Western philosophy and theology have addressed precisely such ultimate questions. It was therefore not considered a challenge by lawyers and courts to distinguish such ultimate beliefs from other opinions. What we see today, for example, is that the new critics of religious freedom argue that this has become increasingly difficult to do. Yet it is good to add that this is in a sense a rather parochial point of view, in that in many other parts of the world even raising such a question is not easily understood. Even in the West, sooner or later the consequences of such a position might become clear, as it implies nothing less than a break with the West's entire philosophical and theological tradition.

Finally, the guidebook asks the question: "[H]ow far should the religious be free to manifest their religion?" A case that comes to mind is *Eweida v British Airways plc*, eventually won by the British Airways employee, on the right to wear a cross necklace. The guidebook suggests a nuanced approach in this matter, implying that the answer to the question differs "according to the kind of manifestation, its significance, its sincerity and its location—where in the social landscape is it happening" (55). An interesting observation the guidebook makes here again is that if one adheres to the idea that religious institutions ought to enjoy a considerable degree of autonomy, then the same will have to apply to more general civil society organizations. In all cases, what is needed is "a particular degree of negotiation, reasonableness and accommodation" (59): "There is no legal algorithm to solve such issues and a simple hierarchy of rights is an inadequately blunt device for sorting them" (60).

What this comes down to is a kind of principled pragmatism that points to "reasonable accommodation" as a way forward (63; cf. McConnell 1985; Horwitz 2016; contra Tushnet 2015). More specifically, the proportionality principle could play an important role in weighing the seriousness of a particular infringement of a right against the importance of the conflicting private or public interest in precisely infringing upon this right. Also, it will have to be accepted that these kinds of questions simply cannot be decided once and for all, but rather constitute an inherent characteristic of any pluriform liberal democracy.

The latter point is obviously of crucial importance in the context of this book, as it touches upon the nature of liberal democracy, and is thus illustrative of the strong links that exist between the concepts of constitutionalism, democracy, and religious freedom. Liberal democracy can be considered as a means of making it possible to live together as a group of people, despite all the religious and other differences. The idea behind it is not to eradicate these differences, nor to have the state suppress all the differences in the name of unity. The idea is rather to tolerate these differences as much as possible, but this inevitably implies both the existence of rules and the provision of accommodations. What the fact that the latter idea is becoming more controversial really demonstrates, therefore, is that the idea of liberal democracy as such is losing support.

The pressing question of "[H]ow should we reconcile religious freedom with equality legislation?" is, again, really a subquestion of the question regarding the scope of the right to manifest one's religion. As the guidebook notes (66),

> This will be morally distasteful to some but that is precisely the sense that we should be experiencing in a liberal, plural society: if we are to take freedom seriously, as opposed to secure it for people, views and practices that are broadly similar to our own, then everyone will find themselves legally accommodating practices that they find morally problematic.

Without doubt, equality legislation, like religious freedom, makes an important contribution to any truly liberal society. As we already noticed in Chapter 1, equality legislation is an important and valuable contribution to a fair society.

> However, if it is administered in a "doctrinaire" fashion, or inequitably, or without due attempts at accommodation, or without a sense of proportionality, it risks burdening some in society unnecessarily. This is not the same as saying that religious people are automatically free from the obligations of equality law, but rather that equality law should be made to serve the common good rather than to pursue more limited social agendas.
> (67)

The latter point is a useful addition to the point made earlier that the intrinsic nature of religious freedom must remain the focus of all legislation and case law. Such a coordinating idea is useful, but at the same time also limited. The boundaries are marked by the notion of the common good. Different human rights have their own groups of proponents, who all tend to believe that "their" specific right automatically takes priority over other rights. There is something about the right to freedom of religion or belief that makes it indeed a right that stands out when compared with all other rights. Contrary to what is sometimes argued, for example, not even the right to freedom of expression is more central to liberal democracy than religious freedom. Before one is able to express an opinion, one first needs to develop an idea, often in community with others. This idea, moreover, is likely to originate in a religious or non-religious worldview, which must thus be protected in order to make freedom of expression substantial.

Even though the right to freedom of religion or belief is therefore special, this obviously does not mean that its intrinsic nature can be pursued without regard to other fundamental rights. Although religious freedom contributes to human flourishing, by helping to make it possible for a person to become fully human, social pluralist theory will also always emphasize that becoming fully human is not an individual matter. This means that by invoking the right to freedom of religion or belief, one always has to take account of the interests of others. The plural nature of society implies that these interests can be different from what one considers to be morally acceptable. Still, just as others in the way they invoke other rights have to be mindful of other people's religious and non-religious beliefs, believers of any kind also have to recognize and respect opposite interests especially when these are equally protected by fundamental rights.

Nones

A few more points can and must be made before closing this chapter. As is clear from the above, a generous approach to the right to freedom of religion or belief does not so much imply maximal but rather optimal religious freedom. Although the limits to the right can to a certain extent differ from place to place, and from time to time, they have historically by and large been determined by the same universal, transcendent truths which also sustain liberal democracy more generally. These truths are referred to in the U.S. Declaration of Independence when it proclaims "that all men are created equal, that they are endowed by their Creator with certain unalienable Rights, that among these are Life, Liberty and the pursuit of Happiness." They can probably continue to fulfill this function, even in the light of the change in religious convictions taking place among, for example, the American population.

Thus, according to data collected by the Pew Research Center, between 2007 and 2014 the percentage of Christians in the population decreased from 78.4 to 70.6 (a drop of 7.8 points), while during the same period the percentage of "nones" rose from 16.1 to 22.8 per cent (an increase of 6.7 points). As we already saw in the Introduction, "nones" are spirituals who no longer wish to count themselves as belonging to a particular religion or denomination. The question is therefore whether they ought to be treated as a religion legally (Movsesian 2014). As the percentage of evangelical Christians has by and large remained stable, it is to be expected that in many cases the nones will be former members of the mainline Protestant churches as well as the Catholic Church.

A shift from adherents of organized religions to nones may not remain without consequences for the support of religious freedom in society. Although many nones will not have been regular churchgoers, they are still likely to have more affinity with organized religious expressions than those who are spiritually fully unbounded. Yet there is also no reason to expect that nones, and indeed people of other persuasions, will not continue to be convinced of the merits of a generous interpretation of the right to freedom of religion or belief.

Contrary to what was widely expected in the 1960s and also in the following decades, the decline of organized Christianity has not led to a full-blown secularization of Western societies. Rather, as authors such as Jürgen Habermas have convincingly argued, we have entered into a postsecular age (2008). As set out in the Introduction, this term indicates that there are not just more secular people in society, but that there is also—and perhaps even mainly—more diversity among the equally significant part of the population that remains religious or spiritual. An approach to religious freedom that is both pragmatic and principled seems particularly apt for such a constellation, although it was also argued earlier that the degree of secularization of Western societies should not be underestimated either.

Separation of Church and State

At this point, it is necessary to refer briefly to the principle of church and state (cf. Garnett 2016). Our understanding of this principle has developed in a way that makes the very idea of communal religious freedom in general and institutional religious autonomy in particular suspicious. To the extent that the existence of a separate right to freedom of religion or belief is still accepted, this concerns its individual dimension in particular. It follows from the general concept of human rights that these can pose certain well-defined limits to state sovereignty. In the case of the right to freedom of religion or belief, the individual conscience functions as precisely such a limit, although even this holds true only under certain conditions. The idea that religious associations, groups, and institutions would enjoy a particular amount of autonomy which sets limits on the sovereignty of the state is considered out of line with Enlightenment liberal thought.

Yet, if one looks more carefully at the history of the principle of church and state, it becomes clear that the principle does not go back to the Enlightenment, but has clear Christian and even biblical roots (Berman 1983). The original idea behind the principle was not so much to protect the worldly authorities from interference by the church, but rather to prevent worldly authorities from interfering in the affairs of the church. This became even more evident during the latter part of the Middle Ages when conflict arose surrounding the authority of the pope and, for example, the Archbishop of Canterbury *vis-à-vis* the worldly authorities. From these and other struggles the idea of freedom of the church arose. This idea meant that the state was not placed above the church, nor was the church placed above the state. Rather, the two were meant to be on an equal level, each in its own way serving the common good.

It is easy to see how the notion of freedom of the church could also today constitute a solid foundation for the right to freedom of religion or belief. Especially since the second half of the twentieth century, during which time the influence of the state has expanded so much, basing the right to freedom of religion or belief exclusively on the individual conscience places individuals by themselves opposite an overwhelmingly strong state. It is also historically more sound to regard the individual dimension of the right to freedom of religion or belief as a corollary of its communal dimension, rather than the other way around as is currently the dominant opinion. What one sees here quite clearly is also how relevant a conservative liberal approach is for specifically religious freedom, although there are certainly also convincing progressive liberal arguments for institutional religious autonomy (Berg 2013). A conservative liberal approach to religious freedom starts from the idea that religious associations, groups, and institutions are sovereign in their own sphere, and thus almost automatically contribute to the notion of limited government.

Seen from this angle, it is regrettable that the principle of freedom of the church as such is not recognized in American or European constitutional law. The notions of a ministerial exception and church autonomy are much more limited to begin with, and even then rather constrained in the case law as we have seen in Chapter 2. What makes the situation even worse is that the principle of separation of church and state is increasingly interpreted in the opposite way. According to Enlightenment liberal interpretations of the principle, the state is deemed to be superior to the church. As a result, whenever faith-based organizations adhere to views that run contrary to the majority opinion in society, these organizations come under pressure to adapt. This pressure can come from the media and public opinion, but eventually also from courts and legislatures. As such, these organizations no longer function as a check on state authority, but the state monitors the faith-based organizations. More importantly in the context of this chapter, the freedom of religion or belief of both religious associations, communities, and institutions and of individuals within these groups is no longer fully guaranteed. This violates the principle of separation of church and state in the original and arguably still highly relevant sense of the term.

An International Right

It will be clear that the notion of the freedom of the church is not restricted to Western liberal states. As a result of migration, it is important, for example, that Christian associations, communities, and institutions outside the West can also enjoy this freedom. The position of the Catholic Church in China is a case in point. This is why the global character of the right to freedom of religion or belief is not just fiction, but of truly fundamental significance to very real people and situations. To the extent that this type of religious freedom is not yet assured globally, this illustrates the need to advance the cause of international religious freedom rather than to give up on the idea of there being an international right to freedom of religion or belief at all. Perhaps in a global context it is more appropriate to focus on the individual dimension of religious freedom to begin with.

There have certainly been, still are and always will be differences in the way the right to freedom of religion or belief is interpreted (see e.g. Zucca 2015). To use the example from the paragraph above, the religious freedom of Christians in China will be different to the religious freedom of Muslims in the West. This is not uncommon, however, and also applies to other fields of law. Furthermore, methods may exist to stimulate convergence in this respect (Ferrari 2016). That the expectations should not be too high, however, is illustrated by the fact that already within the West there remain considerable differences in the application and interpretation of the right to freedom of religion or belief. This holds true for the States Parties to the Council of Europe, despite there being a European Court of Human Rights, and within North America also for Canada and the United States. "Mars-and-Venus-like differences" have, despite attempts at greater cooperation, persisted between United States and Europe as well (Shah 2015; Philpott 2016).

The main point here is not to polarize more than is necessary. It may be fine to have a culture war within Western states on issues such as abortion, but controversy surrounding the right to freedom of religion or belief is a different kettle of fish altogether (Laycock 2014). Similarly, huge differences may exist between Western and non-Western countries on a range of issues, but debates on the right to freedom of religion or belief should not be turned into a clash of civilizations. Real differences exist between the various world religions, and this will also have consequences for the concept of religious freedom. Yet, just as national differences should be accepted and accommodated, so internationally a deep pluralism is not necessarily something to be feared. Intercultural and interreligious dialogue mirror the idea of equal political voice for liberalism within Western states. Any international documents and structures facilitating this type of conversation should be cherished rather than skeptically dismissed.

Ferrari calls this a "reformist" approach, and such an approach at an international level fits in well with the pragmatic approach in the national context suggested above (2016; cf. Glendon 2012). In both cases the approach contrasts with a radical approach such as abolishing the right to freedom of religion or belief altogether. It is one thing to note deficiencies in the way the right is currently applied and interpreted. It is quite another to give up on the right for this reason. This is why the analysis made by some of the new critics of religious freedom is more convincing than most of the solutions they propose for the problems. Even on the smallest scale, such as in families or voluntary associations, it is sometimes difficult to make progress on sensitive issues. Therefore, it comes as no surprise that it is difficult to find common ground nationally, regionally, and globally on a topic such as religious freedom. Just as a culture war about this right itself is not the answer nationally, a clash of civilizations globally concerning this right is not the answer. What is needed is hard work and continued efforts nationally and globally in order to make both societal and world peace possible (Little 2015).

Revolutionary Nature

However, although at first sight it might seem that both nationally and internationally small steps or even holding on to an existing approach will suffice, let there be no misunderstanding how revolutionary mere suggestions like these are rapidly becoming. Scholar of constitutional interpretation Michael Paulsen, whom we encountered in Chapter 1, has developed an interesting theory of religious freedom, called "The Priority of God" (2013). The main idea behind this theory is that no proper theory of religious freedom is possible, unless a society acknowledges the existence of religious truth. If a society recognizes the existence of religious truth, God will of necessity take priority over the state, which must subsequently respect the right to free exercise of its citizens. It is not so much the state that grants this right to its citizens, rather the free exercise of religion is a natural right which precedes the existence of the state.

A second element of Paulsen's theory of religious freedom is that if a state recognizes the priority of God, it will refrain from acting as an arbiter in religious affairs. It will leave it up to its citizens to define religious truth as they see fit. Should a state attempt to enforce religious truth, it is no longer God who takes priority over the state but the state that takes priority over God. On the other hand, if a state recognizes the priority of God, that state will be tolerant in matters of religion, there will be a proper separation of church and state, and citizens can freely enjoy their religious rights. The sovereignty of the state is not absolute, but rather shared.

When both criteria are met, a society acknowledges the existence of religious truth and the state remains impartial in religious affairs, then Paulsen speaks of the liberal concept of religious freedom. There is, however, a second concept of religious freedom possible in societies that acknowledge religious truth. This is when the state is not impartial in religious matters, and instead imposes its own version of religious truth on society. This is a pre-liberal position with respect to religious freedom. The difference with the liberal concept of religious freedom is that there is no tolerance in religious affairs.

These different concepts of religious freedom are not abstract models to Paulsen. On the contrary, he believes that the liberal version of religious freedom was introduced when the United States were founded at the end of the eighteenth century. The United States were, moreover, founded by immigrants who had left their (mostly) European home countries, because at the time these still largely adhered to the pre-liberal concept of religious freedom. Yet the pre-liberal model also still exists currently—for example, in countries dominated by Islamist regimes.

Paulsen's theory does not end here, however. Just as, at least within the West, many countries have developed from a pre-liberal position to a liberal concept of religious liberty, these same countries have recently been undergoing further changes. Because of processes of secularization, several of these countries are no longer able and willing to acknowledge the existence of religious truth. As a result, according to Paulsen, no proper theory of religious freedom is possible anymore. This does not mean, however, that—for example, in the United States—free exercise is no longer possible either.

This third concept of religious liberty can be called a modern one, in that it holds on to the liberal principle of tolerance of the state in religious affairs. However, the nature of tolerance differs from the tolerance that is characteristic of the liberal model. In the liberal model, because God takes priority, the sovereignty of the state is limited. Consequently, the state needs to respect the right to free exercise of its citizens, in principle also when this contravenes the laws promulgated by the state. According to the modern concept of religious liberty, however, the state is considered fully sovereign.

The reason why there will still be tolerance is that many citizens believe it is nice to respect each other's convictions, even when these are outdated, such as in the case of religious believers. However, when believers invoke a right to religious freedom specifically, this will appear to be a bit awkward to fellow citizens. To many people, all opinions should be respected, and the general rights to freedom of expression and freedom of assembly and association suffice for that. There is no longer seen to be a need for a separate right to religious freedom. Also, it is considered unfair when such a right would lead to greater protection than for other, non-religious beliefs.

Yet even the modern version of religious freedom is not quite the end of the story. Paulsen believes that several European countries have already entered the next phase, which he calls postmodern. In the postmodern approach to religious freedom, society no longer acknowledges the existence of religious truth. The difference with the modern concept of religious liberty is that the liberal element of tolerance has, for all practical purposes, disappeared. As a result, the postmodern approach to religious liberty paradoxically resembles the pre-liberal concept of religious liberty.

The difference between the pre-liberal and the postmodern concepts of religious freedom is that whereas in the pre-liberal concept society acknowledges the fact that religious truth exists, in the postmodern version this is no longer the case.

Consequently, the nature of the establishment is different. In the pre-liberal version of religious freedom there is one established religion. In the postmodern version secularism becomes established. As a result, society becomes even less tolerant of the remaining religious beliefs than in the pre-liberal phase. There is only such religious freedom as is fully compatible with the demands of the state.

Paulsen does not explicitly refer to the religious inspiration for the different versions of religious freedom that he distinguishes. It is, however, fair to say that Christianity has been a major influence on the liberal concept of religious freedom as distinguished above. This is not to say that Christianity and liberalism are two sides of the same coin, as we have already seen in Chapter 2. Like other religions, however, Christianity has, as the majority religion in many cases, naturally contributed to society's acknowledgment that religious truth exists. It has also, particularly in its Protestant form, contributed to religious tolerance by the state.

This raises the question of what the future of religious freedom will be. Despite the institutional decline of Christianity, followers of this religion can continue to contribute to the cause of religious freedom by reminding society of the story behind the original treaty and other provisions concerning religious freedom. They will be able to find allies in conservative liberals—in the United States, for example, so-called originalists who wish to stick to the original text of the Constitution and the original intent of the Founding Fathers. It is, however, also important for them to work with those progressive liberals who stick to the modern view of religious liberty.

On the one hand, it seems wise to remain optimistic so as to appeal to, for example, millennials and nones who might not necessarily object to the liberal concept of religious freedom either. On the other hand, it is probably realistic to conclude from Paulsen's article that the chances for a proper grounding and theory of religious freedom have not exactly grown in recent decades. Even though he may be exaggerating somewhat when categorizing European countries in the postmodern category, we saw in Chapter 1 how recent case law suggests that the glass of religious freedom is gradually becoming half empty rather than half full.

Such a development will inevitably entail that the approach to constitutionalism, democracy, and religious freedom set out in this book appears sectarian. In fact, however, although inspired by social pluralist theory, this approach may well be more inclusive and thus less sectarian than the postmodern concept of religious freedom, as is illustrated, for example, by the philosophy of deep equality. This philosophy emphasizes the role of the principles of equality and non-discrimination to the point that not much remains of the right to freedom of religion or belief, or the other classical rights for that matter.

A Different Kind of Transformative Constitutionalism

I have not come across a more comprehensive treatment of this threat than international constitutional and human rights lawyer and religious freedom expert Iain Benson's thesis (2013), which was already referred to in Chapter 1. Building on an impressive number of thinkers from all periods and many disciplines, he argues how such an apparent desire for deep equality should at least be balanced by a commitment to deep pluralism. More concretely, Benson proposes that in order to safeguard religious freedom in the twenty-first century two things are necessary: the right to freedom of religion or belief must be applied and interpreted from an associational point of view, and whenever there is a competing rights claim involving religious freedom, there ought to be a rebuttable presumption in favor of the freedom of religion or belief of the associations, communities, and organizations involved. These proposals originate from two more general starting points—that is, that religions have many goods to offer to society, and that the role of law in regulating religion should be limited. In combination, these two starting points have led him to advocate a principled pluralist approach, a term we have also come across in the context of the concept of democracy.

There is a striking resemblance between Benson's proposals and those made in this book, in that Benson also advocates holding on to liberalism. This is why towards the end of his thesis he also attempts to formulate the limits to such a deep pluralism as he proposes. In addition, his thesis equally highlights the importance of the right to freedom of religion or belief to constitutionalism and democracy, and hence the need to rethink some of the most fundamental concepts of the discipline of constitutional law as they have developed in recent decades. To the extent that religious freedom is or ought to be a major topic in law and religion studies, Benson adopts a broad historical framework. Thus, he argues, law and religion, which were once intimately connected, have now become almost fully separated. Without religious inspiration, the practice of law becomes sterile, however, and any kind of legitimacy of the constitutional system will prove difficult to attain. Religions in turn can also profit from law and the structure—in the good sense of the word—that a legal system is able to provide. In so far as the modern concept of religious freedom has contributed to the separation of law and religion, we are now entering a fascinating postsecular era which potentially will make it necessary to renegotiate the place of religion in the constitutional order in different ways.

Interestingly, if combined with respect for the associational and institutional dimensions of religious freedom as required by the liberal concept of this fundamental right, this will give rise to a different and arguably more appropriate kind of (transformative) constitutionalism than the one we are currently witnessing in the West. As Benson (2013: 172) puts it:

> [A]mbitions towards reformation of society will have to take different forms with foci in different places than the current focus on rights-based litigation. It will, ideally, gradually shift the focus from litigation as a means of forced outcomes to what will likely be genuinely consensual but perhaps, in some ways, slower forms of social development. Focusing on debate and associational change through politics will have obvious benefits as well as what will be perceived by some as drawbacks to their ambitions. The advancement of minorities and equality will continue but the focus will change direction and face, rather than the court-rooms, the more appropriate chambers of

change—legislative chambers and associational meetings and the usual repertoire of active political frameworks. The emphasis will no longer be on legal challenges and outcomes where the advancement of particular agendas rather than associational diversity is presumed to be the important principle. The focus will be, increasingly, on political and civic discourse and debate seeking to change the minds of those in different associations towards larger conceptions of shared goods. Also, and this is key, the search for justice, when it is in the courts (as it will sometimes rightly be) will involve the use of presumptions such as the one suggested with a view to preserving and encouraging diversity within appropriate legal limitations.

Conclusion

These to my mind are deep reflections. They transcend the limited scope of a chapter on the right to freedom of religion or belief. But, then again, this chapter was never meant to be an isolated chapter in the first place. The whole point this book is trying to make is that it hardly makes sense to deal with this fundamental right in an isolated manner. Religious freedom is connected so much with the principles of constitutionalism and democracy as a whole that any discussion of the right should take place in this broader perspective. It is thus only appropriate to consider some of the more general reflections by Benson in closing this chapter on the right to freedom of religion or belief.

In the course of time the discipline of constitutional law has become preoccupied not just with the state as such but also, within the state, with the courts in particular. It is probably fair to say that this trend dates back to at least the post-Second World War era, when constitutional review was introduced in a number of Western European countries. After the fall of the Berlin Wall, the same occurred in various Central and Eastern European countries. This development has—understandably—led to the idea that constitutional review is perhaps the most important characteristic of a democratic constitutional state. Thus, the main task of the discipline of constitutional law became to analyse the case law of these national and international courts. Similarly, it gives rise to the conviction by citizens that in order to claim or defend their constitutionally guaranteed rights, it is necessary to go to court.

This more or less general trend in Western societies certainly also holds true for the right to freedom of religion or belief in particular. The right has become increasingly judicialized. In the process, however, the right paradoxically also becomes more circumscribed. To judicialize a right is to circumscribe a right, as Hirschl would agree (2010). Also, critics can easily point towards deficiencies in the case law in order to make their point that it is impossible to regulate religious freedom in a meaningful way. The critics indeed have a point in that the bigger picture tends to get lost, and lawyers, courts, and even academic specialists get caught up in an ever more complex web of leading and secondary principles and rules. As a result, not only the right to freedom of religion or belief but human rights in general become less accepted by the population.

The solution to this problem is, in the case of the right to freedom of religion or belief, not to give up the idea of religious freedom altogether. Given its strong ties with both constitutionalism and democracy as a whole, this is simply not an option, unless one is willing to sacrifice the idea of liberal democracy as well. This chapter has instead wanted to argue that a generous interpretation of the right to freedom of religion or belief remains necessary. It has used social pluralist theory to provide a solid theoretical foundation for this idea, but it is also possible to call it the liberal concept of religious freedom. What Benson does is to add a constitutional dimension to the argument. It is not just the case that by means of a coordinating idea the intrinsic nature of religious freedom needs to be guaranteed and protected, but also that this can be done best by the legislature and indeed by the private associations in society themselves.

Of course, we cannot do without a judiciary altogether, and there are no serious suggestions in that direction either. But a conservative constitutionalism will stress that the state powers need to be balanced in a way that safeguards the position of the legislature. In addition, it will also emphasize that the powers that be, including the legislature, will have to respect the text of the constitution as well as treaty provisions as they have been approved by the political branches. One can, of course, attempt to formulate the intrinsic nature of religious liberty in an abstract academic treatise, but it will run the risk of remaining too abstract to be of much practical use. One can also search for a formulation of the intrinsic nature of religious liberty in the case laws of different jurisdictions, but these attempts will usually be rather concrete, in terms of the specific circumstances of the case that have given rise to such an elaboration and also because it originates in a particular jurisdiction.

The most successful attempts to formulate the intrinsic nature of religious liberty can therefore be found in existing (inter)national provisions on the topic. To the extent that the current chapter is an appeal to continue to focus on the coordinating idea of religious freedom, the most practical suggestion it can make in this regard is to stick to these regionally and sometimes universally agreed formulations. These formulations were not drafted with the idea in mind that these would necessarily become positive law across the globe. Similarly, there is no reason to abandon these formulations once the societal circumstances within the West appear to be changing. The idea of natural rights is that they apply in all places and at all times, no matter what the exact circumstances are. Although natural rights cannot by their nature be codified, it is submitted that some of the national and international provisions regarding religious freedom do a surprisingly good job in capturing the universal, transcendental truths upon which liberal democracy in general and religious freedom in particular ultimately rely.

Bibliography

Ahdar, Rex and Ian Leigh (2005), *Religious Freedom in the Liberal State* (Oxford: Oxford University Press).

Benson, Iain (2013), *An Associational Framework for the Reconciliation of Competing Rights Claims Involving the Freedom of Religion* (University of Witwatersrand: Ph.D. Thesis).

Berg, Thomas C. (2013), "Progressive Arguments for Religious Organizational Freedom: Reflections on the HHS Mandate," *Journal of Contemporary Legal Issues*, 21(1): 279–333.

Berg, Thomas C. (2016), "What Do Religion's Social Contributions Have to Do with Religious Freedom? Responding to Measuring Faith: Quantifying and Examining Religion's Contributions to American Society," BERKLEY *forum*, September 27.

Berman, Harold J. (1983), *Law and Revolution: The Formation of the Western Legal Tradition* (Cambridge, MA: Harvard University Press).

Burgess, John P. (2013), *Encounters with Orthodoxy: How Protestant Churches Can Reform Themselves Again* (Louisville, KY: Westminster John Knox Press).

Calo, Zachary R. (2015), "Catholic Social Thought and Human Rights," *American Journal of Economics and Sociology*, 74(1): 93–112.

Chaplin, Jonathan (2011), *Herman Dooyeweerd: Christian Philosopher of State and Civil Society* (Notre Dame, IN: University of Notre Dame Press).

DeGirolami, Marc O. (2013), *The Tragedy of Religious Freedom* (Cambridge, MA: Harvard University Press).

Ferrari, Silvio (2016), "Who is Afraid of Religious Freedom? The Right to Freedom of Religion and Belief and its Critics," *Religion and Human Rights*, 11(3): 224–49.

Galston, William A. (2005), *The Practice of Liberal Pluralism* (Cambridge: Cambridge University Press).

Galston, W.A. (2006), "Families, Associations, and Political Pluralism," *Fordham Law Review*, 75(2): 815–31.

Garnett, Richard W. (2007), "Religion and Group Rights: Are Churches (Just) Like the Boy Scouts?" *St. John's Journal of Legal Commentary*, 22(2): 515–33.

Garnett, Richard (2008), "Do Churches Matter? Towards an Institutional Understanding of the Religion Clauses," *Villanova Law Review*, 53(2): 273–95.

Garnett, Richard W. (2012), "Religious Freedom and (and in) Institutions," in: Gerard V. Bradley (ed.), *Challenges to Religious Liberty in the Twenty-First Century* (Cambridge: Cambridge University Press) 71–89.

Garnett, Richard W. (2016), "The Worms and the Octopus: Religious Freedom, Pluralism, and Conservatism," in: Sanford V. Levinson, Joel Parker, and Melissa S. Williams (eds), *American Conservatism: NOMOS LVI* (New York, NY: New York University Press) 160–96.

Glendon, Mary Ann and Raul F. Yanes (1991), "Structural Free Exercise," *Michigan Law Review*, 90(3): 477–550.

Glendon, Mary Ann (2012), "Religious Freedom in the 21st Century: Old Biases, Fresh Challenges, New Frontiers," in: Mary Ann Glendon and Hans F. Zacher (eds), *Universal Rights in a World of Diversity: The Case of Religious Freedom* (Vatican City: Pontifical Academy of Social Sciences Acta 17) 651–64.

Grim, Brian J. and Melissa E. Grim (2016), "The Socio-economic Contribution of Religion to American Society: An Empirical Analysis," *Interdisciplinary Journal of Research and Religion*, 12 (Article 3): 2–31.

Habermas, Jürgen (2008), "Notes on Post-Secular Society," *New Perspectives Quarterly*, 25(4): 17–29.

Hirschl, Ran (2010), *Constitutional Theocracy* (Cambridge, MA: Harvard University Press).

Horwitz, Paul (2009), "Churches as First Amendment Institutions: Of Sovereignty and Spheres," *Harvard Civil Rights-Civil Liberties Law Review*, 44(1): 79–131.

Horwitz, Paul (2016), "Against Martyrdom: A Liberal Argument for Accommodation of Religion," *Notre Dame Law Review*, 91(4): 101–44.

Howe, Mark De Wolfe (1953), "Foreword: Political Theory and the Nature of Liberty," *Harvard Law Review*, 67(1): 91–5.

Koppelman, Andrew (2013) *Defending American Religious Neutrality* (Cambridge, MA: Harvard University Press).

Kuyper, Abraham (1994), *Lectures on Calvinism* (Grand Rapids, MI: Eerdmans).

Kuyper, Abraham (2015), *Our Program: A Christian Political Manifesto* (Bellingham, WA: Lexham Press).

Laycock, Douglas (2014), "Religious Liberty and the Culture Wars," *University of Illinois Law Review*, 2014(3): 839–80.

Little, David (2015), "Human Rights, Religious Freedom, and Peace," a lecture delivered at the opening session of the 22nd Annual Symposium on Religion and International Law, October 4, at the BYU Law School.

Leigh, Ian (2012), "Balancing Religious Autonomy and Other Human Rights under the European Convention," *Oxford Journal of Law and Religion*, 1(1): 109–25.

McConnell, Michael W. (1985), "Accommodation of Religion," *The Supreme Court Review*: 1–59.

McCrudden, Christopher (2012), "Legal and Roman Catholic Conceptions of Human Rights: Convergence, Divergence and Dialogue?" *Oxford Journal of Law and Religion*, 1(1): 185–201.

Monsma, Stephen V. and Stanley W. Carlson-Thies (2015), *Free to Serve: Protecting the Religious Freedom of Faith-Based Organizations* (Grand Rapids, MI: Brazos Press).

Movsesian, Mark L. (2014), "Defining Religion in American Law: Psychic Sophie and the Rise of the Nones," EUI Working Paper RSCAS 2014/19.

Movsesian, Mark L. (2016), "Of Human Dignities," *Notre Dame Law Review*, 91(4): 1517–51.

Napel, Hans-Martien ten (2012), "Beyond *Lautsi*: An Alternative Approach to Limiting the Government's Ability to Display Religious Symbols in the Public Workplace," in: Katayoun Alidadi, Marie-Claire Foblets, and Jogchum Vrielink (eds), *A Test of Faith? Religious Diversity and Accommodation in the European Workplace* (Farnham: Ashgate) 87–99.

Paulsen, Michael Stokes (2013), "The Priority of God: A Theory of Religious Liberty," *Pepperdine Law Review*, 39(5): 1159–222.

Philpott, Daniel (2016), "Bridging Mars and Venus for Religious Freedom," *Arc of the Universe*, July 11.

Rivers, Julian (2010), *The Law of Organized Religions: Between Establishment and Secularism* (Oxford: Oxford University Press).

Rubio-Marín, Ruth (2015), "The (Dis)Establishment of Gender: Care and Gender Roles in the Family as a Constitutional Matter," *International Journal of Constitutional Law*, 13(4): 819–46.

Schall S.J., James V. (2012), "The Speed of Change in the Republic of Rights," *Crisis Magazine*, April 13.

Shah, Timothy (2015), "A Philosophical Basis for Transatlantic Cooperation on Religious Freedom?" *Arc of the Universe*, November 6.

Skillen, James W. and Rockne M. McCarthy (eds) (1991), *Political Order and the Plural Structure of Society* (Atlanta, GA: Scholars Press).

Spencer, Nick (2014), *How to Think about Religious Freedom* (London: Theos).
Tushnet, Mark (2015), "Accommodation of Religion Thirty Years On," *Harvard Journal of Law & Gender*, 38 (Winter): 1–33.
Vyver, Johan D. van der (2001), "Sphere Sovereignty of Religious Institutions: A Contemporary Calvinistic Theory of Church-State Relations," in: Gerhard Robbers (ed.), *Church Autonomy: A Comparative Survey* (Frankfurt am Main: Peter Lang) 645–81.
Williams, Ronan (2008), "Civil and Religious Law in England: A Religious Perspective," *Ecclesiastical Law Journal*, 10(3): 262–82.
Witte, Jr., John and Justin J. Latterell (2015), "Christianity and Human Rights: Past Contributions and Future Challenges," *Journal of Law and Religion*, 30(3): 353–85.
Witte, Jr., and Joel A. Nichols (2016), *Religion and the American Constitutional Experiment* (New York, NY: Oxford University Press, 4th edn).
Zucca, Lorenzo (2015), *Religious Rights* (London and New York, NY: Routledge).

Conclusion: "A Horizon of Beauty"

Introduction

Having reached the end of this book, it is both useful and possible to summarize the argument that has been developed in the previous pages with the help of a limited number of fundamental concepts. These concepts are: pluralism, religious freedom, liberal pluralism, social pluralist constitutionalism, pluriform democracy, and political legitimacy.

How these fundamental concepts relate to one another according to the arguments made in this book is illustrated with the help of the following figure:

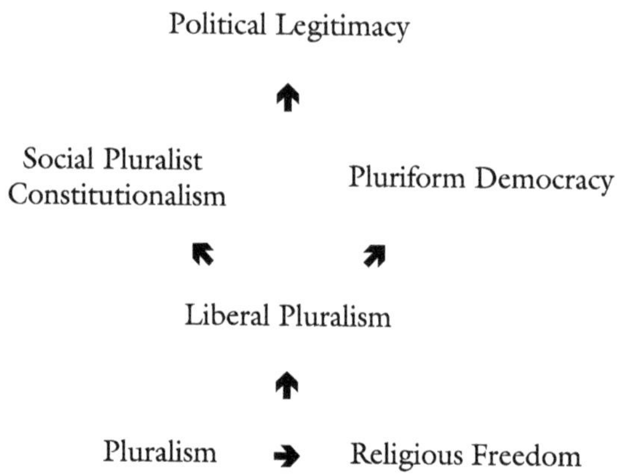

Before adding a few final words about each of the concepts, it should be recalled that the immediate reason for writing this book was the confusion that appears to have arisen surrounding precisely these arguably central concepts of constitutional law, notably constitutionalism, democracy, and religious freedom. Consequently, this book has focused on the associational and institutional dimensions of the right to freedom of religion or belief, and their significance for the proper functioning of our Western liberal democracies. More specifically, it has asked the question to what extent in both Europe and North America communal religious freedom continues to be protected. A second question dealt with in the book was whether the recognition that there are multiple sources of sovereignty in society can actually help to achieve and maintain legitimacy of the democratic constitutional order rather than putting its political legitimacy under pressure.

Confusion

The past 50 years appear to have become an era of change in various ways. This makes it an exciting time for the discipline of constitutional law. Change is not necessarily only to be interpreted as a negative threat to an existing situation. Change can also be for the better. There is no reason to assume that we have somehow come to the end of either human or indeed constitutional development. What can be expected, though, is that change brings about a certain measure of confusion, as it is not immediately clear what the new order of things is going to be. Also, it may not be immediately clear which existing constitutional concepts ought to be retained, and which new concepts or interpretations of existing concepts could perhaps be introduced into the political order. It is to this process that this book has aimed to make a contribution as far as the concepts of constitutionalism, democracy, and religious freedom are concerned.

In order to do so, it has proven necessary to adopt a theoretical framework, or so it was argued. The book has made clear that this framework is social pluralist theory. This theory originally stems from both the Catholic and Protestant traditions and conservatism. It is hoped and expected, however, that several of its core ideas make sense to the reader in a way that makes it possible to, at least partially, subscribe to them without necessarily also buying into the underlying more or less comprehensive doctrines. Roman Catholicism and orthodox Protestantism are certainly examples of comprehensive doctrines. Conservatism is a considerably less clear example of such comprehensive doctrines, which may help even more.

To the extent that the core ideas of the theory do not immediately make sense, the book aims to function as a conversation opener rather than as a conversation stopper. A renewed discipline of constitutional law can only profit from a fair measure of academic debate, in which participants are more open about their underlying assumptions than has been the case for a while. If the discipline is truly going to become more theoretical, interdisciplinary, and comparative in its approach, it is almost inevitable that such debate will arise and further contribute to the flourishing of the discipline. The book is therefore an open invitation to debate issued to my colleagues inside or outside the field of constitutional law who disagree with its contents, to indicate why and to what extent its arguments may need to be revised.

The book wishes indeed to be theoretical in its approach precisely by adopting a theoretical framework such as the social pluralist one. It is also interdisciplinary in the sense that it wishes to be principally open towards possible contributions that other disciplines can make to reflect on the way the concepts of constitutionalism, democracy, and religious freedom have developed in recent decades. By adopting such a principal openness to other disciplines, it has actually appeared that many worthwhile contributions on the topic of liberal democracy are currently coming from ethicists, legal and political philosophers, and theologians in particular. The book is comparative in the sense that it uses these often theoretical insights as a mirror in order to reflect on the current state of our Western liberal democracies. It is also comparative in that it sometimes points towards differences and similarities between Europe and North America, albeit not in a systematic manner.

One final introductory remark is that neither the degree of change nor the amount of confusion must be exaggerated. It is probably true that every generation is likely to believe that the changes in their time are greater than ever before, and that as a result the challenges before them are also greater. Yet, looking back at the history of the disciplines of constitutional law and politics, it is also easy to see that these have had to confront major challenges before. It may be the case that at least some academics feel lost and overwhelmed. This can, however, at least in part be the result of a perceived need to abandon earlier insights, which have in fact stood the test of time. Of course, adopting a social pluralist perspective also means resorting to wisdom that has gradually built up during centuries of constitutional development. It is also simply not possible in this area to start all over again, even if we wanted to.

Pluralism

Looking at the state of liberal democracy from a social pluralist perspective, it is almost inevitable to begin by noting that many societies today have become plural societies in a very real sense. This includes Western countries. It is true that Western societies, like other societies, have to a certain extent always been plural societies. They are currently becoming even more plural, however, because of immigration, for instance. Again, this change should not be exaggerated, also because the degree of pluralism existing in the world has hardly increased. The change is mainly that this pluralism is becoming more evident in individual countries, whereas in the past it was (also) visible in different countries.

Although the plurality of society manifests itself in a number of ways, it is characteristic for a social pluralist framework to focus on religious diversity. To the extent that human beings can be regarded as primarily spiritual beings, plurality also means first of all that a wide or at least widening variety of worldviews is represented in society. According to the same social pluralist approach, this plurality of worldviews is not considered to be something that it is inherently good in itself and therefore to be conserved, for example. It is rather accepted as a fact of life, as something that is apparently part of the way things are or have been created, as some would say.

It is true that many of these Western societies, to which this book has limited itself, have also undergone processes of secularization throughout the second half of the twentieth century in general and since the cultural revolution of the 1960s in particular. However, contrary to what was widely expected, by social scientists in particular, this has not resulted in a complete homogenization of these societies from this perspective. Rather, it is more accurate to speak of a postsecular constellation, in which the secular part of the population has certainly increased. In certain countries this group may now even be in the majority or will be in the (near) future. Even in these cases, there are also religious and other minorities to be found in society.

Moreover, the diversity in society by which Western societies have always been characterized may paradoxically have deepened in recent decades after all. This is in part because of the new groups of migrants entering these countries, whose religions have not yet in all cases been "domesticated" to the extent that this holds true for Christianity, for example. On the other hand, and partly in response to the arrival of Muslims in particular, the secular part of the population may itself have radicalized as well. Just when they thought that as a result of the process of secularization a privatization of religion was within reach, their dream was rather roughly disturbed. This explains why they may—understandably—have become even more aware of who they are and what they have to offer to society. From a social pluralist perspective, this is a lot indeed, as secular humanism is regarded as a similar worldview to, for example, Judaism or Islam. Just as most religious worldviews can potentially make valuable contributions to society as a whole, secular humanism can also do so.

In fact, it is not quite clear how useful even the use of the term "secular" is exactly. To the extent that the term suggests that being secular is the very opposite of what it means to be religious, this is rather misleading. Perhaps we would be better advised to put it this way: Most people are trying to make sense of their lives; many of us do so in a transcendental manner, others look for meaning in what is immanent. Even when looking at the religious–secular divide in this way, it is still possible to note that Christianity is gradually losing the majority status it has long enjoyed in Western societies. These societies are increasingly also composed of "nones" and adherents of other world religions, notably Islam.

Religious Freedom

The finding of Western societies being characterized by pluralism as such is not, or at least should not be, something that can only be made from a social pluralist perspective. The same holds true for the finding that this plurality is, in part, of a religious nature. The difference with other theoretical approaches therefore probably begins with the relative importance that is being attributed to religious differences within the general context of plurality in society. Yet it has in previous decades often been treated as a leading question in legal and political philosophy: how a political order can in particular deal with differences in comprehensive doctrines. It is hardly an exaggeration to note that in the revitalization of legal and political philosophy that has taken place, thanks to the work of Rawls among others, this question has played a major role.

A more distinctive step which social pluralist theory can therefore propose is to regard a separate right to freedom of religion or belief as a necessary consequence of the plurality of worldviews in society. Yet this is an almost automatic consequence of attributing so much weight to the fact that human beings are essentially spiritual in nature. If it is the very essence of a human being that she or he is a spiritual being, then it becomes clear that in order to become "fully human" such a person must be able to live according to her or his worldview. This obviously holds true with regard to their private lives. Yet, to the extent that such worldviews are truly comprehensive doctrines, as they tend to be, this principle will apply to all domains of life. More specifically, to the extent that a difference is or can be made between the private and public sphere as we have become accustomed, a person must also be able to live according to her or his deepest convictions in public life.

An interesting thing to note at this point is that this right to freedom of religion or belief already comes up in social pluralist theory at this early stage—that is, before liberalism enters the stage. This is an expression of the idea that the right to freedom of religion or belief is a natural right—that is, it is not introduced by a political theory such as liberalism, but human beings can be regarded as possessing the right no matter what political theory is adhered to by the majority in a given society. What one sees here is that social pluralist theory is principally open towards a transcendental dimension of human existence. Nor can this transcendental dimension of human existence be regarded as a relatively unimportant or irrelevant aspect of social pluralist theory. In current debates surrounding the right to freedom of religion or belief, the very nature of this right is precisely what is at stake. Is it a right that has been granted by a particular political theory or constitutional system, and can it therefore also be taken away again by worldly authorities? Or is it a right that itself has transcendental origins, with which human beings have been endowed ever since they were first created, and therefore exists whether a constitutional system wishes to recognize this or not? The United States Declaration of Independence subscribes to the latter view, and this is an insight with potentially very practical and thus real consequences also for twenty-first-century political orders.

It also deserves to be noted that from the perspective of social pluralist theory, there has always been a universal dimension to the right to freedom of religion or belief. In the way the right was presented earlier, no distinction was made either between different religions or between different regions of the world. If people are essentially spiritual beings, and there is a plurality of worldviews in society, it is not possible to argue that, for example, only Muslims should or would possess the right to freedom of religion or belief in a given society. Nor does it make sense that only in the West are citizens entitled to freedom of religion or belief. In fact, not a single distinction is defensible in terms of who is entitled to the right to freedom of religion or belief, as long as it concerns "ultimate beliefs."

On the other hand, there is room for a different interpretation of the right with respect to different religions or different regions. The same plurality that exists with respect to the worldviews of human beings can be applied to interpretations and applications of the right to freedom of religion or belief. Even if it is correct that the right to freedom of religion or belief historically originated in the West and in a culture dominated by Christianity, this does not imply that other religions in different regions of the world could not benefit from the same right. There is nothing special about the right to freedom of religion or belief compared with other provisions of international law, in the sense that the interpretation and application of all such provisions will vary depending on the circumstances.

It is also conceivable that the right to freedom of religion or belief may vary from time to time. To the extent that religion is not static but a dynamic phenomenon, which tends to develop over time, the protection that adherents to the different religions require will also change. Fundamental rights are not goals in themselves, however, but serve particular purposes. Therefore, it is only to be welcomed when a fundamental right demonstrates that it possesses the flexibility to adapt to changing needs. It only becomes dysfunctional when its interpretation and application become fixed, for example, in legislation and case law and these no longer meet the demands of society. Having said that, the main aspects of the right have probably been covered by the phrase "teaching, practice, worship, and observance" as contained in Article 18 of the Universal Declaration of Human Rights adopted by the United Nations in 1948.

Liberal Pluralism

It is at this stage that the question arises as to what a suitable answer from constitutional law could be regarding the plurality of worldviews in society. This is, again, the question that has been raised by Rawls and several other legal and political philosophers in recent decades. The answer that social pluralism gives to this question differs in part from the answers provided by at least some liberal thinkers, although there is fortunately and not surprisingly also common ground that can be discerned. As we have concluded in virtually every chapter, it is probably fair to say that at least two kinds of liberalism exist.

According to the first kind of liberalism, which can be labeled the progressive form of liberalism, the democratic revolutions of the seventeenth and eighteenth centuries mark a radically new beginning in constitutional history. This form of liberalism stresses the importance of a concentration of public powers in the state. It is also a more comprehensive kind of liberalism in that it wishes to progressively implement its core values such as equality in society, even with respect to citizens who do not subscribe to these values. It is important to stress that such an ideological fervor is recognizable for those who study religions, as many religions also wish to proselytize. When applied to the state level, such fervor can become more problematic, in the case of liberalism as well as that of religious worldviews. It can hardly be considered illegitimate, though. When a religious group constitutes the majority in society, it can legitimately influence legislation and even the constitutional framework of a given society. This is not a hypothetical situation, as it had been the case in many Western countries for the better part of the twentieth century. At that time, religious groups indeed constituted the majority in society and thus also in politics, and hence were able to influence legislation—for example, with respect to Sunday opening hours of shops in Europe.

Since the cultural revolution of the 1960s, Western societies have gradually changed, and in certain cases there are now secular rather than religious majorities in society and politics. This means that government policies and legislation will undergo the influence of this shift. This is the way democracy functions. It does not come as a surprise therefore that religious groups now complain about particular measures, just as in the past the secular part of the population did not welcome the religious influence on government policy and legislation. To the extent that there is a difference, this difference consists of the fact that progressive liberalism also potentially threatens to affect the constitutional liberties of religious groups. As we saw, progressive liberalism aims at concentrating all public power in the state. Thus, it tends to regard society as consisting of individuals and the state. The fact that mediating structures perhaps also exist, which even have powers of their own, is not evident to progressive liberals to say the least. To the extent that progressive liberals acknowledge the fact that these groups exist and claim rights, they will tend to object to this.

This is the principal difference between progressive liberalism and a more conservative kind of liberalism. This second kind of liberalism does not see the democratic revolutions of the seventeenth and eighteenth centuries so much as a radical break in world history. On the contrary, according to this kind of liberalism, these revolutions marked the crystallization and codification of developments that may have been under way for centuries. Constitutionalism is thus not seen as an invention of liberalism, but as an idea that has slowly but steadily developed within religious traditions such as Judaism and Christianity. This also implies that more room exists for mediating structures in society, as *mutatis mutandis* was the case in the Middle Ages, for example. Moreover, in the type of constitutionalism that this kind of liberalism favors, these institutions of civil society play a crucial role.

There are several other ways in which the difference between these two kinds of liberalism can be described. One way is with the help of the concepts of negative and positive liberty. Therefore, progressive liberals will favor positive liberty, which has to be actively pursued. Conservative liberals, on the other hand, stick to negative liberty, in the sense of freedom from state intervention in private lives and indeed the lives of the different religious associations, groups, and institutions that exist in society. Progressive liberals are also sometimes called Enlightenment liberals, as the Enlightenment ideals of liberty, equality, and fraternity constitute their political programme. Conservative liberals represent a diversity or Reformation type of liberalism, in which the freedom of conscience plays an important role, whereas Enlightenment liberals will emphasize the importance of individual autonomy.

No matter which labels are used, it will come as no surprise that from the point of view of social pluralist theory the second kind of liberalism is to be preferred. Political theorist William A. Galston, who advocates this second kind of liberalism, has used the term liberal pluralism for it. As Galston points out, within liberalism in recent decades there has been a development towards the first kind of liberalism. This is in a sense unfortunate. Because of the changing world-views in society, there is already a more or less gradual but major shift taking place in many Western societies from the religious majorities of the past towards new secular majorities. On top of this change now comes a development among secular liberals in the direction of a more comprehensive type of liberalism.

Given the fact that we are currently witnessing a postsecular constellation, in which religious minorities continue to be represented in Western societies, a more political kind of liberalism appears to have a better chance of preserving peace in society. We will come back to this later on. For now, it is equally important to note that liberal pluralism is better able to accommodate the reality of mediating structures existing in society. As in the case of the view that human beings are essentially spiritual beings, anthropology plays a role. As social pluralist theory regards it as only natural that citizens organize themselves in groups, it is advisable for the dominant political theory in a given society to respect this fact of life.

Social Pluralist Constitutionalism

One of the great fruits of liberalism from a constitutional law point of view is the notion of constitutionalism. In fact, liberalism and constitutionalism are so strongly linked that by a reference to the concept of constitutionalism, a reference to liberal constitutionalism was usually intended. Other types of constitutionalism, which differed from liberal constitutionalism, were usually referred to as authoritarian. It is only recently that legal scholars have begun to realize that there are actually different forms of constitutionalism and that liberal constitutionalism is only one such form. For example, a distinction can be made between liberal and illiberal constitutionalism.

Within the broad category of liberal constitutionalism different forms of constitutionalism can also be distinguished. One possible distinction is between political and legal constitutionalism, depending on where the primacy among the various state powers lies. In the case of political constitutionalism the primacy lies with the political institutions; in the case of legal constitutionalism the primacy belongs to the judiciary. It is submitted that a different distinction within liberal constitutionalism relates to the two forms of liberalism just identified.

Thus, one form of liberal constitutionalism departs from the idea that all sovereignty in a liberal democracy rests with the state and that therefore the only necessary type of separation of powers is the one between the legislature, the executive, and the judiciary. A second, more conservative, form of liberal constitutionalism sees the democratic revolutions of the seventeenth and eighteenth centuries as less of a break in constitutional history. It is therefore willing to acknowledge that public power may still be dispersed between different state and non-state actors in society. It considers that the relevance of this distinction between state and non-state actors in society is even increasing, given the degree to which the power of the state has grown in Western societies since the Second World War. Consequently, a form of separation of powers between state powers only no longer suffices. What is needed to check the power of the state is a kind of balancing act between the state powers on the one hand and non-state actors on the other hand, in addition to a form of separation between the state powers.

More specifically, this second type of liberal constitutionalism is characterized by two core ideas. The first idea is that, in between the state and the individual, a variety of mediating structures indeed exist. This starts with the family in which a person is born and which has a considerable impact on the worldview she or he will adopt. But the list continues with schools and other educational institutions in which the character of a person is formed further. After school comes work, and with work come numerous other organizations. Of course, there are also civil society associations which do not directly relate to work.

Given the generally increasing academic interest in the role of civil society, perhaps this does not seem to be a very important insight. Yet within public law the focus has traditionally been on the state and the individual. It is only relatively recently, under the influence of the processes of Europeanization and internationalization, that this is starting to change. Because of Europeanization and internationalization, constitutionalism is becoming transconstitutionalism. It appears as though scholars engaged in transconstitutionalism are more open towards the role of non-state actors in the global arena, in addition to state actors. In transnational constitutionalism such non-state actors play an important role—for example, in the context of separation of powers. It is likely that these and similar insights will also have an impact on national constitutional law and thus promote a fuller understanding of constitutional realities also within national societies.

The second core idea of the second type of liberal constitutionalism builds on the first. It is not just that, in addition to state actors, the role of non-state actors is emphasized more. These non-state actors will, in order to perform their proper role in society, also need to be provided with a certain degree of institutional autonomy from the state. It is here that constitutional law becomes directly relevant. For example, in the context of the right to freedom of religion or belief it is important to also acknowledge that a communal dimension to this right exists. This communal dimension can, as we have seen, be further divided into an associational and an institutional dimension.

As constitutionalism generally aims to limit the role of the state, to protect the freedom of its citizens, the obligation of the state to respect the autonomy of non-state actors is also formulated as a negative obligation. There is a presumption that non-state actors are entitled to a certain degree of autonomy. It is only in the event that a state nevertheless wishes to intervene in the internal life of such an organization, that it has to provide arguments for doing so. It is possible that such arguments will justify the particular intervention. The presumption that non-state actors are entitled to a certain degree of institutional autonomy is rebuttable. As such, the freedom of religion of associations, groups, and institutions does not differ from the religious freedom of individuals. Individual freedom of religion or belief can also only be enjoyed within certain constitutional limits, notably the constraints of public order within a given state. As in the case of individual religious freedom, it is crucial, however, that these limits on the actual exercise and manifestation of religious freedom are not imposed in an arbitrary manner. This is one thing that this second kind of liberal constitutionalism is likely to be more sensitive to than the first type of liberalism. It is for this reason that the second type of liberal constitutionalism has been baptized social pluralist constitutionalism in this study.

Pluriform Democracy

The second great contemporary characteristic of a liberal constitution is the notion of democracy. Of course, the history of democracy precedes the rise of liberalism. Yet the idea of democracy has been incorporated in the idea of liberal democracy to the extent that it is now hardly possible to conceive of a liberal constitutional order without a democratic component. Within the category of democratic regimes a distinction is made between democratic regimes that are also characterized by a form of (liberal) constitutionalism and democratic regimes that are not. However, what interested us most in the context of this book is a distinction between different forms of liberal democracies.

As in the case of constitutionalism, it turns out that the different forms of liberalism distinguished earlier also affect the character of democracies. In the case of democracies, on the one hand there is a model of democracy that tends to exclude religious discourse from the public and parliamentary debate. It does so by formulating demands that participants in such debates have to meet in order to make legitimate contributions to the decision-making process. Public reason liberalism is the name for this type of democracy. This name stems from the work of John Rawls, who developed the notion of public reason. As set out in Chapter 3, the concept was meant to facilitate a dialogue between different reasonable voices in the political debate. It is also a concept that anticipates that it is possible to reach a conclusion after a rational debate. That conclusion will (have to) be accepted by all the different participants in the preceding debate.

The alternative to public reason liberalism has been called equal political voice liberalism. Again, the differences between the various comprehensive doctrines in society are taken as the starting point. However, the various participants in the public and parliamentary debates are not required to meet the standards of public reason. Instead, all participants can make the arguments they wish in the language they prefer. In addition, it is not necessarily anticipated that an agreement will be reached. At the end of the debate, there will therefore need to be a vote. Those who vote against are likely to disagree strongly with the outcome of the decision-making process.

This is exactly where the second characteristic of this democracy model, which is known as the pluriform democracy model, comes in. Because it is not likely that an agreement will be reached, it is vital that the decision-making process is characterized by constitutional limits. Of course, the same holds true for public reason liberalism. Still, the relevance of the constitutional limits becomes even greater in a pluriform democracy. It is also likely that the pluriform democracy model raises the bar even higher for any majority that wishes to intervene in the internal autonomy of private associations, groups, and institutions. This is mainly what the constitutional limits are about. The limits concern primarily classic fundamental rights, such as the freedom of religion or belief, the freedom of expression, and the freedom of assembly and association.

Regarding the institutional autonomy of civil society associations, there is a clear parallel with what was said above in the context of social pluralist constitutionalism. However, whereas in the context of constitutionalism the presumption in favor of institutions of civil society is formulated in a negative manner, respect for the institutional autonomy of faith-based organizations is more of a positive requirement when discussed in the context of democracy. A pluriform democracy actively promotes and facilitates the founding of civil society associations, as it is aware that society consists of more than individuals and the state. In a pluriform democracy it is important for citizens to be able to live according to their deepest convictions in societal spheres other than the state. Therefore, the fact that multiple sovereignties exist in society is not regarded as problematic, but rather as a solution to the fact of a deep pluralism.

Political Legitimacy

It has often been argued that maintaining a stable political order in a divided society is a difficult, if not impossible, task. Nevertheless, it is submitted that the forms of constitutionalism and democracy set out above will contribute to the legitimacy of the political order. This is the considerable societal relevance that the current proposals possess. The envisaged "liberal peace," moreover, has both an internal and an external dimension. Internally, it is likely that the different groups in society will be able to live together and reach political decisions without being discriminated against or having to resort to violence. Externally, the expectation is that constitutional democracies of the kind envisaged in this book will not easily resort to military force against other constitutional democracies or against any other state for that matter, perhaps even less so than majoritarian democracies that are less accustomed to reconciling differences.

The reason to submit that the types of constitutionalism and democracy presented above will contribute to internal peace is that these are aimed at enhancing the legitimacy of the political order. Given the pluralism of society, a specific type of liberalism is needed in order to be acceptable to the different groups represented in society. This liberal pluralism then leads to distinctive forms of constitutionalism and democracy, respectively. Social pluralist constitutionalism leaves room for multiple sovereignties existing in society. Pluriform democracy is characterized by a lively public square. Moreover, the political decision-making process is constrained by constitutional limits, which guarantee the rights to freedom of religion or belief, freedom of expression, and freedom of assembly and association of all associations, groups, and institutions represented in society to the greatest extent possible.

Political legitimacy is without doubt also the aim of other political and constitutional theories, notably the work of Rawls. Yet, judging by some of the literature that has come out of religious groups such as Christians, Jews, and Muslims, it is not likely that these are willing to accept the criterion of public reason imposed on them by such theories. One only has to look at the criticisms of a naked public square which have been raised over the past decades to realize that the chances of success in terms of legitimacy for such an approach are rather small. It can hardly be a coincidence, moreover, that the alternative to public reason liberalism in the form of equal political voice liberalism has been put forward by a Christian philosopher.

Nevertheless, it must be stressed again that it is hoped that the arguments developed in this book will not only appeal to the various religious groups. As it is broadly in accordance with a conservative vision of man and society, readers of all persuasions could be attracted by the "horizon of beauty" which is arguably evoked by the proposals (Francis 2013: 15; Berg 2015). Certainly, many liberals will be able to subscribe to these ideas, in particular to the extent that they adhere to the type of diversity liberalism as defended by Galston, among others. As is the case for other groups, it may not be their ideal form of government, but it certainly could be perceived by many as the best achievable.

The same by and large holds true for the aim of peace between constitutional democracies. Empirical evidence for this "liberal peace" is already convincing. It is surprising that this evidence does not weigh more strongly for the new critics of religious freedom. To the extent that their criticisms are driven by ideals of a greater freedom, it is unclear what this greater freedom would look like exactly. Internally, even now there is not much demand for greater religious freedom in Western democracies, other than that different groups feel that they are disadvantaged by a liberalism that is no longer willing to accommodate them. Externally, there are strong correlations between the degree to which religious freedom is guaranteed in a given country and the protection of other political rights.

What remains relatively underdeveloped in the approach set out in this book is how it can also more explicitly promote the common good. Part of the pluralism which the model takes as its starting point is that different groups in society wish to contribute to the common good. Various groups also have rather outspoken ideas about what this common good might look like. In a different context, in which they would possess the majority in society, these groups would feel tempted to implement their particular version of the common good. This can go quite far—for example, that all legislation and other political decisions have to undergo an ultimate sharia check.

The proposals put forward in this book do not include the possibility of implementing any particular common good in full. In fact, part of the idea behind the proposals is that in order to preserve peace, it is necessary that all groups abstain from imposing their own particular version of the common good on the whole of society. As a result, however, the role of the state can easily become restricted to patrolling the constitutional boundaries. Since these are formulated negatively, there is hardly a positive role to be played by the state. This, however, runs contrary to the ideas of at least some of these groups about what role the state should play in promoting the common good.

There appears to be no easy way out of this dilemma, except by noting that it can well be regarded as a major contribution to the common good that the final result of the proposals is to contribute to both the internal and external peace. Otherwise, it is up to the different groups themselves to make sure that how they act in private, whether individually or collectively, reflects their vision of the common good. In fact, this is what refraining from drawing too sharp a distinction between private and public good comes down to in this respect—that is, that it is not just up to the state to promote the common good but rather to the whole of society. In this view, it is not up to the state to pursue all kinds of substantive goals itself, but rather the state makes it possible for civil society associations to do so.

Democratic Ethos

Finally, there is one more "problem" with the conclusions of this book. The problem, or rather the weakness, is that the success of the model depends on the moral engagement of citizens. As noted earlier, equal political voice liberalism demands that citizens are willing to engage with one another and also respect each other's convictions. It is also necessary that citizens abide by the constitutional limits set on the political decision-making process. This is a weakness to the extent that the state cannot "introduce" such an ethos, although it can help to create the conditions under which a democratic ethos can grow and be maintained. These conditions include a willingness to respect the institutional autonomy of religious associations, groups, and institutions in society which are able to stimulate the growth of such an ethos.

It cannot come as a surprise that such institutions include the family, schools, and other institutions of civil society that were mentioned earlier. It is here that the foundations are laid for a democratic and constitutional order in the first place. It is also here that any changes to the current functioning of the Western political orders ought to begin. It is here, finally, that the only real safeguards against extremism have to be created.

Religious extremism has not been part of the narrative of this book thus far. The explanation for that is not a kind of naivety of which adherents of the type of liberal democracy as advocated in this book are sometimes accused. Religion is not inherently good, and nowhere in this book has this been argued. Nor is religion inherently evil, and this book has very much set out from the point of view that religion is simply a fact of life that is not likely to go away anytime soon. It is one of the main sources of the pluralism that has given rise to the (potential) problem that this study has wanted to address.

To the extent that religious extremism exists, it is doubtful whether forms of militant democracy will be of much help. In recent years the threat of religious extremism has mainly, though not exclusively, come from political Islam. The idea that such extremism can be eradicated by simply forbidding particular religious associations, groups, and institutions is probably more naive than to advocate the type of liberal democracy set out here. The roots of religious extremism lie deeper, and it is beyond the goals of this book to deal more extensively with that topic and what to do about it. What the proposals in this study envisage is that many believers from all faith traditions will find it easier to connect to the political order in which they live. Paradoxically, it is by creating as much space as is reasonably (and also unreasonably) possible that the legitimacy of European and North American political systems can arguably be enhanced.

It is not the case that the situation with respect to the legitimacy of these systems is in any way dramatic yet. Otherwise, the findings of empirical political scientists and others looking at the topic would be different. The first chapter put it this way: we find ourselves *in medias res*—that is, in the midst of a development. That chapter dealt specifically with religious freedom. But, as we have seen, this right is of fundamental importance to constitutionalism and democracy as a whole. Being in the midst of a development leaves open the question which direction the development will take. It could proceed along the current lines or the direction could also take a different course.

Regarding the question of how exactly the development will continue, this study ends on an optimistic note. To the extent that being fully human means that a person is able to live out his or her deepest beliefs, religious or other, both in private and in public, a form of liberal democracy which is designed to make precisely that possible may continue to appeal to citizens, independent of their persuasions. That includes people of younger generations, such as millennials, and indeed the "nones." Not belonging to an institutional religion is not the same as not being religious, nor does it mean that one is necessarily opposed to the idea of religious freedom for those people who do adhere to particular religious or other beliefs. It may be the case that "nones" find it harder to imagine what a right to freedom of religion or belief is good for exactly, but the whole idea of a liberal democracy depends on the willingness of citizens to tolerate beliefs and manifestations of belief that one does not subscribe to, does not understand or is even—sometimes strongly—opposed to.

Nor is it the case that Enlightenment liberals are the main opponents. As has been stressed time and again in the previous pages, their political actions are to a large extent legitimate and they will not easily resort to persecution or violence, as this runs contrary to their convictions. In that sense, the threat from populism is perhaps greater at present. Up till now, the West has managed to deal with extremism and terrorism, however difficult this may have been. Secularization by itself is not a direct threat, as it only leads to different majorities in society and politics, and thus to changes in legislation and case law. It is only when increasing numbers of citizens no longer appear to subscribe to either religious or non-religious worldviews, and a kind of nihilism sets in, that one could become concerned about the future of liberal democracy.

It is yet another illustration of the close links between constitutionalism, democracy, and religious freedom that populists also tend to target the right to freedom of religion or belief of, for example, Muslims. In doing so, the contrast between such ideals and the horizon of beauty which the current study has wanted to point towards becomes all the more clear. There is ample reason for gratitude that, despite increasing criticisms, this form of liberal democracy has nevertheless survived thus far. Moreover, care should be taken not simply to equate populism with nihilism, and also to attempt to remain in dialogue with populists, if only because it is realistic to do so given the developments within Western electorates since the turn of the century in particular.

Anticipated Criticisms

In closing, I would like to return to the issue of the methodology followed in this book by replying to some of the anticipated criticisms that the book may receive. For instance, some readers may find the text too *normative*. They will argue that the discipline of constitutional law, or political science for that matter, does not allow for such a normative perspective. Perhaps they also believe that in this way the book runs the risk of not reaching the audience it wishes to reach. They might well say that the book is "sectarian" by adopting a social pluralist theoretical framework, as this is influenced by a religious tradition, among other things. Such religiously inspired frameworks do not comply with the principle of separation of religion and science.

I have addressed this concern in various parts of the book already, starting with the Introduction. Therefore, I can be relatively brief here, although it is worthwhile to come back to the criticism at the very end of the book as well. As I see it, the discipline of constitutional law is at least in part a normative discipline. Its central concepts of constitutionalism and democracy, which are also central concepts in this book, aim to structure and legitimize the liberal democratic state in a particular way. As a result, many constitutional lawyers engage on a regular basis in evaluating whether, and to what extent, liberal democratic states live up to these normative ideals in practice.

The normative character of the discipline of constitutional law is strengthened further by recent attempts to make it more theoretical in character. What these attempts reveal even more is that many of the central concepts of the discipline, such as constitutionalism and democracy, are essentially contested concepts themselves. It all depends on your democratic theory, for example, whether a political order can be characterized as democratic or not. As we have seen, the same applies even for the concept of constitutionalism.

In fact, it is one of the strong points of the new critics of religious freedom that they have pointed out how "biased" the right to freedom of religion or belief really is. As the book has argued, the critics are at least partially right when stressing the Christian, and even Protestant, origins of the right as it is formulated today. This does not preclude other religious and non-religious traditions from embracing the right, and in the process the interpretation and application of the right can develop further. It is crucial, however, that the various traditions actively engage with the right, in order for it to remain a living right.

Given that there is, to a certain extent, a theological background to concepts such as constitutionalism, democracy, and religious freedom, it would somehow be strange to exclude religious perspectives to them by means of a theoretical framework. Other, perhaps more common, theoretical frameworks are not necessarily less sectarian and are sometimes even more so. Having said that, the current study has also made an effort to make clear that the social pluralist perspective bears quite some resemblance to a more general conservative theoretical framework, if only because conservatism is one of the three trends within social pluralist theory.

This brings me to a second criticism—that the book is too *conservative* in character. The first thing I can say here is that I have to admit that this is indeed the case. As I indicated earlier, during my fellowship in the United States I finally came to realize and accept that this label indeed describes my position to a certain extent. Of course, this is not exactly a common position in academia, either in mainstream law schools in the United States or at home in Europe. The Netherlands in particular is a country in which the term remains rather taboo.

But what is conservatism? Anyone who tries to find an answer to this question will soon discover that there are so many varieties that the general label "conservative" does not provide much clarity about someone's position at all. Moreover, I would not want to be associated with many forms of conservatism. That is why in this book I have chosen to use the social pluralist label instead. Although much lesser known to most people, it clearly indicates that the kind of conservatism I mean is the type that is closest to Catholic social teaching and neo-Calvinism. As neither Catholic social teaching nor neo-Calvinism are altogether conservative, this already indicates that social pluralist theory can also be progressive in outlook. In fact, in at least one handbook on social pluralist theory the label "progressive Calvinism" is used rather than neo-Calvinism.

This also more generally holds true. Even to the extent that social pluralist theory can be called "conservative," the effects are nevertheless sometimes actually progressive. For example, it may be conservative to point to the importance of character building when raising children. However, if this is done with a view to maintaining liberal democracy, this can simultaneously be called progressive. What is more progressive: to ensure that a liberal democratic regime can continue to exist and flourish, or to ignore the basic requirements that are needed in order for such a regime to remain in place?

Having said that, the book is based on the idea that a distinctive conservative approach to constitutionalism, democracy, and religious freedom is conceivable. This approach can perhaps be best illustrated by contrasting it with the approach taken by the new critics of religious freedom, who take issue with virtually all aspects of the right to freedom of religion or belief. They do not seem to realize that in doing so they may well put the liberal democratic order as a whole at risk. Or they do realize, but do not care, because they have difficulty with liberalism in any case.

In contrast, a conservative approach to constitutionalism will begin with the grateful acknowledgment of the many good things that liberal democracy has brought in the past. This does not imply a blindness to any possible criticisms—on the contrary. Precisely because of the esteem in which liberal democracy is held, conservatism can put it under close review. That is in fact what this book has also attempted to do. Although some Christian theologians and other thinkers have opted out, it is characteristic of the social pluralist approach that it continues to support liberal democracy despite its many flaws.

Some readers will no doubt also be critical of the fact that the book is *not sufficiently empirical*. At this point, it should first be admitted that originally the idea was indeed partly to present a more or less detailed overview of the relevant case law regarding the associational and institutional dimensions of religious freedom. There remains room for such an analysis, especially when performed in a historical and comparative manner. It could be worthwhile taking a closer look at the foundations of the notion of institutional religious autonomy, especially since these are still valid today. It could also be instructive to explore similarities and differences between the jurisprudence of American, Canadian, and European courts, as well as between the various European jurisdictions.

However, generally speaking, such analyses of the case law abound, whereas far less often attempts are made to develop a theoretical framework in order to interpret the case law. In light of the more or less fundamental criticisms of the right to freedom of religion or belief, I thought it would be appropriate in this case to undertake precisely such an attempt to develop a theoretical framework rather than simply describe what the different courts are saying. Given the fundamental matters at stake in the case of communal religious freedom, it is first of all important to sharpen one's focus, before delving into the details of the case law.

Having said that, it should be stressed that the "empirical" part of this book is not confined to the first chapter. The second and third chapters, on constitutionalism and democracy respectively, also contain empirical assessments of the state of both. These assessments are based on secondary sources from various disciplines. Especially when such sources from various disciplines by and large present the same picture, this is something to note. Also, it should be remembered that the various disciplines use different methodologies when looking at the state of, for example, constitutionalism and democracy.

What this means is that the social sciences cannot claim a monopoly with regard to empirical research. We have already seen that ethicists sometimes employ a different approach. Legal and political philosophers often also start from empirical observations, however. Thus, it is not simply for the discipline of constitutional law to adopt social scientific research methods in order to become more academic, as is sometimes advocated. But it is important that legal scholars are informed about social scientific research. This is precisely one of the risks when undertaking a historical and comparative study of (just) the case law of various jurisdictions. Sometimes without realizing it, one runs the risk of presenting a particular problem as primarily or even only a legal issue. On the other hand, social scientific research sometimes loses sight of the legal dimensions of a problem which are usually also involved.

Is the focus of the book not *too narrow*? Constitutionalism and democracy are obviously broad concepts, but is the combination with religious freedom not therefore regrettably limited in its perspective? This criticism is one that I have become accustomed to ever since I specialized in the field of religion and politics. I also noticed that this criticism was mostly voiced in Dutch and European circles, where the assumption apparently existed that religion no longer had anything to do with politics. To the extent that there was still some doubt possible, this certainly ought not to be the case, or so it was believed. It is one of the reasons why I was pleasantly surprised, when I attended an Annual Meeting of the American Political Science Association, to discover that the religion and politics section was actually one of the largest and liveliest of all.

The problem did not completely disappear when I switched from religion and politics to law and religion. Again, the impression in my home country, and also within the broader European context, was that somehow religion does not belong to the core business with which law school curricula ought to be concerned. Once again, this impression was removed upon the founding of the International Consortium for Law and Religion Scholars in 2009, and similar networks and organizations. At the time of the completion of this book, the field of law and religion is thriving, with its own infrastructure including journals and publication series.

Some readers may, on the contrary, find the topic of the book *overly broad*. Is it not too ambitious to deal not just with religious freedom in general but also with its relationship to constitutionalism and democracy in one and the same book? It is true that with both constitutionalism and democracy the fundamentals of the entire discipline of constitutional law are covered. Certainly, in my view, when religious freedom is added to these concepts, the treatment becomes almost all-encompassing. There is little of any real importance within the discipline that does not somehow relate to one or more of these concepts.

In writing the book I did indeed discover that I was touching upon numerous aspects of constitutionalism and democracy that I could not go into any further because of space and time restraints. This is in part a reaction, however, to many studies in the field which can be considered to be rather narrow in approach. It is relatively easy to lose oneself in the details of a particular topic, trying to analyse the increasingly specific case law. Often Ph.D. students, for example, are encouraged to leave the deeper questions aside, in order to keep the topic manageable. Although this may certainly be defensible in certain cases, it ought not to become an excuse for those questions to be ignored by the discipline as a whole. As such, my book arises from the positive notion that we are encountering a number of problems to which the discipline of constitutional law has a contribution to make, among others. It has been argued, for example, that the discipline of political science is not making the contribution to solving societal problems that it could be expected to make.

Having said that, the true focus of this book remains the right to freedom of religion or belief. It is only in order to illustrate the broader significance of this right that the book also touches upon the topics of constitutionalism and democracy. This explains why the treatment of these latter two topics remains limited to their connection with the topic of religious freedom. This is exactly why I am already looking forward to exploring one or more aspects of either constitutionalism or democracy in my future writing. Without specifically looking for connections with the right to freedom of religion or belief, this opens up entirely new avenues of research. At the same time, it is anticipated that the theoretical perspective developed in this book will also prove useful in that context.

Some reviewers of the original proposal for this book believed the proposal to be on the *theoretical* side. To a certain extent this is, of course, the case. When one attempts to develop a theoretical framework in order to study a particular problem, rather than focusing on the problem itself, this can without doubt be called theoretical. In this sense, some of the courses I have taught have also been on the theoretical side. They served the purpose of making students aware of the importance of a particular problem and the deeper questions that it raised.

I do believe that there is a need for such a theoretical approach. In our age there is so much material readily available, not just in books and journals but also on the internet. What is missing, however, are the tools needed to properly interpret this constant stream of information. In a sense, it is precisely this overkill of information that makes a theoretical approach almost a necessity. Without the tools to interpret new information, both scholars and students are likely to lose their way in the most recent refinements of the case law and legislation. This also holds true for the area of religious freedom. Thus, in a very real sense there is nothing more practical than a good theory, as the saying goes, when it comes to the right to freedom of religion or belief.

It should be noted, however, that in a very real sense this study is equally one big pointer towards the actual case law in the area of religious freedom. One of its central arguments is that it is worthwhile continuing to protect the right to freedom of religion or belief roughly in the way that is done today. At first sight, it may seem strange that this case law itself is not studied in more detail first. However, there are other studies that attempt to do precisely this. The purpose of this study is rather to point out why this should continue to be done, and why these attempts to put religious freedom into practice ought to be evaluated more positively than the new critics of religious freedom, among others, tend to do.

In that sense, the study shows no contempt whatsoever for what is done in practice by numerous courts and other actors, governmental and non-governmental, to contribute to the protection of the right to freedom of religion or belief. If anything, it is hoped that the book will be read by these actors and serve to make clear to them, in so far as is necessary, why their contributions are so valuable. It is one thing to write a theoretical book, but it is quite a different matter to do the dirty work of trial and error in specific cases of trying to find a way from the facts to the interpretation and application of the law. In fact, one of the theses of this book is that these practitioners often do a better job in promoting the kind of constitutionalism and democracy as envisaged in this book than academics, although all involved would certainly also do well to be aware of some of the criticisms raised in recent academic work.

Is the book too *Dutch* in outlook? This is possible. Every author leans on his own background. Without doubt, my nationality plays a role in how I look at the world, just like an American author's eyes are biased as well. Even having lived abroad for one or two years and regularly having attended conferences elsewhere, this does not mean that one really gets to know a country like one's own home country.

Still, one needs to be precise. I have heard it said to me, for example, that the position on religious freedom which I defend in this book is only the natural position to take when one is born and works in a Western country such as the

Netherlands. A thesis like this suggests a kind of parochialism on the part of the author which I reject. As I explained in the introduction, my views originate in a theoretical perspective which is not determined by geographical factors. In fact, without denying that cultural differences do exist, I would claim that this particular perspective is applicable globally.

However, a true comparison between Europe and North America with respect to issues surrounding the right to freedom of religion or belief would indeed require a much more elaborate effort than I have made for the purposes of this book. This was a conscious choice, as such a systematic comparison between America, Canada and Europe is not what this book is about. Of course, had this been the purpose of the book, I would have had to explore the differences between various European countries as well, and indeed between national jurisdictions in Europe and the European Court of Human Rights. One would also have had to pay attention to differences and similarities between the European Court of Human Rights and the European Court of Justice, especially since the European Union has adopted its own Charter of Fundamental Rights. Considering North America, it is clear that the United States and Canada, despite geographical proximity, differ considerably as well.

Even with respect to what the purpose of the book is—that is, looking at the question of the significance of the right to freedom of religion or belief in light of the notions of constitutionalism and democracy—differences obviously exist between Europe and North America. I have not delved into these differences either. Instead, I have raised some questions which, despite all these differences, the three jurisdiction might have in common when looked at from an abstract level. It is clear that this brings us back to the criticism dealt with before, namely that the book is too theoretical. My only defence would be that if the comparison between Europe and North America truly were made first, then a sequel book would have been needed to deal with the questions raised.

The book is founded, however, on the idea that Western countries have enough in common to make possible a general theoretical argument as put forward in this book. This is illustrated by the fact that, outside the West, Western countries are often perceived as having more in common than Westerners themselves assume to be the case. Interestingly, this perceived commonality also often relates to topics such as those treated in this book. Thus, although within the West itself it is often stressed how secularized countries have become, from a distance the West still looks like a distinctively Christian part of the world. Also, with respect to the right to freedom of religion or belief, as we have seen, it is frequently noted that this is a Western invention. In this respect, it is rather difficult to discriminate between American, Canadian, and European influences.

To the extent that the book is specifically Dutch in outlook, this was not regarded as a major problem from the outset. It is true that, with respect to developments such as secularization, the Netherlands is probably ahead of other European countries and in particular the United States. However, there are so many cultural and historical ties binding the Netherlands and the United States and Canada that these countries are unlikely to be heading in completely different directions. Of course, for a while the idea has existed that the United States is the exception to the rule that all Western countries are to a greater or lesser extent secularizing. At the time of writing the book, it seemed more likely that the United States is only following European trends, be it a few decades later than some European countries themselves started their makeovers.

Final Remarks

So, having summarized the book's main argument and having responded to some anticipated criticisms, how can the central questions the book began with be answered? To what extent does communal religious freedom in both Europe and North America continue to be protected? The first three chapters have attempted to provide an answer to this first question. An article by Paulsen (2013), referred to in Chapters 1 and 4, can conveniently be used to structure the answer. I did not come across this article until a rather late stage of my research for this book, but it is striking how well the main findings of this study fit into its framework.

It should be remembered that Paulsen distinguishes a liberal conception of religious freedom, according to which it is widely assumed that religious truth exists in a society and the state is tolerant towards the various faith and other traditions. According to Paulsen, the United States has developed in the direction of a modern conception of religious freedom, which no longer recognizes religious truth although the state remains tolerant. In such a situation communal religious freedom will also continue to be protected, although it is likely to become more controversial, as it constitutes a threat to state sovereignty which has become absolute.

On the basis of the (admittedly limited) empirical evidence gathered within the context of this study, it is not possible to confirm Paulsen's thesis that several European countries have adopted a postmodern conception of religious freedom. This conception does not only no longer recognize religious truth, but also implies a considerably less tolerant state, as secularism becomes the established "religion." On the basis of the analysis presented in Chapters 1 to 3 it cannot be ruled out either that Paulsen's thesis is correct or that future developments may prove him right, however. In fact, such a diagnosis would fit with the conclusion of Chapter 1, that the glass of religious freedom is currently half empty rather than half full.

Can the recognition that there are multiple sources of sovereignty in society help to achieve legitimacy of the democratic constitutional order rather than putting its political legitimacy under pressure? The development from a liberal conception of religious freedom to a modern conception of this right makes this second question rather pertinent at this moment in time. The answer to this question has to be in the affirmative, to the extent that such a recognition of multiple sources of sovereignty is characteristic of the liberal conception of religious freedom. This religious freedom conception has prevailed in the West during the previous two centuries and contributed to the legitimacy of its political orders. The fact that the modern conception of religious freedom presupposes absolute state sovereignty arguably puts the legitimacy of the political order at risk. Certainly, a further development in the direction of a postmodern conception of religious freedom would even strengthen this trend.

This leads us to the main argument the book has tried to make. Religious freedom has historically been regarded as a natural right which precedes the state. A liberal democracy is thus obliged to grant generous protection to the right to freedom of religion or belief. Such generous protection implies that the sovereignty of the state remains limited, because it is shared with religious and other associations, groups, and institutions in society. Similarly, in conjunction with other fundamental rights, religious freedom ensures that religious believers enjoy equal political voice.

Due to the processes of secularization, a different kind of liberalism is arguably gaining ground across the West. This more progressive liberalism sees religious freedom as a positive right granted by the state. As a result, state sovereignty becomes absolute, and the autonomy of religious and other associations, groups, and institutions comes under pressure. In addition, under the influence of the notion of public reason, religious political voices are being excluded from the public square.

In response to this development, the current book has made a case for the classical liberal position with respect to religious freedom. In light of the current pluralism in society, this position paradoxically appears to be more conducive to maintaining the legitimacy of the political order than the alternative of the establishment of secularism. Yet, at a point in time in which liberalism as a whole has come under pressure globally, and even within the West, what is vital is for conservative and progressive liberals to look at what they have in common rather than what divides them. The differences with both premodern and postmodern conceptions of religious freedom are greater than those between the liberal and the modern conceptions of religious freedom. The principal issue of whether state sovereignty is absolute or not can, as has been the case in the past, remain undecided. What suffices, I hope, is a shared conviction that no legitimate liberal democracy is conceivable without generous protection of religious freedom.

Bibliography

Berg, Thomas (2015), "Francis and Religious Freedom Arguments," *Mirror of Justice*, October 7.

Francis (2013), "Evangelii Gaudium: Apostolic Exhortation on the Proclamation of the Gospel in Today's World," November 24.

Paulsen, Michael Stokes (2013), "The Priority of God: A Theory of Religious Liberty," *Pepperdine Law Review*, 39(5): 1159–222.

Index

www.ingramcontent.com/pod-product-compliance
Ingram Content Group UK Ltd.
Pitfield, Milton Keynes, MK11 3LW, UK
UKHW011016180926
475701UK00004B/774
* 9 7 8 0 3 6 7 2 2 4 2 0 2 *